SITTING BULL
IN
CANADA

by Tony Hollihan

© 2001 by Folklore Publishing
First printed in 2001 10 9 8 7 6 5 4 3 2 1
Printed in Canada

The Publisher: Folklore Publishing

Website: www.folklorepublishing.com

National Library of Canada Cataloguing in Publication Data

Hollihan, K. Tony (Kelvin Tony), 1964–
  Sitting Bull in Canada / by Tony Hollihan.

(The legends series)
ISBN 1-894864-02-6

1. Sitting Bull, 1834?-1890. 2. Dakota Indians—Wars, 1876.
3. Dakota Indians—Saskatchewan—Government relations. I. Title.
II. Series: Legends series (Edmonton, Alta.)

E99.D1S57 2001   978.004'9752'0092   C2001-902356-4

Photography credits: Every effort has been made to accurately credit the sources of photographs. Any errors or omissions should be directed to the publisher for changes in future editions. *Photographs courtesy of* Arizona Historical Society, Tuscon (p.80, 25624); Centennial Archives, Deadwood Public Library (p.262); Denver Public Library, Western History Dept. (title page & p.273, X-33214; p.277, B-422); Glenbow Archives, Calgary, Canada (p.52, NA-1196-7; p.57, NA-1193-4; p.105, NA-2631-1; p.108, NA-652-1; p.123, NA-742-1; p.124, NA-3811-2b; p.131, NA-1060-1; p.158, NA-1151-1; p.182, NA-1406-229; p.189, NA-5091-1; p.209, NA-2003-49; p.245, NA-343-1; p.253, NA-1183-2); Library of Congress, Prints & Photographs Division (p.71, USZ62-78505; p.266, USZ62-113198); Montana Historical Society, Helena (p.97, 943-884); National Anthropological Archives, Smithsonian Institution (p.22, 83-15549) National Archives of Canada (p.102, C-6513; p.118, C-62596); National Archives, Still Pictures Branch, College Park, MD (p.43, 111-B-4693; p.59, 111-SC-95986; p.67, 111-B-1769; p.73, 999-ANSCO-CA-10; P.76, 77-HQ-264-801); National Library of Canada (p.112, C-17038); RCMP Centennial Museum (p.199); State Historical Society of North Dakota (p.259, C0320); *The American West in the 19th Century,* by John Grafton, 1992, Dover Publications (p.41; p.236)

PC: P5

Contents

For Benjamin, who rocks with the best of them.

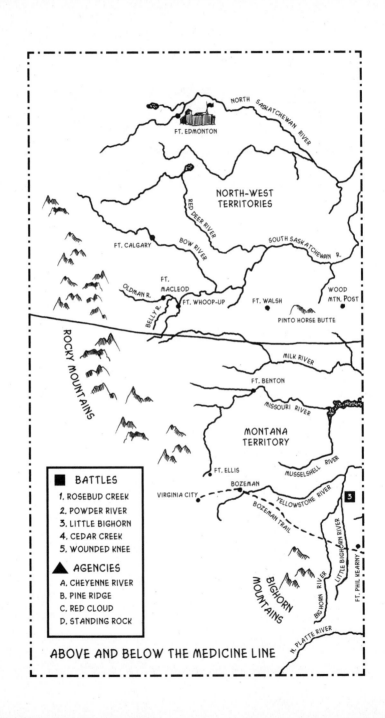

ABOVE AND BELOW THE MEDICINE LINE

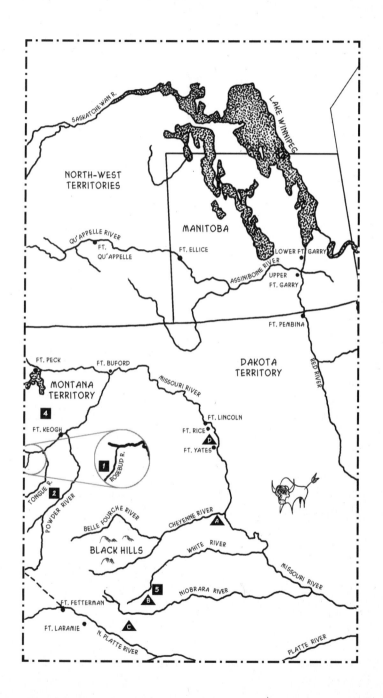

Prologue

"There's a body 'ere and it's Sioux, that's for sure," called Gabriel Solomon.

Major James Walsh, Superintendent of the North-West Mounted Police force at Fort Walsh, was content to listen as his scout described the grisly find.

"I don't think he's been dead long."

"Was he killed here?" asked Walsh.

"Don't think so. His wounds are old an' festered. Smell terrible," added Solomon as he threw the buffalo robe back on the body.

"Well men, we know the Sioux have been here. Trail leads east. We won't find them any sooner by thinking about this poor chap." Walsh spurred his horse and it trotted away from the White Mud River. Soon the flowing waters were lost behind Pinto Horse Butte. There was no sight of the Sioux before nightfall and Walsh gave the order to make camp.

They were moving again with the sun's rising, a strange sight indeed. Even with the backdrop of spring's colorful offerings, their scarlet tunics were an unsettling presence. Of the seven in the party, five were in the full dress of the Mounted Police—Walsh, Sergeant McCutcheon and three constables. The other two were scouts, dressed in the fringed buckskin that would've fit in anywhere on the plains. They weren't riding long when the sheltering hilltops began to move.

"Indians!" shouted Solomon. "Look! Their numbers grow!"

"I see them. Keep riding. A slow, steady pace," advised Walsh. "Are they Sioux?"

"Hard to tell from 'ere, but they could be." *Thank God for my Sioux momma*, Solomon silently thought.

The party rounded a bend and before them lay a large Native encampment. They dismounted and started to walk towards the tipis. They didn't get far before a group of Native braves stood before them and blocked their way. They were Sioux all right. And they looked every bit the fierce warriors that the Sioux were reputed to be. The leader of the group was bare from the waist up, save for the cartridge belts that crossed his chest…and the paint splashed upon it. The party weren't looking at the paint, though. No, their eyes were drawn to the weapon in the warrior's hand. Three feet of stout ash, with three sharpened blades of steel protruding from one end and dangling feathers that an imaginative man might have seen as dripping blood. It was a fearsome instrument…even for the unimaginative.

Walsh smiled.

"Spotted Eagle, my friend," he said as he stepped forward to embrace the man.

"Long Lance, it is good to see you," replied the Sans Arc chief.

"We are looking for Sitting Bull. Is he here? We wish to speak to him."

"This is the camp of Sitting Bull. It is good you are here, for he wishes to hear your words. Come," said Spotted Eagle as he led the Mounties into the camp. "You know, Long Lance, no white man has ever dared to enter the camp of Sitting Bull. And with good reason, for he would not leave it alive."

Walsh replied without missing a beat.

"I do not fear for my safety. I am a Mountie, a representative of the Great White Mother's council in the east. I've got a job to do." *And, by God, it'll be done*, he thought to himself.

Spotted Eagle directed the Mounties to a large lodge at the center of the camp. Surrounding it were several Sioux, whom Walsh took to be the band's headmen. After they stood, the shortest of them limped towards the Mounties. He took Sergeant McCutcheon's hand and shook it vigorously.

"I am Sitting Bull. Welcome to my camp."

The surprised sergeant stuttered an answer.

"Ummm, g-glad to be here…chief."

Walsh stepped forward.

"I am Major James Walsh, the Queen's head chief in these parts." Léveillé, one of the scouts, translated.

"Ahh, Meejure, the one called White Forehead," replied Sitting Bull.

Walsh nodded. Sitting Bull had apparently been in contact with the other Sioux bands Walsh had already approached.

"I've come to tell you about the Great White Mother's law."

"Please tell, for I wish to hear."

"You know that you are in the territory of the Great White Mother?"

"Yes. We know it well. I was raised in these parts with the Red River half-breeds. My grandfather fought here with the Great White Father."

"We've got laws here that must be obeyed by whites and Indians alike. There's no killing and no stealing. And that includes horses. Women and children are not to be harmed. Most importantly, you are not to go back to the United States and wage war upon the Americans and then return to Canada. Should that happen the Americans will not be your only enemies."

"I buried my weapons before I crossed the Medicine Line," said Sitting Bull. "My heart is no longer bad."

"I am glad to hear it. Obey the laws and no harm will come to you," advised Walsh.

Perhaps this is a Medicine House, where one can be safe and live without fear, Sitting Bull thought to himself. He took the measure of the man standing before him in the scarlet jacket. It was a powerful color for the Sioux, a good omen. Perhaps he and his people could finally rest.

CHAPTER ONE

A Boy Becomes
a Man

Wakan Tanka was angry with the people.

"Unktehi!" called Wakan Tanka. "Unktehi, I do not like the way things are. Flood the land. It is time to try again."

Even though the water monster was a great and powerful spirit, Unktehi trembled before Wakan Tanka, the Great Mystery, and did as asked. Slowly, the waters rose. Within days, the waves rolled above the head of the tallest brave. Not long after, only the highest branches of the mightiest poplars could be seen. The people were forced to climb mountains of *Paha Sapa*, but even as they did, the water continued to rise. At the top of the range, there was a ravine into which the people slipped, hoping for protection. But the water surged forth, filling every crevice, every fissure, drowning some and dashing others against the rocks. Their blood turned the mountains red.

A great spotted eagle, Wanblee Galeshka, watched the rising water from his nest far above. His sharp eyes fell upon a maiden clinging to the rock face. She was the most beautiful woman he had ever seen. The eagle leaped from his nest and, with a few powerful strokes of his wings, swept down upon the maiden.

"Pretty girl," called Wanblee, "catch hold of my legs and I will take you to safety."

She did so and, slowly, Wanblee climbed the steep clouds back to his nest high atop *Paha Sapa* (the Black Hills). The waters continued to rise, but they never reached his tree home.

In those days, people and animals were much closer than today and soon Wanblee took the young maiden as his wife. In time, she bore him two children, a boy and a girl. When the waters receded, Wanblee took his family down from his nest to the earth far below.

"You are the only ones left. Go and make a nation," he commanded them. When they were man and woman, the children of Wanblee and the maiden gave birth to a people known as the Lakota. The People of the Eagle took to wearing an eagle feather in their hair as a mark of respect for the great warrior Wanblee who had saved them.

Wakan Tanka favored the Lakota and over the years they prospered and divided. As the centuries passed, the Lakota spread across the land of the *Paha Sapa*. Occasionally, the pressure of competing tribes or the search for game forced them to move. Never, however, did their journeys take them far from the sacred *Paha Sapa*.

By the middle of the 19th century, three distinct branches of Lakota had emerged. Despite the divisions, they continued to share a common language, acted as military allies and often shared each other's hunting grounds.★

★ Those of Wanblee's people who lived in the east called themselves Dakota, those in the west, Lakota. The Dakota/Lakota came to be popularly known, especially by the white man, as Sioux, a corruption of the Chippewa word for enemy. This book will use the popularized name of Sioux.

In the Minnesota woodlands to the east lived the four tribes known as the Santee. Existing as a mostly semi-sedentary people, they fished and hunted and harvested wild rice, all without the use of horses. The Yankton and Yanktanoi lived on the prairies and hunted the buffalo on horseback. Many of their customs and practices, however, were similar to the Santee.

In the western Dakotas, in eastern Wyoming and Montana and on the southern plains of Canada lived the third branch, the Tetons. These were true Plains people, nomadic in their lifestyle. By the late 18th century, they had fully adapted to the "big dog" brought by the white man. Indeed, the horse became central to their way of life, trans-forming it. Walking gave way to riding, allowing the Teton to increase their geographical range. A man's wealth came to be measured by the number of horses he owned. The Teton didn't raise their own horses because their winters were too cold. Instead, they stole the animals from nearby tribes, either in hand-to-hand combat or in a stealthy raid. Thus, warriors with many horses were also seen as coura-geous. Since all Teton sought to be brave, in time there wasn't a tribe on the Plains that did not fear them.

But success in battle demanded more than bravery; it required skill. From a young age, the Teton practiced rid-ing bareback, without using their hands. The same riding skills that were used to bring honor as a warrior were nec-essary to garner respect as a hunter. For the Teton, the hunt centered on the buffalo. Nothing was more important to Teton culture than the great shaggy beast of the Plains. The buffalo shaped their lives. Its meat provided food, its hide warmth and shelter, its sinews and bones equipment, its blood paint and its dung fuel. The buffalo was also a sacred and mythical animal that served as the foundation for much of the Teton's spiritual and ceremonial life.

Among the seven tribes of the Teton were the Hunkpapa, "the Campers at the Entrance of the Circle." Their homeland was the area west of the great Missouri River, below the mouth of the Yellowstone River. Dominated by expanses of rolling prairies, their land was punctuated with wooded plateaus and the occasional refreshing green valley. The rich environment provided everything in the way of animal life, vegetation, shelter and fuel necessary for a varied and fulfilling existence.

It was a lifestyle that came under increasing attack in the few decades following the mid-19th century. An unfamiliar and strange presence, the white man, challenged their practices, their beliefs, their way of life. The hairy-faced newcomers wanted the land of the buffalo for themselves. They wanted an end to the honorable Teton ways of fighting and stealing (though many of them hardly seemed reluctant to engage in such practices themselves). To the Teton, however, the land, the buffalo hunt, intertribal warfare and the accompanying rituals were as food and air; they gave life to the people.

Wakan Tanka did not abandon his people in these turbulent times. He sent a leader who commanded the attention of a continent, whose name became synonymous with that of his people. From the Hunkpapa came Sitting Bull.

Heavy gray clouds filled the sky and a harsh wind blew from the north, taking the very song from the birds. Buds that had begun to spring from the trees hesitated. Her-Holy-Door decided early that she would build her fire in the tipi rather than outside. As she prepared the family's meal, her young son sat beside her, comfortable on the buffalo robes that covered the ground. In his hand, he held a small bow, skillfully made by his uncle, Four Horns. An arrow rested on the ground beside him.

Her-Holy-Door watched the boy for some time. He examined the bow, turning it over, plucking the sinew and rubbing the wood. Other boys would have notched the arrow and sought to fire it. Not her son. Never had she seen one so deliberate yet so young. Before he did anything, he spent many moments thoughtfully considering what should be done. His behavior had earned the young boy a nickname. Although his formal name was Jumping Badger, he was known by all as Slow.

"Mother, tell me a story."

"What would you like to hear?" she asked as she stirred pieces of buffalo meat in her pot.

"A warrior's tale."

"I needn't have asked," she laughed. "Listen to the story of Itunkala the mouse and Igmu the cat."

"Yes!" he nodded. It was one of his favorite stories. He placed his hands in his lap and fixed his eyes on his mother.

"Itunkala was a young mouse. He dreamed of wearing black paint and of having many horses. He wanted to tell his stories of coups taken. Only he could not wear black paint. And he had neither horses to count nor stories to tell. He was not yet a warrior," she explained.

"Determined to change this, he went to his mount, Washin the bullfrog. Off he rode in search of his enemy. Along the way, Itunkala plucked a sturdy blade of grass to use as his coup stick. 'Washin,' he cried, 'today we will take the scalp of Igmu!'

"Itunkala used all the skills he had learned as a young mouse to find his enemy. Finally, he came upon him in a great clearing. 'Igmu,' he shouted, 'stand to fight. I am not afraid of you.' With that, he rode Washin hard towards Igmu.

He struck the enemy with his blade of grass. 'Ha, ha!' he cried. 'I have counted first coup!'

"But that was not enough for Itunkala. He wanted a trophy. So back he rode, this time with his knife. With a great slash, he cut a whisker from Igmu. 'Your scalp is mine, enemy. Beware the mighty Itunkala!'

"The victorious brave rode back to camp," continued Her-Holy-Door. "He directed Washin right into the middle of the camp, holding the whisker high in the air. 'Today I am a warrior!' he called to all. 'Pretty girls, prepare me a feast!'

"The girls all rushed out of their lodges to see this new warrior. They were surprised by what they saw. Finally, one of them asked, 'Itunkala, where is your tail?'"

"In Igmu's stomach!" shouted Slow, rocking backwards in laughter.

"Yes," agreed Her-Holy-Door. "But no sacrifice is too great for victory."

As they finished the story, the flap that covered the entrance of the tipi opened. In stepped Slow's father, Sitting Bull. He stepped towards his wife.

"Four Horns agrees. It is time for Slow to learn the skills of a man, of a warrior," he said.

Her-Holy-Door nodded. She tried to hide her sadness. Since his birth, Slow had been part of her world. For seven summers, from the cradleboard of infancy through his first steps as a toddler to the strong young boy he was now, Slow had been her responsibility. Now, that duty would be his uncle's. Four Horns would prepare him to become a brave. It was the way of things, but Slow was her only son and it was not easy to accept.

Slow heard what his father had said and was excited. A smile illuminated his already broad face. He liked Four Horns, who was a powerful leader of his people, the Hunkpapa Sioux, and who had counted coup many times.

"Jumping Badger, gather your belongings and go to the tipi of Four Horns," directed his father.

Slow did as requested. Before leaving, he embraced his mother, his older sister Good Feather and his father.

"I will be a warrior," he stated as he left the dwelling.

Over the next few years, Slow spent many hours with Four Horns. Gone were the carefree games of playing camp and hide-and-seek. While such games provided the basis for the skills Sioux needed as adults, Slow had to become a warrior. The ability to quickly break camp, for example, was necessary for the Sioux to master, because the possibility of ambush was a constant reality. Slow learned how to track animals and men, how to use the bow and arrow and how to ride a horse. Four Horns was steeping him in the ways of warriorhood.

"A true warrior," Four Horns explained, "knows more than how to kill the enemy and to bring home food for his family. He must be brave and generous. He must display fortitude. He must seek wisdom. Not all Sioux reach the point where others can say they are these things. Only those who are special, only those blessed by the Wakan Tanka, the Great Mystery, reach that place. Still, all strive to do their best."

Slow's first step towards manhood came at the age of ten, when he was finally able to exercise his skills.

"You have learned much. You are fast and strong. It is not often that the other boys best you in competition. You have proved your worth among them. Today," his uncle informed him, "you will put your skills to a true test. You will hunt buffalo."

It was high summer and the great buffalo herds were near the encampment, so they would not be difficult to find. But to bring one down...that was a challenge! The mighty animals had been blessed by Wakan Tanka. They were strong and not easily killed. As his uncle said, it would be a real test.

For years, Slow had been the observer, watching what his uncle did, reflecting on his actions and memorizing them for future use. On this day, Four Horns observed. He remained silent as Slow, riding his gray cayuse, led them to the herd. He followed as his nephew slipped downwind from the beasts. He watched as Slow measured the herd, selecting the best position from which to strike. Four Horns looked upon the herd and knew it would be a difficult kill. The buffalo were tightly bunched, and the wily and tough bulls patrolled the fringes.

Slow sat for a long time watching the herd; so long, in fact, that Four Horns thought he might be reluctant to continue. Again, he looked at the boy. Perhaps Slow was too young for his first buffalo hunt. He had been taught well, but the great beasts were many times his size and sometimes struck fear into the hearts of even the most experienced hunters. Still, Four Horns held his tongue and waited. It was more than their shared blood bond that led Four Horns to believe that the boy showed great promise…it might simply be that he was uncommonly patient.

Four Horns did not have to wait much longer; a handful of buffalo broke off from the main herd. At that moment, Slow drew an arrow from his quiver and notched the shaft against the sinew of his bow. With his legs wrapped tightly about his cayuse and his hands on his weapon, he jabbed his horse sharply with his feet and darted towards the buffalo.

"Yip, yip, yip, yiiii!" he cried, as he rode towards his prey. Closer, closer he rode, until he was near the main body of the herd. Finally, he let his arrow fly. Its flint point embedded itself in the chest of the animal; it gave a great bellow and fell. Slow had brought down his first buffalo!

Four Horns rode over to Slow, who stood by his kill.

"Why did you shoot at the bull?" he asked. "The cow was an easier target."

"There was a calf, uncle. To kill the mother would be to kill the offspring. Both will return again."

Four Horns nodded.

"I will wait here. You return to camp and tell the women to come and prepare the meat."

Slow rode back to camp and made his way to his father's tipi.

"Mother, I have killed a buffalo. Four Horns waits with it. Come back with me to dress the meat."

Her-Holy-Door quickly gathered what she needed to perform the task.

"And, mother, ensure that the best piece of meat is given to Spotted Doe."

Spotted Doe had fallen on hard times. She had lost her husband during the last winter and was left alone with three children. The cries of their hunger could often be heard at night.

"Yes, my son," nodded Her-Holy-Door, quietly pleased with the generous nature of her son.

Not long after his first buffalo kill, Slow was presented with another opportunity to display his skills. Village Center, the tribe's foremost arrow maker, arranged a contest. He would give a bow and a set of arrows to the boy who shot the prettiest bird. Among the Hunkpapa, there was little as welcome as a competition, so Slow set out with the same great enthusiasm as the other boys.

Slow spent some time thinking about the prettier birds that called the trees around his camp home. The sparrow and crow were bland. The magpie had tail feathers that glimmered blue and purple in the sun's rays, but it was far too easy to kill. The woodpecker had a great crown, but it was also far too easily killed. The meadowlark's beautiful

song did not match its appearance. The cardinal had possibility. The blood red color of its feathers was much
respected.

As he gazed at the trees contemplating, his eyes fell
upon an oriole. With feathers of yellow, orange and
brown, it was indeed beautiful and could fly like no other
bird. Here was a worthy prize. His mind made up, Slow
trailed the oriole.

Even with Slow's skill, the oriole was a challenge to
bring down. By mid-afternoon, half his arrows were
gone, and still he remained empty-handed. It was then
that he stumbled upon some other boys also engaged in
the contest.

"No!" shouted Crossed Rabbit as he held his bow in his
hand and glared up at the tree. "Look. My favorite arrow
sits there on the branch. I can't win the contest without it. I
will give one of my best arrows to whoever retrieves it," he
declared.

Slow took the challenge. He drew his own best arrow
and let it fly at Crossed Rabbit's. Both arrows fell to the
ground, but Crossed Rabbit's broke in the process.

"Look what you've done!" he cried in disbelief. "My
best arrow, broken. Slow, you must pay for it," he
demanded, his voice rising with each word.

With that, a great argument ensued. Some of the boys
sided with Crossed Rabbit, while others claimed that Slow
had met his end of the bargain. They were on the verge of
blows when Slow came up with a solution.

"Crossed Rabbit, take my best arrow and be done with it,"
he said, giving the arrow to him. With that, he walked away.

Later that night, Village Center prepared to judge the contest. Before he could begin, however, one of the boys spoke.

"Village Center, there is something you should know."
The boy explained what had happened.

"By giving away his best arrow, Slow prevented what surely would have been a great fight," he concluded.

Village Center was quiet for a moment, then he spoke.

"There are many ways to measure victory. Sometimes it is found in compromise. On this day, Slow has demonstrated something of what it is to be wise. The bow and arrows go to him," he decided.

Slow was still a young boy, but those who took notice saw in him the first stirrings of exceptional manhood.

Slow, wearing only the yellow paint that covered him from head to toe and a trailing assortment of threaded, colorful beads, sat atop his cayuse and waited. The Sioux war party had finally caught up to the small band of Crow they had long been following. The Crow were camped in a nearby coulee, unaware that their enemy was about to strike. Slow had accompanied war parties before, but as a boy his role was mainly to perform assigned errands. He was always an onlooker when the fighting took place.

Slow found it difficult to watch battles from afar. He was tired of the games of youth and longed to become a man. He wanted to rush into the fray and count coup. But he was a thoughtful boy, and his temperament would not allow such a rash course of action. Instead, he patiently watched and learned and came to know what it was to be a brave in battle. Many times, he relived in his thoughts what he had seen. He gave great consideration to the strategies and practices of his Sioux brothers. He prepared himself for the time when he would fight with them. That time had come.

Earlier in the day Slow's father, Sitting Bull, had spoken to him.

"Jumping Badger, Four Horns tells me that you have learned well. Today, you have a fast horse. Show me that you are brave."

With those brief words, Sitting Bull gave his son a coup stick and left. Little was more important in battle than the coup stick, because counting coup was the mark of the warrior. Less significance was given to the killing of an enemy than to the man who first touched him.

As he waited for the cry that would signal the attack, Slow rubbed his hand along the long piece of hard ash. He prayed quietly to Wakan Tanka, the Great Mystery. He did not ask for success, but rather humbly requested that his courage not fail. A whistle pierced the silence and the Sioux were off.

When they reached the edge of the hill that gave way to the coulee, the Sioux shouted their war cries and rushed down the slope towards the Crow. Surprised, the Crow took a defensive position, spreading out quickly. The Sioux outnumbered them and, sensing defeat, some of the Crow braves mounted their horses trying to escape the ambush. Slow caught sight of one riding for the open end of the coulee and exploded in pursuit. Surely the confidence of the fleeing Crow grew as he looked back at his assailant. Slow's youthfulness suggested he had little to fear. The Crow confidently fired an arrow, but it flew past its mark. More anxious, he dug his heels deeply into his mount, urging it on.

Slow felt the breeze of the arrow as it passed, but did not break his stride. His horse was a fast one, well distinguished in the buffalo hunts and Slow was a good horseman. Riding as one, the pair was soon close enough to smell the enemy's fear. Slow reached out, extending the coup stick as far as he could and hit the brave on the arm. With that, he gave a great whoop, a signal for others to witness his achievement.

Sitting Bull's own drawing of his first coup
at age 14 in a battle with a band of Crow

Slow continued his pursuit until the two horses rode abreast. Slow lifted the tomahawk that he held in his other hand and brought it thundering down on the Crow's head. The Crow fell from his horse, stunned. Before Slow could dismount, another Hunkpapa pounced on the Crow. He pulled the hair of his enemy tight and, with a quick pull of his arm, dragged his knife across the forehead. With a tug, the scalp was his. So was second coup.

When the battle was over, eight Crow lay dead. Not one Sioux was injured. Sitting Bull made his way to Slow and embraced him.

"Son, today you are a warrior. Today you are a man."

The celebrations began in earnest when the war party returned to camp at Powder River. Sitting Bull ordered that there would be a great feast. There was dancing and eating and the telling of heroic deeds of long ago, until Sitting Bull asked for silence.

"Today we celebrate the birth of a warrior. When we sit around our fires at night and tell the stories of counting coup, each warrior is left to tell of his deeds before Wakan Tanka. Only the great warriors have their stories told by others. Though he has seen only 14 summers, we have a great warrior. I have seen it in my dreams. Let me tell you of how Jumping Badger counted his first coup."

Sitting Bull's words hung heavily in the air. The celebration turned solemn. Everyone knew that Sitting Bull was a dreamer, one of the few in the tribe visited by spirits who brought powerful messages. They listened closely as the wise leader retold Jumping Badger's exploits. Slow had counted coup early in life, much sooner than most. Already, his bravery was evident. When Sitting Bull finished, he directed a few braves to bring horses into the gathering.

"In recognition of my son's bravery, I give these horses away." He walked around his people, distributing the animals to those who needed them until only one, a magnificent bay, remained. Then, he walked to his son.

"Jumping Badger, I place this white eagle feather in your hair as a symbol of your first coup. I give you the bay horse, a warrior's horse that has served me well."

Sitting Bull dipped his hands into a small pot. When he withdrew them, they were black. He painted his son until there was not a trace of his copper-toned skin. When finished, he spoke again.

"This is my son, a warrior of the Hunkpapa Sioux. He is no longer naked. From this day on, I am Jumping Bull. This warrior's name is Tatanka Iyontanka, Sitting Bull."

No greater honor could be bestowed on the young brave. The much-respected Sitting Bull had given his name to his son. But it was not just any name; it had come to Sitting Bull during a strange visitation. The father, then known as Returns Again, was in camp with three other braves when a great white buffalo bull, whom all were certain was the embodiment of the Buffalo God, had approached them and spoke. Only Returns Again understood what had been said. The Buffalo God had given him permission to use the name.

None failed to understand the importance of the name itself. The buffalo was a sacred animal for the Sioux, respected and revered. It was known for its endurance, hardiness and implacability. A sitting bull would not be moved.

"Sitting Bull, I give you this shield. May it protect you in battle," Jumping Bull said.

With trembling hands, the young warrior took the shield from his father, marveling at its beauty. The young brave lost himself in its intense colors. Scarlet, green, dark blue and brown provided the backdrop against which stood a man-bird, a visitor to his father's dreams. Sitting Bull's fingers played gently against the taut buffalo hide that served as the canvas for the holy man who had drawn the figure. There was no give. From the willow that served as a frame hung four eagle feathers, meant to remind a warrior, among other things, of the four cardinal virtues to which all Sioux aspired: bravery, fortitude, generosity and wisdom.

"My people, I give you the warrior Sitting Bull!" exclaimed Jumping Bull.

A great cry arose. Some whooped, others whistled and still others shouted. All knew they were witnessing something special.

Over the next year, Sitting Bull never missed an opportunity to meet the enemy in battle. Like all Native peoples, he was steeped in the history of his tribe. He knew that the Sioux possessed a war record unmatched by any of the Plains peoples. They were a feared tribe and, through that fear, had earned great respect. The expectations of his people were high and, when Sioux warriors descended on the enemy, Sitting Bull was never a reluctant participant. His attitude earned him the red eagle feather, much prized among warriors, since its cost was injury in battle.

He wasn't long 15 when Sitting Bull was engaged in a skirmish with the Flathead. The Sioux were ambushed and, though they were outnumbered, they refused to retreat. Surprised by this stand, the Flathead dismounted. Using their horses as cover, they rained down a volley of arrows and bullets on the Sioux.

Sitting Bull called to his friends.

"Brothers, I will run the daring line."

All knew Sitting Bull's intent. He would ride his horse between the opposing forces, well within range of the Flathead. There was nothing strategic about running the daring line. It was simply a way of demonstrating one's bravery. Not all warriors had the courage to do it.

With the calls of his friends at his back, Sitting Bull rode into the middle of the battle. He refused to bend low and use his horse's neck as a shield. The Flathead had a good target, but their arrows and bullets failed to find their mark…until Sitting Bull was near the end of the line. A ball struck him in the foot and, although the pain was great, it wasn't enough to make him withdraw from the battle. Only when night fell did the Flathead finally retreat.

Once they were again in the main camp, Sitting Bull was honored at another celebration. In recognition of his battlefield wound, he was given the red feather. The two feathers that he wore proudly in his hair were symbols to all of a singular young man.

But, the Hunkpapa began talking about more than his courage. During a battle with the Crow, Sitting Bull and his Sioux war party had taken a Crow woman. The practice among Native peoples was to adopt captured women into their tribe. In time, they were seen as full members of the community. It was discovered, however, that this captive was a crazy woman and sexually promiscuous in her behavior. The Hunkpapa women would not accept the Crow woman and decided instead to kill her as an enemy. Death came neither easily nor quickly to condemned enemies. She would be burned alive.

Sitting Bull opposed the Hunkpapa women. Death in battle was one thing, as was the torture and killing of a warrior. There was honor in such things. Where was the honor in torturing a woman? But Sitting Bull held his tongue. Although he was gaining a reputation as a brave warrior, he was still a young man. Youth commanded neither respect nor authority among Native peoples.

Frustrated, he watched as the women piled the brush that would serve as the crazy woman's funeral pyre. His eyes fell upon those of the captive, who was tied tightly to the stake at which she would be burned. What he saw in those eyes is unknown, but it was enough to prod him into action, action he knew would bring the disapproval of many. He drew an arrow from his quiver, pulled it tightly against his bowstring and let it fly towards the Crow. The arrow pierced her heart and she died instantly.

The Hunkpapa women screamed and wailed at the turn of events, but Sitting Bull simply turned and walked away. Only 17, he knew something of compassion. He also knew that one cannot turn from what is necessary and right.

The Hunkpapa were camped near a small stand of cottonwoods. As they went about their daily tasks, sounds filtered through the trees, mere fleeting whispers, heard by chance and not by design. Though muffled, one might discern the occasional word of a song, the rattle of a shaker or the shuffling of dancing feet. Everyone knew that in the clearing just beyond the cottonwoods danced Sun Dreamer, the great Hunkpapa shaman. His world was that of visions and prophecy, and his doings were mystical. Few had the courage or curiosity to eavesdrop willfully on the activities of Sun Dreamer.

Eventually, he emerged from the trees, the smell of smoke from the sacred red pipe heavy upon him.

"My brothers," he called, "see my hand. It is black." He raised it for all to see. "It is a sign. We will meet the Crow within a day."

Sun Dreamer's prophecy was met with enthusiasm from those gathered. They had been traveling for many days in search of their traditional enemies so that they might raid their horses. None was surprised when later that night, two scouts returned to say that they had sighted the Crow just down river.

Using the darkness of night as cover, the Hunkpapa slipped into the Crow encampment and made off with many horses. By dawn, the Crow were in pursuit. Hampered by their prizes, the Hunkpapa moved slowly. Realizing they would not be able to escape the trailing enemy, they decided to stand and fight. The Crow were surprised when they climbed over a rise and found the Hunkpapa waiting. They paused to consider this unexpected turn of events.

Three of the Crow, perhaps angrier than the others or simply more rash, made a courageous rush at the Hunkpapa.

One rode into the gathered Hunkpapa and counted two coup before he made his escape, while the second shot and killed one of his enemies. A warrior just as brave challenged the third Crow, who was alone between the opposing forces.

Sitting Bull dismounted his horse with his rifle and shield and shouted, "I am Sitting Bull. I come to fight!"

When the Crow saw Sitting Bull, he brought his mount to a sudden halt. Sitting Bull's reputation as a great warrior had not yet spread across the land, but the Crow could see that the Hunkpapa warrior wore a regal headdress. Blackened buffalo horns, still attached to the fur from the beast's head, appeared to extend from his ears. Long, black crow feathers reached to the sky. Dark strips of ermine streamed down his back. A dark red wool cloth decorated with feathers lay on his shoulders. But it was the long trailing sash that caused the Crow's breath to freeze in his throat. He had seen such warriors before; he had heard stories of their bravery. Here was a rider of the Strong Hearts Society.

The Strong Hearts Society was the most prestigious one of all the Hunkpapa war societies. It consisted of some 50 of the Hunkpapa's bravest. From among them, two were chosen to be the sash bearers. These two warriors pledged to ride into battle and to stake their sashes into the ground. They would remain so lodged until one of their own freed them. The act indicated to everyone that the sash bearer would not retreat; he would fight until there was victory or death.

The Crow dismounted and ran towards the Hunkpapa, for he, too, was brave. As the distance between the two warriors closed, the song of Sitting Bull trumpeted his determination.

"Comrades, whoever runs away, he is a woman they say. Therefore, through many trials, my life is short."

Sitting Bull's voice was deep and betrayed no fear. But as he drew closer to the enemy, he knew he had reason to be cautious. His foe was no mere warrior. The Crow wore a red shirt trimmed with ermine, the dress of a chief. In his hand, he clutched a flintlock rifle.

Suddenly, the Crow dropped to one knee and raised his rifle. Sitting Bull fell to the ground and took shelter behind his shield. The shield may have provided some protection against arrows, but it was no barrier to flying lead. He heard the retort of the gun and then felt the sharp pain in his left foot. He dropped the punctured shield and took aim at the Crow. Sitting Bull's bullet struck him in the chest. He limped over to the Crow and slipped his knife into the man's heart. Certain of victory, Sitting Bull retrieved his horse and joined his newly inspired brothers in a full attack on the Crow. Those of the enemy left alive soon scattered.

Sitting Bull's foot was poorly treated and failed to mend properly. His sole was permanently contracted and thereafter he walked with a limp, but he never saw it as a limitation. He could still run fast. And, to the Hunkpapa, his limp was a reminder of his great bravery. So unquestioned was his courage that he was soon elected the leader of the Strong Hearts, an uncommon tribute for a man in his mid-20s. He did not disappoint. Over the next few years, he led raids on opposing tribes greatly increasing Hunkpapa hunting territory.

Sitting Bull demonstrated more than courage in battle. His compassion for others often brought on the disapproval of confused friends. During a winter not long after he was injured, Sitting Bull went on a raid against the Hohe (Assiniboine), who called the land north of the Missouri River home. The fall hunt was long completed and there was plenty of food for the coming winter months. Restless, the Hunkpapa braves set out for adventure.

When they reached the river, they found a tipi on its shores. Smoke lazily rose through the small opening in the top.

"We are Sitting Bull's boys!" came the call as the warriors attacked the lodge.

Fearful of the cry, a man, a woman clutching a baby and two children ran from the tipi. The man stood and let loose an arrow that missed its mark. Before he could notch another, he was on the ground, his bright red blood pooling in the white snow beneath him. Soon, his wife, their baby and one of the children lay with him. Enemies were enemies, regardless of sex or age.

The oldest boy, perhaps 11, found himself on the frozen river. Valiantly, he fired his arrows at the Hunkpapa. He had not the skill to succeed and his small arrows would not have inflicted much damage had they hit their target. Three Hunkpapa quickly counted coup on the boy, but they left the kill for Sitting Bull. When he reached the boy, he stepped from his bay horse, Bloated Jaw.

The young Hohe had no reason to believe that his fate would be any different that of his family's. But, rather than cower, he leaped towards Sitting Bull and embraced him.

"Big brother," he cried, "save me!"

The action had a profound effect on Sitting Bull, who had no brother and had recently lost a son during childbirth. He stood still for a moment.

"Do not kill this boy. He is my brother. Let him live!" he proclaimed.

His compassion was not shared by all, so an argument over his decision erupted. The others finally agreed that Sitting Bull's wishes would stand until they returned to camp. Once there, a consensus was reached. Sitting Bull would be allowed to adopt the boy, a common practice among Plains Natives. A great feast was held and Sitting

Bull gave away many horses. Those who feared that the presence of a potential enemy might cause problems soon learned their concerns were groundless. The boy had many opportunities to return to his people but always chose to stay. For this reason, he was named Stays-Back. He fought many battles at Sitting Bull's side and his bravery, like his adopted brother's, was unquestioned.

With this act of compassion, Sitting Bull's reputation among his people grew. Stories that once focused on his courage also began to praise his generosity. His ways, many suggested, were those of a great chief. However, none was truly aware of the depths of his generosity, depths revealed on a day of great personal tragedy.

The burning summer sun blanketed the ground with a stifling heat. The lazy songs of the birds, the heavy smell of the grass and the trees and the thick still air comforted the moving Hunkpapa. All, that is, save one. Jumping Bull, Sitting Bull's father, endured a toothache that had only worsened with time. He was an old man, so the aches and pains of age were challenges to bear. He longed for relief.

As the band traveled, summer's embrace made them less vigilant. From the shelter of the trees, enemies were watching. They saw that the Hunkpapa were unprepared and they struck.

"Ambush!" came the cry. "Crow!"

The words still rang in the air when two young Hunkpapa were brought down with arrows. Soon, chaos reigned. Eventually, the Hunkpapa warriors gathered together and charged the enemy. The Crow fell back. One remained and faced the Hunkpapa.

"He is mine!" called Jumping Bull, running to the fore before anyone else could act. The Crow jumped from his horse and ran towards the old man. As Jumping Bull raised his bow and arrow, he was driven backwards by a bullet that hit his shoulder. Regaining his balance, he continued to charge, until the two stood face to face. The Crow pulled his knife, while Jumping Bull reached for his. His fingers were not as nimble as they once were and, as he clawed for the weapon, the Crow plunged his blade into Jumping Bull's chest. He fell to his knees, unwilling to yield. The Crow drove his knife into Jumping Bull's skull, ending the struggle.

Sitting Bull was told of his father's fight, but the old man was dead before he arrived. Sitting Bull took off in hot pursuit of the Crow and, reaching him, killed him with one blow of his lance. He then cut the body to pieces. Incensed at the death of Jumping Bull, and perhaps ashamed of their failure to match his courage, the Hunkpapa attacked with renewed enthusiasm. Though they were outnumbered, few Crow remained alive to flee. Three women were particularly unfortunate and were taken captive.

With their emotions still running high, the Hunkpapa wanted to kill these women to avenge Jumping Bull's death. When they saw Sitting Bull, his clothes torn, his braids cut and his face wet with tears for his father, they were more determined than ever. Preparations were being made when Sitting Bull spoke.

"Do not kill these women. Let them live and treat them well. My father was a warrior and death is his."

After four days of mourning, the Hunkpapa held a great victory feast. Sitting Bull joined the celebration as the new head of his family. His wish regarding the women was fulfilled. By summer's end, they and the horses given to them as gifts were returned to their people.

〰〰

Sitting Bull sat in front of his tipi with his young nephew, One Bull. He had taken on the responsibility for the boy's education, just as Four Horns had done with him. It was the moon of the chokecherries, June, and a hint of winter lingered in the breeze.

"Listen, One Bull," he said as he placed his hand on the boy's shoulder. "What do you hear?"

"It is the meadowlark, Uncle."

Sitting Bull answered the bird's call so perfectly that the bird responded in kind. Few Hunkpapa had his ability to mimic as effectively the sounds of so many birds.

"If you listen carefully, you will learn to understand what the meadowlark says. There is great wisdom in the bird's song."

After a few moments of silence, Sitting Bull rose and stepped towards a covered tripod that stood near the opening of his tipi. He lifted the fur that covered it. Carefully, he took the object that lay beneath and walked to One Bull. He sat next to him.

"Nephew, you know this is my peace pipe. I will be smoking it soon," said Sitting Bull.

One Bull looked at the precious object. A wooden stem sheathed with bird skins and decorated with dangling eagle feathers extended from a polished red catlinite bowl. He knew enough to realize that smoking the pipe was a serious matter, done only before important ceremonies.

"I want to tell you the story of Ptesan-Wi, the White Buffalo Woman, and the Sacred Calf Pipe. It is good to remember such things before it is smoked."

Sitting Bull crossed his legs and gently placed the pipe in his lap.

"Long ago, before the Hunkpapa had horses, the Teton came together and camped. Though it was summer and animals should have been plentiful, none could be found. Search as they might, the scouts always returned with bad news."

One Bull knew how serious that could be.

"One day, the scouts climbed to the peak of a hill. Able to see far into the distance, they hoped they might find game. They were disappointed. They were about to return to camp when one of the braves called that he saw something. It was far away and they had to squint to determine what it was. It was a person. As the figure drew closer, they saw that it was not just any person. Instead of walking, the being floated. The person was holy. The person was Ptesan-Wi," explained Sitting Bull.

"Soon, the braves realized that the figure was a woman. Her beauty was greater than any ever witnessed. Long, shiny blue-black hair fell straight near two red dots on her face. Her dark eyes bespoke an unknown power. She was dressed in a white buckskin outfit, so white it glowed in the midday sun. Her clothes were decorated with colorful designs of porcupine quills, so intricate that they were well beyond the ability of Lakota women to make. In her hands, she carried a large bundle.

"When she arrived at the hilltop, one of the scouts was so taken by her beauty that he reached out to touch her. Immediately, a cloud descended upon him and snakes devoured his flesh. Only his white bones remained on the ground. The others stood still properly."

One Bull nodded at his uncle, his eyes wide.

"'I bring something good for your people,' she said. 'Go back and tell your chief to set up a medicine lodge and to make it holy for my arrival.'

"The scout returned to camp and the preparations were made. When Ptesan-Wi arrived, the chief spoke. 'Sister, we are glad you have come to teach us.' Pleased, Ptesan-Wi accepted his invitation into the medicine tent. Once there, she opened the bundle. It contained the *chanunpa*, the Sacred Calf Pipe. She raised it before those in the tipi, grasping the stem with her right hand and the bowl with her left. It has been held that way ever since," informed Sitting Bull.

"Ptesan-Wi told the Teton of the importance of the pipe. 'The red bowl is from the *Paha Sapa*,'" said Sitting Bull, as he held the pipe before One Bull. "'The stone from which it is made is red from the blood of your ancestors. It represents your own flesh. The bowl also represents the buffalo, the sacred animal created by Wakan Tanka to hold back the great waters of the sun's descent. Look closely and you will see seven circles. They represent the seven campfires of the Teton. The stem represents all that grows on the earth. The twelve feathers that hang from it are from Wanblee Galeshka, the eagle, a wise and sacred bird who is Wakan Tanka's messenger.

"'The skull and backbone of the *chanunpa* form a living being. When you smoke the *chan-sahsa*, the red willow bark, it creates the breath of Tunkashila, the great Grandfather Mystery.' As she said this, Ptesan-Wi placed a dry buffalo chip on the fire. When it glowed red, she took it in her hand and lit the pipe. Soon smoke drifted skyward. 'Use the *chanunpa* when you wish to communicate with the Wakan Tanka.'

"Ptesan-Wi stood. 'Use the *chanunpa* wisely,' she cautioned. 'Respect it and it will lead you to where you must go. I will see you again.' With that she slipped out of the tent. Once outside of the camp, she turned into a buffalo and disappeared.

"Ptesan-Wi was true to her word. She returned many times to tell the Teton what was good and necessary, and of the ceremonies that we must perform to show respect to Wakan Tanka and to the created world," concluded Sitting Bull.

"Uncle, it is true then? You smoke the *chanunpa* because you are to dance before the sun?" asked One Bull.

"Yes," replied Sitting Bull. "It is my time."

The Sun Dance honored Wi, the sun, the great spirit who reigned over the world of the living and the dead. The celebration was a lengthy affair, lasting 12 days. Over that period, ritualized ceremonies reinforcing the Hunkpapa ideals and mores were performed. The greater part of the Sun Dance was devoted to the preparation of the dancers and to the dance itself. Those who participated subjected themselves to self-torture in the belief that such sacrifice would be looked upon favorably by Wakan Tanka.

The self-torture was endured in stages, including frenzied dancing to the point of exhaustion, the ritualized cutting of arms and the skewering of the chest and the back. The men were suspended until the skewers ripped through their muscle and flesh. The culmination of it all was a communal dance. When completed, the band was renewed, its shared sense of identity reinforced.

The Sun Dance held particular importance for Sitting Bull. Many believed that he was a *wichasha wakan*, a holy man. He could communicate with animals and, like his father before him, had the gift of prophecy. But one could not truly be a *wichasha wakan* until one had endured the self-sacrifice of the Sun Dance. To give one's body was a statement before the community of both willingness and readiness.

The sun was low in the sky, and the sinews that suspended Sitting Bull between the sacred poles were taut. Though blood seeped from the wounds on his chest, the buffalo bones linking him to the sinews had not yet torn loose. His raw, red arms hung limply at his side. As Wi journeyed across the sky, his mind drifted.

He was a boy again, sleeping in the shelter of a great tree. As he dozed, he heard the thumping of a woodpecker. It called to him, "Lie still, lie still." He did as he was told.

When the bird stopped, he opened his eyes. Above him stood a huge grizzly. It was close enough for the boy to smell its rancid breath, to feel the tickle of its coarse fur. He closed his eyes and remained still. He had been taught that a grizzly doesn't bother that which it believes is dead. The lesson was true and, after some time, the bear ambled off. The boy stood and sang to the bird, who remained attached to the tree's trunk, watching.

"Pretty bird, you saw me and took pity on me. You wish me to survive among the people. O Bird People, from this day you shall always be my relatives!"

Suddenly, a new memory appeared. He was older now, walking in the woods when he came upon an injured wolf, its breath ragged. Two arrows protruded from its bloodied flank.

"Boy," called the animal, "help me and all will know your name."

Carefully, Sitting Bull dislodged the arrows and treated the wounds. As the animal limped away, Sitting Bull sang his song to the wolf tribe. "Alone in the wilderness I roam; with much hardships in the wilderness I roam. A wolf said this to me."

As the song died away, Sitting Bull found himself in another place, a dark place. The dying embers of a fire glowed and gave an eerie countenance to the *wichasha wakan* who sat next to him. The man remained silent as the boy told him of his vision. Sitting Bull listened carefully when the *wichasha wakan* finally spoke. The whispery voice of the frail man traveled like a feather on the breeze.

"You have dreamed of much. You have seen the buffalo. The thunderbird has visited. You are blessed by Wakan Tanka," he concluded, as he painted the boy's face with streaks of lightning. "Your honor is great. But your responsibilities are greater."

With the words of the *wichasha wakan* still echoing, the piercing bones ripped free of his flesh. With a gasp, Sitting Bull fell to the ground, exhausted. It was finished.

Only in his mid-20s, Sitting Bull had achieved much. Accolades as a warrior and a hunter long since garnered now commanded even greater respect. He was a holy man. All recognized him as special, one with the ability to communicate with Wakan Tanka as well as the created world. No one in his community doubted his power. Brave, generous, fortuitous and already wise, he was all that the Sioux sought to be.

CHAPTER TWO

A Great Leader Emerges

"The Indians killed my cow!" shouted the man. "I want compensation. I want a new cow! Or else I want cash! I haven't led that animal halfway across a continent to have it killed by some red-skinned savage!" he bellowed, his face reddening with each word. "Gggod...yes, goddamn it! I want satisfaction!"

"Let me get this straight, sir," replied Second Lieutenant Hugh Flemming, the commander of Fort Laramie. "You're part of a Mormon emigrant train headed for Utah. The Indians slaughtered one of your cows."

"It's as simple as that."

"Fine. When the Indian agent returns, I'll have him look into it and then we'll assess damages."

"Hell, sir! That's not good enough," interjected Second Lieutenant John Grattan, who witnessed the complaint. "Forgive me for speaking so frankly, but the Indians have been nothing but trouble. They're harassing American citizens as they travel west, with their begging and pilfering. It's not been three years since they signed a treaty right here in this very office, pledging that they wouldn't cause problems. Some treaty. They've been snubbing their noses at us ever since. I'd say it's about time someone bloodied those noses."

Grattan took Flemming's continuing silence as an invitation to plead his case further.

"Last year, you yourself led a detachment that killed three Sioux and captured two others, all in response to an errant bullet that didn't come within a yard of anyone."

"An errant bullet fired at a member of the United States cavalry, Grattan. I don't need reminding. We'll wait until the Indian agent returns," Flemming concluded.

Later that day, Chief Conquering Bear arrived at the fort. Under the 1851 Fort Laramie Treaty, he was the one responsible for ensuring that the Natives obeyed its terms because the Americans demanded a supreme chief. He was uncomfortable with the duty, because the Sioux had no hierarchy of command that granted anyone such a position; nonetheless, he took it seriously. He explained to Flemming that the cow had wandered into a Brulé Sioux camp and, as there was no owner apparent, a visiting Miniconjou killed it for food. He reminded the commander that the Miniconjou had not signed the treaty. Still, he was willing to make reparation for the loss and offered some ponies as compensation.

The offer was inadequate. By the next morning, Flemming found himself swayed by Grattan's argument that it was necessary to take quick, decisive action against the Natives. He authorized a detachment under Grattan's direction to set forth and arrest the brave who killed the cow. Flemming could not have chosen a more poorly qualified officer to command the operation.

Grattan was only a year out of West Point and was known to brag that, with a few dozen good men, he could

A drawing for *Harper's Weekly* of a wagon train camp;
white settlers provoked the Natives by crossing their land
in the journey to the farmlands and gold fields of the West

rid the plains of the red men. When he set out on his
mission, Grattan learned differently; he never returned to
Fort Laramie. Finding the Brulé camp, he arranged his
men in an attack formation. As they made ready to force
the perpetrator's surrender, a shot rang out. Who fired it
was never determined, but there was no doubt that when
the smoke cleared, no white man was left alive.

News of what was officially described as a massacre quickly reached Washington. Though there were eyewitness accounts of Grattan's ineptitude, they fell on deaf ears. From the start, officials had their sights set on punishment. Brigadier General William C. Harney, a tough veteran of southern warfare with the Natives, was dispatched west. His mission was clear: teach the western Sioux a lesson and don't be soft about it.

Less than a year after Grattan's troop had been wiped out, Harney was in the heart of southern Teton Sioux country. Unfortunately, it was a band of Brulés that his force of 1200 men first stumbled upon. For Harney's immediate purposes, they were as good as any other red men. Under the cover of a white flag, Harney launched his attack. When the echoing crack of the last rifle faded, 86 Sioux were dead. All this over a wandering cow! The Sioux found the response difficult to understand and decided that it was best to hand over the brave who had killed the cow to military authorities. As a sign of his goodwill, Harney pledged future protection of the Natives against the western-bound settlers. The Sioux understood this pledge to mean that no white men, save licensed traders, would be permitted to cross their territory except through two designated routes.

In the years that followed, Harney's pledge was ground into the mud by the turning wheels of the settlers' wagons. When a government surveying party arrived at the sacred Black Hills, the Teton Sioux forced them to retreat, finally understanding the necessity of taking matters into their own hands. At about the same time, the Santee Sioux in eastern Minnesota were reaching the same conclusion.

The white men rolled through Minnesota like a prairie tornado, without warning or mercy. Since the day in 1849 when Minnesota became a territory, settlers had campaigned the federal government for greater access to Native lands.

General William C. Harney (the Hornet),
who tried to bring the Sioux into submission

Their lobbying had amounted to little until 1862, when the
new president, Abraham Lincoln, signed the Homestead
Act. The act authorized the granting of a homestead of
160 acres of public lands to settlers who lived on the land
and improved it for five years. Thousands packed up and set
out for the Overland Trail through the northern territories,
the homeland of the Santee Sioux.

The Santee were already ornery. In the early 1850s, they had agreed to confine themselves to a narrow strip of land north of the upper Minnesota River. In return, they were to be given food, equipment and money for trade goods. The annuities rarely arrived on time, and when the money did show up, unscrupulous traders and Indian agents often charged outrageously high prices, robbing the Santee of what was rightfully theirs. Hungry and demoralized, Chief Inkpaduta led the Santee in an uprising that killed 40 white people. He remained free only because the troops of the closest American forts were preoccupied with the Mormon War.

Later, in the spring of 1862, four Santee killed three men, a woman and a girl while the whites and the Natives were engaged in a target competition. Emotions on both sides ran high and only a spark was needed to ignite the situation. It came in the words of an oafish trader, whose opinion of Natives was hardly unique.

It happened that spring when the annuities were again late in arriving. The winter had been a harsh one. Little Crow, chief of one of the Santee Sioux bands, had heard that some traders were giving away trade goods on the promise that annuities would be handed over to the Indian agency once they arrived. He took some of his braves to a local trader, who was far from cooperative.

"What the hell do I care if the winter's been tough on ya? Screw what other traders is doin'," he barked. "Only tradin' I do is when there's cash on the barrelhead. I ain't in this business fer my health, ya know."

"Our people won't make it much longer," replied Little Crow. "Already the hungry children cry themselves to sleep. The weakest have died. Others will soon see their ancestors. I am begging you..."

"Beg all ya want. If yer hungry, eat grass. There's plenty of that. Ya know, you folks is nothin' but a problem. Killin' and beggin'. Soon enough, though, I won't have to deal with the likes of you anymore anyway. A railway's being built that's gonna come right through here. If ya think there's been lotsa whites now, well, ya ain't seen nothin' yet. Get yer stinky red hides outta here and don't come back less'n ya got some money."

Little Crow was a peaceful man, long opposed to war with the white strangers. Despite mounting pressure from his young braves, he had counseled against violence. But even he found it difficult to accept what the trader had said. The white man would be increasing in number! He foresaw a future that held only more of the same suffering and discrimination. He would have to act before those whites arrived. The time, he knew, was right. The northern forts were empty; the blue-coated Long Knives had gone south to fight amongst themselves. On April 18, 1862, the Santee Sioux gave in to their anger and began to fight back.

Their first target was the agency that employed the offensive trader. Once he was killed, his mouth was filled with hay as a reminder to others to treat the Santee with greater respect. From there, they rolled down the valley of the Minnesota River, destroying the town of New Ulm. Other Sioux joined the struggle and quickly there was violence west to the Dakotas and south into Iowa. Soon, some 800 whites lay dead; only 100 of them were soldiers. Hundreds more were taken prisoner, many of them facing an agonizing future that would have them wishing they were dead.

It took a few weeks for the Americans to organize an appropriate response. Alexander Ramsey, the governor of the Minnesota Territory, hired trader and one-time colonel, Henry H. Sibley, to counter the assault. In late September, Sibley defeated Little Crow at Wood Lake, Minnesota. Four hundred Santee were brought before a commission to defend their actions; some 300 were sentenced to hang.

However, President Lincoln intervened personally, introducing a notion of justice to the proceedings. Ignoring the public outcry in Minnesota, he decided to review the reports dealing with the condemned Santee himself. Finally, he decided that only 38 should die. On December 26, the sentence was carried out. Minnesotans saw the bravery of the Santee, as the warriors sang their death songs while nooses were slipped around their necks. Those Santee not killed were sent to a reservation in Nevada. Others, who had escaped Sibley's clutches, fled north to Canada.

Whether it was a deterrent or not, the punishment failed to satisfy the frontier's sharp appetite for revenge, and Colonel Sibley continued to cut a dark red swath westward. His assault eventually led his troops into Hunkpapa territory. The Hunkpapa had not yet engaged the white newcomers in warfare. They had witnessed attacks to the south and to the east and felt the growing pressure of that violence squeezing them. By the mid-1860s, it had arrived at the entrances of their tipis. War seemed inevitable.

Sitting Bull guided his horse to the top of a bluff overlooking the Upper Missouri River. Reaching the crest, he brought the animal to a stop. While the horse grazed on the high grass, Sitting Bull scanned the horizon. An onlooker, had there been one, likely would not have been impressed by the short man, his lower body bent to the shape of his horse and two long black braids extending from a sharp, deep part in the middle of his head. Sitting Bull would not have cared. In the distance, he could see the palisades of

Fort Rice, not far to the west along the Cannonball River. To the south, he could see the Hunkpapa, one of a handful of Sioux tribes, camped in the lower valley. He held his place for some time, since he had much to consider.

General Alfred Sully had sent runners to the Teton tribes requesting that they come to Fort Rice to discuss peace terms that might avoid future bloodshed. Sitting Bull trusted Sully no more than he trusted any white man; trust had to be earned and none of the strangers had yet made the effort. The two had met previously in battle at Killdeer Mountain in the summer of 1864. More than 2000 soldiers attacked the Teton encampment, killing more than 100 Sioux. Months later, they fought to a standoff at the Battle of the Badlands. But Sully's show of force was enough to convince many Teton that it might be a good idea to follow the eastern Sioux's example and negotiate terms.

Sitting Bull opposed any such strategy. As leader of the Strong Hearts society, he advocated war. But he was learning that the war of the white man was a strange affair. He had been taken aback when he first encountered them in 1863. Until that point, he had been content to pursue a policy of peaceful coexistence with the soldiers of the Great Father—the American president. As long as he could hunt the buffalo and live as his ancestors had, he saw no need to fight. But when General Sibley had marched into Hunkpapa territory in pursuit of fleeing Santee Sioux, the Long Knives had attacked his hunting party. Sitting Bull retaliated.

He quickly discovered that fighting them was not like fighting the Crow or other Natives. They stood their ground, carrying their attack with big guns and repeating rifles. Their warfare was just shooting, without the personal contact so important to the Sioux. For the Sioux, there was more honor and greater courage displayed when a warrior

struck the enemy with a hand or a coup stick. When fighting the Long Knives, the charge of a brave warrior was met
with a bullet rather than a countering enemy. Firing rifles
from a distance was a dull affair indeed. Bullets could be put
to much greater use hunting than killing the enemy. Sitting
Bull did not enjoy fighting on these terms.

Still, he had no desire to capitulate, for that was what
negotiation apparently meant to the white men. He found
himself in the minority. Other Sioux, particularly those
who lived near the white man's forts and had become
dependent on their trade goods, were more willing to seek
peace. Sitting Bull thought he might accept peace if it
meant the white men would leave him and his people to
their traditional lands and way of life. But, he knew that
achieving such an agreement was unlikely. The word of
the white man was not to be believed. He rode down from
the bluff and back to camp, convinced that the only course
left open was resistance.

His case was strengthened when he arrived at camp only
to discover that Sully's troops had reached Fort Rice and
promptly killed the 300 Sioux living nearby. And these
were the tribes who wanted peace on the white man's
terms! Immediately, Sitting Bull stripped to his loincloth,
splashed black coloring upon his body and walked through
his camp, slashing his arms with his knife.

"Revenge!" he cried with each step, blood streaming
from the wounds. "We must avenge our brothers and sisters.
Join me and ride on Fort Rice!"

Once he made his way through the Hunkpapa camp, he
moved into the other camps. Soon, he had attracted
300 warriors to accompany him on his revenge expedition.
Painted in red, with only his eagle-feathered headband and
loincloth as coverings, Sitting Bull led the charge. Astride
his favorite war-horse, Bloated Jaw, he struck at the fort's

trading post. Soldiers flooded out from the garrison to repel the attack. The Long Knives met with success when the hot shells of the howitzers began to rain down on the Sioux. At the end of the day, more Sioux than soldiers were dead, but even the latter conceded that the Natives had fought valiantly.

Not, however, Sitting Bull. He counted coup at the trader's post, made off with two horses and then withdrew, choosing not to fight in the battle. It is difficult to understand his course of action. Clearly, fighting the Long Knives was still new and distasteful to him. His domestic situation might also be considered. In his lodge were two wives, three children, his mother, his sister and her son. Sitting Bull was responsible for them all and he was surely aware that his death would bring hardship to them. In fact, his mother, who carried some influence over him, had advised him to be wary in battle. He had proven himself; let the younger braves carry the fight.

But the reason may be as simple as a fleeting vision of Wakan Tanka advising against participation. Sitting Bull never defended his course of action, despite the shame and disgrace that fell upon him. Up to this time no one had doubted his courage. After the battle at Fort Rice, there were those who described his conduct as cowardly. It was a serious charge against a war chief. For his conduct, he was whipped and his two stolen horses were killed. Never again would he let anyone have the opportunity to question his bravery.

Later, it was discovered that the massacre of the Sioux camped around Fort Rice had not happened. They had simply moved on, allegedly after hearing rumors of Sully's intent to attack. The Sioux's armed response derailed any peace talks. If Sitting Bull had his way, they would remain so.

In the summer of 1865, his force of 300 braves successfully engaged General Patrick Connor's 1000-man contingent near the Powder River. And when Sitting Bull wasn't involved in large-scale skirmishes (which were rare), he ravaged the army's lines of communication in guerrilla-style attacks, introducing chaos to the Dakota territory surrounding the northern forts. Mail carriers knew that every time they rode from a fort, their lives were in danger.

Sitting Bull, however, refrained from attacking white settlements. He had no problem with the white settlers if they left the Sioux and their hunting grounds alone. But to interfere with either was to bring down his wrath. He rode the warpath to maintain a way of life. In his eyes, the demands of the Sioux were easy enough to meet: close all roads in Native territory, stop the steamboats, remove the forts and expel all whites, save the traders. The demands were nothing more than what had been promised by the white man in treaties signed in Wyoming and Minnesota. If the Great Father delivered on those promises, Sitting Bull would happily lay down his lance. He wanted only peace, a wish he voiced on more than one occasion.

As Sitting Bull waged war on white encroachment, his destiny was about to take a dramatic turn, one orchestrated by his Uncle Four Horns, long a chief of the Hunkpapa and a respected leader amongst all the Sioux tribes. Four Horns was displeased and disturbed with what he saw happening in Sioux territory. It wasn't so much the rolling waves of white men that were rising in force; it was the poor response of Sioux leadership to the new threat. He himself might have taken a more active role, but time had taken its toll on his energy. The situation called for new leadership.

The solution Four Horns contemplated was revolutionary. He envisioned a supreme chief of all the Sioux, one who would make decisions on all matters, especially those of war and peace. Four Horns would lead the way by abdicating his own position. But he knew that even with his own example, it would be difficult for others to accept. Although the Sioux shared bonds of language and culture, the tribes were as diverse as they were similar. Never had the independent tribes united under the leadership of one man. But, as Four Horns well knew, the situation was unique. Never had they been confronted with such a threat.

In addition, Four Horns believed that he held a trump card: Sitting Bull. He saw his nephew as ideal for the position. His record as a warrior was nearly unblemished. Young braves looked up to the leader of the Strong Hearts. Older Sioux were impressed by his thoughtfulness, seeing wisdom beyond his 36 years. All were in awe of his ability to prophesy. But perhaps his most appealing characteristic was his resilience in the face of white encroachment. He held most dearly to the principle that there should be no contact with the whites, except with licensed traders.

In 1867, Four Horns called for a gathering of the Teton Sioux. A matter of great importance needed to be discussed. Soon, six of the tribes, a few Yanktonai Sioux and some Cheyenne were camped on the lower Powder River. The Hunkpapa chief proposed his plan. Only one-third of those present supported Sitting Bull's position regarding the white man. But all were only too aware that fighting as autonomous tribes had met with little success. With the enthusiastic support of important chiefs such as Crazy Horse and Gall (men who would remain key allies of Sitting Bull throughout the years), agreement came quickly. Only the Brulés and the southern Oglala, neither present, refused to recognize Sitting Bull as their chief. The decision was followed by an elaborate ceremony of investiture.

Sioux chief Gall (1840–1894), one of the delegates that
Sitting Bull sent to negotiate the Fort Laramie Treaty of 1868

Sitting Bull sat in his tipi while preparations were made.
Eventually, four chiefs went to his lodge. Before its
entrance, they unfurled a buffalo robe. They went into his
tipi and escorted him out onto the shimmering fur. Each
then took a corner of the robe and carried Sitting Bull to
a lodge built for the ceremony. He rode not as a king who

rules, but a man who serves. Once he was placed in a position of honor, Four Horns spoke.

"Today, we have a new chief and renewed hope. It is his responsibility to ensure that the Teton are well fed, that the miseries of want do not throw their long shadows across our tipis. When you say fight, we will; when you say make peace, we will lay down our bows and arrows. We will smoke the Sacred Calf Pipe so that Wakan Tanka may bless our decision."

Four Horns removed the pipe from its tripod and lit it. He held the stem towards the earth so that it might hold them well. He presented it to the four winds so that they might not blow cruelly. Finally, he held it towards the sun so that its light might guide their way. The pipe was then passed around the circle, from right to left, in the direction of the sun's journey. All puffed deeply, exhaling the smoke with a prayer that their decision would be looked upon favorably by Wakan Tanka. Finally, the pipe was given to Sitting Bull.

"Use it to pray for our people," advised Four Horns.

Sitting Bull took the pipe and remained silent as those who wished to speak did so. Stories of his life were told, rekindling memories of acts of bravery, generosity and courage, characteristics that defined the man. Others reminded him to think always of the welfare of his people, especially the poor. Fly high like the eagle, others suggested, the wise chief of all birds. Black Moon, who had taken on the responsibilities of Sun Dreamer, suggested that Sitting Bull always consult with Wakan Tanka.

Crazy Horse, leader of the northern Oglala, was installed as Sitting Bull's second-in-command. Although years younger than Sitting Bull, he had long devoted himself to fighting the white man. In fact, his only possessions were his war-horse and weapons. His reputation as a warrior was exceeded only by Sitting Bull's.

Sitting Bull was presented with a bow, 10 arrows and a flintlock rifle. More importantly, he was given a spectacular war bonnet. It consisted of a beaded headband, ermine pendants and a crown and tail of double eagle feathers that stretched to the ground. Every feather represented a coup of the man who had contributed it. It was a fitting symbol of the Teton Sioux's courage.

Sitting Bull was guided from the lodge and led to a magnificent white stallion. Once he was lifted into its saddle, a line formed behind him consisting of the four warrior societies, all dressed in their finest clothes, with their shields held high and their eagle feathers standing proud. They chanted as he rode, falling silent only when Sitting Bull spoke. His words came in the form of song.

"Ye tribes, behold me. The chiefs of old are gone. Myself, I shall take courage."

A new beginning for the Teton Sioux had taken shape.

The Black Robe rode towards the Hunkpapa camp. Father Pierre Jean De Smet was old, his white hair and creased face betraying his years. He had spent many of those years among the Natives of the Plains and his efforts had earned him respect among those people. When he asked Sitting Bull to meet with him to discuss peace, the chief agreed. He would not turn down an opportunity for peace.

De Smet's small escort of 80 friendly Sioux were some two weeks out of Fort Rice and headed towards the fork of the Yellowstone and Powder rivers, the location of Sitting Bull's camp. Long before they reached the camp, Sitting Bull was aware of their impending arrival. A few miles from camp, De Smet was met by a delegation of 400 Hunkpapa warriors, led by Sitting Bull himself. The priest stopped and unfurled his flag. Though none of the Sioux could read the name of Jesus, all felt comfortable with the drawing of the Virgin Mary, for it reminded them of the White Buffalo Woman.

Sitting Bull left his warriors and rode to the priest. They shook hands.

"Sitting Bull," said De Smet, "the Great Father wishes to make peace. He wants you to live amongst your people on your own lands, as free men."

"The soldiers of the Great Father have waged war upon us. I have killed many of them," confided Sitting Bull. "But as bad as I have been towards them, I am willing to be just as good."

"If you are good," continued De Smet, "the Great Father promises rations so that your people will never want."

"I have my own plans for my people," countered the Hunkpapa chief. "If they follow what I say, they will never be hungry. Wakan Tanka has bestowed the bountiful land that provides for us. All that is wanted from the white strangers are their traders—no soldiers, no settlers. Come, I will listen."

Sitting Bull signaled his warriors, and the four chiefs who had accompanied him rode over to meet the priest. They led De Smet into the camp. He marveled at the sight of 600 Hunkpapa tipis arranged in a great circle, simple yet impressive against the vivid green grass of the valley. Sitting Bull took the priest to his own lodge, in the middle of the circle. He posted a guard of 20 warriors and spoke loudly so that many might hear.

"See that the Black Robe gets plenty of food and drink. He must stay in his tipi and no harm must come to him or his goods." Some of the Hunkpapa would have enthusiastically slipped a knife between the ribs of the white man.

"Tomorrow, the great peace council will meet," he informed De Smet.

Mid-morning, De Smet was taken to a great lodge that covered half an acre. He sat on one of the four buffalo robes that were at its center. Sitting Bull, Four Horns and Black Moon, another important Hunkpapa chief, joined him there. Other chiefs sat nearby, while the rest of the lodge was filled with their warriors. Outside, some 5000 Sioux gathered.

The council began with a dance of many warriors dressed in their finest apparel. When Four Horns noticed sweat glistening on their skin, he waved for the dancing to stop. He then lit his peace pipe. After completing the ritual offerings, he took the pipe to the seated men according to rank. Starting with De Smet, all took a few puffs. Once all were united before Wakan Tanka, Black Moon addressed the visitor.

"Speak, Black Robe. Our ears are open and we are ready to hear your words."

De Smet said a short prayer and began his speech.

"I am glad that you have agreed to let me speak. I have brought tobacco so that you will know that my words are true. The war between your people and those of the Great Father must stop. Think not only of yourselves, but also of your children. The Great Father means you no harm. He will help you. He wishes you to leave the past and to bury your hatred for the whites. He wants peace. His chiefs wait for you at Fort Rice."

Though he did not say it, the impetus for his peace offer was largely Sioux successes in battle. The activities of Sitting Bull in the north and the Ogala chief Red Cloud in the south had resulted not only in bloodshed for the whites, but also in unexpectedly large military expenditures. A willingness to end Native hostilities had broken out among officials in

Red Cloud (1822–1909), Sitting Bull's southern
counterpart in the Sioux fight against white encroachment
into the Black Hills; he disagreed with Sitting Bull's leadership

Washington. Whether the Sioux would be as willing to turn
the other cheek, a concept alien to them, was another matter.

The Sioux remained silent as Black Robe stood and
unfurled his banner.

"This is the flag of peace. As a measure of my sincerity
and good wishes for your people, I will leave it with you.
Please consider it a blessing from God, Him from whom all

blessings come. Avoid bad thoughts for they lead to bad actions. Always remember that peace must reign in your land. Only goodwill come from that. I will continue to pray for your good. Now, I am ready to listen."

Black Moon rose and began to speak for his people.

"I am glad that Black Robe has come. His words are what my heart wants. But my heart is scarred with the many wounds ripped open by the Great Father's people. We do not want war with them, but they brought it to us. Our land is red with blood and the animals do not come as they once did. The smell of death is offensive to them. Our land is marred by the roads built by the white man. Our trees no longer stand as they once did. The white man has built his forts on our land. The white man ruins our land.

"I have said it before," he continued, "I do not wish to sell the land that my father lived and died on. I like to trade, but I do not want annuities; I do not want gifts. I do not wish to see our land filled with whites. Some are good, but too many are bad. They treat us badly. We accept your tobacco and your advice. In a sign of peace we extend our hands before Wakan Tanka."

Black Moon fell silent and turned to his people.

"Let the past be forgotten," he concluded.

When Black Moon was seated, Sitting Bull stood and addressed the assembly.

"Black Robe, I thank you for praying to the Great Spirit for us. When I first saw you coming, my heart was filled with hatred, as I remembered the past. I commanded it to be silent and it was. When I shook hands with you, I was glad.

"I have always been a fighting fool. My people have made me so. When the wars with the white man started, they were confused. They believed that the whites caused

General William T. Sherman and commissioners
in council with Native chiefs at Fort Laramie, Wyoming
to discuss terms of the Fort Laramie Treaty of 1868

their problems and they became crazy. They pushed me forward and I have done many bad things to the whites. They
are responsible. Now, before them all, I say welcome to the
messenger of peace.

"I have said what can be said. My people will return
with you to Fort Rice to meet the white chiefs. We will
make peace. If the Great Father wishes to be my friend, I
will be his friend."

Sitting Bull shook hands with De Smet and he was met
with the thunderous applause of those assembled.

As the applause died down, he stood again.

"My friends, I have forgotten two things. I will not sell any of our land. And the forts of the white men must be abandoned."

Saved for the last and therefore doubly emphasized, Sitting Bull's concluding remark struck at the heart of the matter. His conditions were nothing more than what he had always wanted.

Sitting Bull did not journey with De Smet to Fort Rice. Instead, he sent a delegation of lesser chiefs led by his friend Gall, instructing him to refuse all presents and to hold fast to his insistence that the forts be removed and that the steamboats be stopped. On July 2, 1868, Gall and his delegation met with three commissioners and signed the Fort Laramie Treaty on behalf of the Hunkpapa Sioux.

It was a victory for Sitting Bull and the Teton Sioux, though, undoubtedly, there were aspects of the treaty they could not grasp fully. It is not even clear whether Sitting Bull understood that Gall's signature bound him to its terms, as the American government contended. The treaty established the Great Sioux Reservation, located in the southwestern quarter of the Dakota Territory. It extended south to the Nebraska border, east to the Missouri River, north just above the Grand River and west to the Little Missouri River and the Black Hills. At Red Cloud's insistence, it stipulated that the American forts on the Bozeman Trail be abandoned and that the trail itself be closed.

Most important was the clause barring whites both from settling on the territory and passing through it without prior consent of the Sioux. While the government would provide rations, the Sioux could hunt legally on any land north of the Platte River, as long as there were enough buffalo. When the buffalo were gone, the Sioux agreed that they would relinquish their right to occupy any territory outside the reservation. For their part, the Sioux were required to keep the peace. Sitting Bull got what he wanted. As long as the white man obeyed the terms of the treaty, he would not raise his lance against them.

For the most part, Sitting Bull kept his word. Save an occasional raid on the cattle herds of the northern forts, his war activities over the following years were confined mostly to skirmishes with other tribes. These were the battles of old, honorable fights to protect or to expand hunting grounds. In a particularly intense battle near Big Dry Creek on the upper Yellowstone River in the early winter of 1870, 30 Crow were killed. Although Sitting Bull counted three coup, he mourned after the fight, because his youngest uncle, Looks-for-Him-in-a-Tent, was killed. An encounter with the Flathead near the Musselshell River a few months later also proved memorable.

Four of the Teton Sioux tribes had gathered near the mouth of the Rosebud River. Many people were assembled when Sitting Bull rose and proclaimed that a vision approached. As he walked away, he sang. Soon, he returned and lit his pipe. His eyes followed the smoke as it drifted to Wakan Tanka. Finally, he spoke.

"In two days, there will be a battle. Many enemies will die, as will some Sioux. I saw a ball of fire approach me. It disappeared when it reached me."

Scouts returned with the news that the Flathead were camped nearby, encroaching on the Sioux buffalo grounds. Sitting Bull prepared a plan of attack.

"Our young warriors will ride fast horses to the enemy. When the Flathead see they are few in number, they will give chase. They will be led back to the older warriors, who will remain hidden. They will be trapped."

The plan was met with great enthusiasm. It worked as conceived and only three Sioux died, a small number compared with the Flathead losses. However, Sitting Bull, as he prophesied, was injured. An arrow passed through his fore-arm. The wound healed well. Sitting Bull's reputation as both a war chief and a *wichasha wakan* grew.

Evening arrived and with it, the surveyors called it a day. There were 20 of them, all employed by the Northern Pacific Railroad and charged with identifying the best route the company could take through Dakota and Montana. The surveyors weren't alone. Under the command of Major Eugene M. Baker, a military escort of nearly 500 soldiers out of Fort Ellis accompanied them. It was 1872 and, by then, building railways was an enterprise that had the full support of the American government, which was convinced of both the necessity and inevitability of western expansion in any form.

The surveying crew made its way back across the Yellowstone River, opposite the mouth of Arrow Creek, where the base camp was situated. They settled into another meal of beans and pork and began discussing the subject that was on all their minds.

"It's damn pretty country out here."

"Yeah, it's pretty, but is it safe?"

The surveyors knew they were in the northern heart of Teton Sioux country. The fertile plains rolling from the Yellowstone teemed with animals. In fact, the Sioux knew it as the Elk River. It had not always been their territory. Not so long ago, the Crow had called it home. Many Sioux had died in the struggle to gain control of it, and they weren't about to let it slip from their fingers.

"One of the officers was telling me that the Sioux aren't pleased to see us here. Said that a Sioux chief named

Spotted Eagle met with Colonel Stanley in the spring. The chief said he knew that the surveyors meant that a railroad was coming."

"Pretty sharp!"

The comment elicited an uneasy chuckle from the handful of men.

"The Indian continued to say that his people had never agreed to allow a railroad through the territory south of the Yellowstone. Claimed the treaty of '68 didn't allow it."

"Does it?"

"Hard to say. Could be argued that it's unceded territory. The Indians, at least, think it's theirs. Before Spotted Eagle left, he threatened that his people would tear up the railroad and kill its builders until the last Sioux was dead."

"Shit." That seemed to sum it up for all and the terse comment was met with silence.

Unknown to the surveyors, the Sioux were aware of Baker's every movement. As they tracked west, Sitting Bull was regularly apprised of their approach. The day after the army set up camp near Arrow Creek, the Sioux set up their own camp nearby, but far away enough to remain undetected. A council was called to determine a course of action.

"We've gathered to fight the Crow," said Sitting Bull, "but it seems we have a greater problem. The Long Knives are above the Elk, where they have no right to be. They are a grasping people. They always want more. We have allowed them to march along the Missouri. But now, they are at the banks of the Elk. Tomorrow, it will be the rivers that flow to it."

Sitting Bull spoke to a large gathering. In addition to the Hunkpapa were the chiefs of the Oglala, Sans Arc, Miniconjou, Blackfoot, Brulés and Cheyenne. Sitting Bull's close allies, Gall and Crazy Horse, were present. All were attentive, keenly aware that the lands surrounding the Yellowstone were as important to them as the blood that had been shed in taking them from the Crow.

"We have promised not to fight, but they have broken treaty. Those without honor will listen only to force," said Sitting Bull.

"It is soon time to hunt the buffalo. Perhaps our bullets are better used there," suggested one.

"If the white man comes, there will be no buffalo," countered Sitting Bull. "But perhaps it is best to speak with the Long Knives first." The suggestion was met with murmurs of agreement, which were quickly silenced by the sharp cracks of gunfire. A brave soon stood at the entrance of the lodge.

"Come," said Sitting Bull. "What has happened?"

"Young warriors, Brulés and Hunkpapa, have attacked the Long Knives' camp."

Sitting Bull smiled, his broad face alight.

"The courage of youth. It seems our decision is made." With that, the council dissolved.

Throughout the night, the Natives and the army exchanged shots. As they settled into defensive positions to await the light of day, there was little in the way of casualties. One unfortunate Hunkpapa was Plenty Lice. He rode the daring line and was killed. The Sioux watched as the Long Knives threw his lifeless body on a campfire. They bristled at this sign of disrespect.

Morning found Sitting Bull and Crazy Horse atop a bluff overlooking the battlefield.

"The Long Knives are well hidden," said Crazy Horse. "Our braves cannot reach them among the dense brush."

"Yes," agreed Sitting Bull. But he was less concerned with the position of the soldiers than he was with the actions of his own men.

"Our braves continue to run the daring line. There is no need for it. They have proven their courage. Look! It is the same group. They run for a third time!"

Crazy Horse squinted his eyes against the rising sun.

"They are not any braves, Sitting Bull," he said as he recognized them. "They are followers of Long Holy."

Sitting Bull sighed. Long Holy claimed to have had a vision, which he interpreted to mean that those who rode with him were cloaked by a magic invisible blanket that prevented bullets from striking. Again and again, Long Holy rode his followers between the opposing forces. A few were hit, but none were killed.

"It is enough," declared Sitting Bull. "Their courage has become foolishness. I cannot allow our young men to be wounded or to die. I will stop this."

Sitting Bull rode down the gentle slope of the bluff to the Sioux line of the fight.

"Brothers," he called. "Your courage is not in doubt. No longer run the daring line. The shedding of your blood does us no good."

"Is this the great Sitting Bull who speaks?" challenged Long Holy. "Perhaps he forgets what it is to be brave. Age and blood upset a man's stomach easily."

"He talks a good fight," said one of the braves. "He's always talking, saying how it should be done." Some of the braves were upset at Sitting Bull's unsolicited advice. Young men preferred actions to words and saw him as increasingly nosy and bossy. "I am young, but I would rather my eyes see than my ears hear."

Rumblings suggested that many others agreed.

Long Holy and others had questioned his courage. Sitting Bull's position as the Teton chief demanded no doubt remain. He dismounted, took his pipe and tobacco from a pouch on his horse and, with his weapons in hand, walked to the open land stretching between the opposing forces. There he sat, his two eagle feathers identifying him as a simple Sioux warrior, little different than his brothers.

"Other Sioux who wish to smoke, join me," he said.

It was a challenge as much as an invitation. Soon, four others joined him, two Sioux and two Cheyenne. Sharp-eyed watchers might have noticed that their journey was taken on shaky legs. When they arrived, Sitting Bull filled the bowl of his pipe and, with the use of his flint and steel, lit it. Placing the stem between his lips, he contentedly took a few long, deep drags. He passed it to his companions, whose trembling hands and short quick puffs suggested they were more aware of the small clouds of earth kicked up around them by the enemies' bullets than was Sitting Bull. The pipe made a few rounds before the ball of tobacco was spent.

Once it was, Sitting Bull picked up a stick and cleaned out the bowl. He placed it back in his pouch, rose and walked slowly back to the admiring Sioux line, his limp emphasized for effect. He hadn't taken a few steps, when the others rushed past him, deterred neither by courage nor disability. One left in such haste that he forgot his weapons. He chose not to retrieve them.

When Sitting Bull arrived, he was greeted with silent awe. Who had ever seen such an act of bravery? Was there a coup counted that displayed such courage? What words could describe his daring? To a people who placed great value in a man's willingness to risk his own life in the face of great danger, Sitting Bull's action was unmatched. It served to solidify his authority among the Sioux further.

Finally, Sitting Bull broke the silence.

"It is enough. Today's fighting is over."

None questioned his decision. Their morale intact, the Sioux pulled back. The Battle of Arrow Creek was indecisive;

General William Tecumseh Sherman (1820–1891),
Civil War hero and, later, the army's general-in-chief

neither side could claim clear victory. However, the fighting had deepened the surveyors' fears. They subsequently refused to go south of the Yellowstone and made hurried measurements near the northerly Musselshell River before quickly heading back to Fort Ellis. Spotted Eagle's prediction hadn't quite been met, but the Sioux could claim, with some truth, that their first blow against the Northern

Pacific Railroad—and everything it stood for—had been successful.

However, success was a relative term and, in this case, it was short lived. The episode and others like it only strengthened American resolve. General William Tecumseh Sherman, General-in-Chief of the American army, gave voice to that determination before Congress in early 1873.

"The Northern Pacific Railroad is a national enterprise. We are forced to protect those who survey and construct it against the most warlike Indians on the continent. They will fight for every foot of the line." Left unspoken, of course, was the American willingness to engage them in that battle, regardless of where the line might go.

Sitting Bull, for his part, concluded that he would no longer engage the white man unless he brought the battle to the Sioux. "Let the white man come," he confided to Crazy Horse. "If he comes shooting, I will shoot back; if not, I will leave them be."

But the soldiers and surveyors continued to come. In the late summer of 1873, the opposing forces met near where the Bighorn River joined the Yellowstone River. Again the fighting proved inconclusive, with few losses on either side. But the Battle of the Yellowstone was an important one. The series of skirmishes with the Sioux supported Sherman's prediction, and eastern financiers were reluctant to continue to press west in the face of the huge costs involved. For the time being, the rail would not extend past Bismarck in the northern center of Dakota.

The encounters around the Yellowstone had done much to raise Sitting Bull's reputation among the white population. Increasingly, his name was recognized, not as the brave warrior he was known to be among his people, but rather as the most savage of Native chiefs. By the end of 1873, the Americans no longer talked of making peace with Sitting Bull.

Finally, the Battle of the Yellowstone introduced the Sioux to a Long Knife who would play a crucial role in their future: Lieutenant Colonel George Armstrong Custer.

CHAPTER THREE

The Fight for Paha Sapa

Spring had arrived on the Missouri River and Fort Abraham Lincoln was at the mercy of the heat and the mosquitoes that came with it. It was damned uncomfortable. Only the recent order from General Sheridan that the men would be moving south to explore the Black Hills brought any relief. But the departure date was still weeks away and Lieutenant Colonel George Custer, charged with leading the exercise, was irritated. The bugs and the weather were bearable, but somehow the Natives had discovered the army's plans and the continuous stream of Sioux intent on dissuading his Seventh Cavalry from its exploratory mission was trying his patience. He bit his tongue and listened to the appeals of yet another one.

"The Black Hills are *Paha Sapa*; they are sacred," explained the Sioux emissary. "They are our home. They have been since the beginning."

"I've heard the story, chief. Great flood, eagle, a bloody strange marriage…," sighed Custer. "Fact is that times have changed. But you're right about one thing. Plenty of mystery

Paha Sapa, the Black Hills, sacred home of the Sioux

surrounds those hills and Americans want to know what's in them."

"The Laramie Treaty places the Black Hills in the Great Sioux Reservation," objected the Sioux.

"Well, now, if you folks'd read that treaty, you'd know that the American government can send its officials onto that reservation whenever it wants. Sorry chief, there's nothing you can do about it. Good day." Custer looked down at some papers on his desk, ending the conversation.

The expedition to explore the Black Hills set out in early July 1874, marching south to the band's rendition of *The Girl I Left Behind Me*. At the front of the column, on his favorite bay horse, was Custer. He cut a dashing figure, his long blond hair falling to his shoulders beneath a slouch hat pinned up on the left side. A generous and unkempt mustache gave no hint of a mouth. Fringes hung from the arms of his buckskin jacket and lustrous black riding boots reached up to his knees. The butt of a pistol extended from a belt and the tip of his long sword fell beneath his heel. Here was the kind of adventure he wanted, and he was ready.

Some 15 years earlier Custer had graduated from the prestigious military academy at West Point, but only just. Three more demerits added to those he'd already accumulated and he would have been unceremoniously shown the door. He'd been an officer for only a couple of days when he faced his first court-martial for dereliction of duty. Memories of his often less-than-stellar behavior faded when he won honors for himself in the Civil War. Nature made him flamboyant, courageous and enthusiastic, and design put the characteristics to effective use. He'd never met a politician or a ranking officer he didn't like and rarely was he unsuccessful at currying their favors. Before long, his abilities caught the eye of General Philip Sheridan, who would become one of his greatest supporters. Still in his early 20s, he was made a brevet major general.

When the Civil War ended, Custer accepted a posting on the Plains, certain that in the subjugation of the Natives he would find the glory he so desperately sought. Promoted to the rank of lieutenant colonel, he was sent to Fort Riley,

George Armstrong Custer (1839–1876), commander
of the Seventh Cavalry, which was wiped out by Sitting Bull's
warriors at the Battle of the Little Bighorn

Kansas, to serve with the Seventh Cavalry. It wasn't long
before he was again arrested for disobeying orders (he went
AWOL to visit his sick wife). His case wasn't strengthened
when it was revealed that he didn't hesitate to shoot desert-
ers who sought flight rather than suffer his long forced
marches. In November 1867, he was suspended from the
army for one year.

He could thank "Custer's Luck," as the soldiers had come to call Custer's uncanny ability to land on his feet, that General Sheridan had been made commander of the Department of the Missouri. Sheridan was charged with bringing the southern Plains Natives under control. Initially, the campaign went poorly and his troops suffered losses. To turn the tide, Sheridan believed it necessary to bring in officers whose desire to fight was unquestioned. He applied for Custer's reinstatement. In the fall of 1868, Custer joined Sheridan at Camp Supply on the Beaver Creek, anxious to polish his tarnished reputation. He didn't have to wait long.

Sheridan gave him command of the Seventh Cavalry and ordered him south to the Washita River. He wasn't sent to parley. The soldiers found the Native camp during the night and surrounded it. When dawn arrived, Custer directed the band to begin playing *Gary Owen*, his favorite fighting song. As the notes filled the air, the attack began, and it wasn't long before the camp was wiped out. Later, it was discovered they had attacked Black Kettles' Cheyenne, a band friendly to the Americans. Neither the army nor westerners gave that a second thought, because the Seventh Cavalry's crushing victory brought peace to Kansas.

The years that followed Custer's triumph at Washita saw no other events quite so grand. Eventually, he was transferred to Fort Rice to protect the surveying crews of the Northern Pacific Railroad. Through 1873, the Sioux nipped at his flanks, although injury and theft were never more than minimal. Still, combined with the Sioux efforts on the Yellowstone River, the Native offensive was enough to halt plans for the railroad's western expansion. The Sioux victory had an unforeseen result. It gave the army an excuse to reconnoiter in the Black Hills, a mountainous region cloaked in the unknown and subject to tantalizing rumors of gold.

By late July, the Seventh Cavalry had reached the outskirts of the Black Hills, a name that does disservice to both their great size and rich colors. Even a quick glance at the land that rolled to the base of the hills was enough to convince Custer that it was well suited for grazing. The many stands of oak and poplar provided ready building material and fuel. The peaks towered over hidden valleys and, before their majesty, even a pragmatic military man like Custer stood in awe. They cradled blue lakes of clear, alkali-free water and fresh streams feeding the Cheyenne River. Colorful flowers blossomed on the shorelines, ran across open grasslands and scurried up the hillsides. Everything about the Black Hills suggested they were well suited for agriculture. Animals were plentiful and Custer could easily appreciate why the Sioux considered it so dear.

As he wrote of these enticing details in his official report, he knew it would be difficult to stop the arrival of settlers, who would surely want access to the uncommonly inspiring region. When he included his discovery of gold, he knew it would be damn near impossible.

Custer was right. Despite his caution about the amount of gold he'd found (carefully noting that the need for a more detailed study of the local geology meant there was no good reason for a miner to expect to get rich), the discovery took on a life of its own. Greatly exaggerated, word spread like a prairie fire. Gold fever boiled men's blood and, within a year, over 1000 prospectors were toiling in the Black Hills. More were en route along what the Sioux called "Thieves Road," the trail that Custer took on his expedition. The army took the position that the miners shouldn't be there. Its policy was based more on practical concerns than legal ones. It didn't want to cause

A panoramic view of the U.S. army camp
during Custer's Black Hills Expedition of 1874

trouble with the Sioux. The army prevented some miners
from arriving and expelled others found there. Despite its
desire and its efforts, neither of which could be described
as zealous, the miners kept coming, and soon, irresistible
pressure was exerted on the federal government. The message was clear: do what had to be done, but get control of
the Black Hills.

There was, of course, a problem. The government was aware that the Laramie Treaty of 1868 gave the Sioux title to the Black Hills. To address the troubling legality of the situation, the Allison Commission was established and charged with extinguishing Native title to the region. In September, the commissioners arrived at the Red Cloud Agency, just below the southwest corner of the Great Sioux Reservation near Camp Robinson. There, they sent word to the agency Natives—those who had entered into agreements with the American government and had chosen to live on the reserve—that they wished to discuss terms for purchasing the Black Hills. The assumption was that agency Natives would be more willing to deal than would be the more independent hunting bands.

Some Sioux, a few hundred out of the 10,000 that represented the entire population, were willing to listen. Red Cloud of the southern Oglala, who disagreed with both Sitting Bull's leadership and his aggressive attitude, was one of those.

"Surely you are aware that Americans are currently in the Black Hills," said one of the commissioners. "That is not likely to change. We are presenting you with an opportunity, one that will see you justly compensated for the territory. The offer is six million dollars."

"The Laramie Treaty says that the Black Hills are ours forever," replied Red Cloud. "My people fought for that and it is only fitting, as they have always been ours. But I am a realistic man, and although the changes that come are difficult to accept, accept them I will. For seventy million dollars."

"Seventy million!" exclaimed the commissioners in concert.

"That is hardly reasonable," barked one.

"Reasonable or not, it is my price," concluded Red Cloud.

His demand ended the discussions. The commissioners returned to Washington, incensed and frustrated. In their report, they suggested that the government should fix a fair price for the Black Hills and present the offer to the Sioux as a *fait accompli*. The government was caught between a rock— the desire of settlers for access to the region—and a hard place—their word that the Black Hills belonged to the Sioux. In late 1875, President Grant called a meeting of his senior generals and Native officials. They quickly settled on a plan of action, one giving recognition to the new order in the West.

"It seems, gentlemen," concluded the president, placing his hands on the table and rising above those seated around him, "that the only solution is war."

"It is easily justified," agreed one of the generals. "The Sioux have been raiding in the territory around the Yellowstone for some time, violating the '68 Laramie Treaty."

"Though," reminded another, "those Sioux did not sign the treaty."

"A Sioux is a Sioux, goddamn it!" bellowed another. "The president is right. The Indians will not succumb until they feel the full might of the United States."

"It's settled then," said Grant. "We will keep in effect the order barring miners from the Black Hills, but we will make no effort to enforce it. Their mounting presence will soon put an end to the nagging disputes over possession. We will also demand that all Sioux hunting bands return to the reservation. Once there, they can be made dependent on annuities and trade goods. A dependent people are a pliant people."

"The order needs teeth, sir," said Zachariah Chandler, the Secretary of the Interior. "What will we do if the bands refuse to return? Sitting Bull's hostility towards Americans is well known and it is likely he will not obey the directive."

"You direct the commissioner of Indian Affairs to notify all Sioux and Cheyenne living off the reservation to return before January 31. Should they fail to do so, they will be considered hostile Indians, enemies of the American government. The army will be charged with compelling all hostiles to obey."

When February arrived, Sitting Bull, as expected, had not returned to the Great Sioux Reservation. He and the other Sioux who had rejected the American government's demands were immediately labeled hostile. Within days, the government declared war on them.

In March 1876, General George Crook, "Three Stars," as he was known to the Sioux because of his insignia of rank (one star on each shoulder and one on his hat), set out from Fort Fetterman, just north of Fort Laramie. Only months before, he had been transferred from the American southwest, where he had enjoyed success containing the local Natives on their reserves. With him went one of the largest military forces yet to ride against the Sioux. The new government directive that identified the followers of Sitting Bull and Crazy Horse as hostile Sioux to be conquered was still fresh in his mind. Crook was in search of Crazy Horse's band of Oglala. Unknown to him, his scout directed him to the Cheyenne camp of Two Moons, near the mouth of the Powder River.

Two Moons and his band were peaceful Natives, yet Crook attacked. The Cheyenne held their own, but were ultimately forced to abandon their camp, which was subsequently burned by Crook's men. Refugees and at the mercy of winter's cold grip, the Cheyenne stumbled into

General George (Three Stars) Crook (1828–1890), who
attacked Two Moon's peaceful band of Cheyenne, thinking it
was Crazy Horse's band of hostile Oglala

Crazy Horse's camp. Upon their arrival, the two chiefs met
and Two Moons described the encounter.

"We do not want to fight the Long Knives, but they
have brought the battle to us," proclaimed Two Moons.
"The stand of Crazy Horse against the white invaders is
well known. Now the Cheyenne stand with you."

"We welcome you with open arms. Let us go and see Sitting Bull," said Crazy Horse.

When the Oglala and Cheyenne arrived at the Hunkpapa camp, they were greeted enthusiastically. Well fed and given new supplies, the arrivals marveled at the generosity of the Hunkpapa. The mood turned black, however, when Sitting Bull was told of the unprovoked attack. The chief became incensed.

"Who are these Long Knives!?" he shouted. "They agree that *Paha Sapa* is ours forever and then they demand to own it. Money they will give us for food. I get my food from *Paha Sapa* and do not need what the Long Knives offer. It is known that I accept no price for them. And when they learn of this? They attack! They are not to be trusted!"

"My brothers," he continued, "we are as islands in a lake of white men. If we continue to stand separately, they will destroy us all. We must unite. Since meeting with the Black Robe, I have raised my lance only in self-defense. I have been patient and put up with much. Well, now the Long Knives have come shooting; they have brought war. War they will have," he concluded.

Sitting Bull dispatched runners to every Sioux, Cheyenne and Arapaho camp west of the Missouri River. He beseeched them to join with him and engage the Long Knives in one great battle on the Rosebud River. Many responded to his call, and the spring of 1876 saw the trails leading to Sitting Bull's camp flowing with Natives. The sight was testament both to the respect he commanded and to their desperation. Although not all who heard his plea came, there were nearly 500 lodges gathered, representing some 1000 warriors.

In late spring, Sitting Bull called a war council. He was chosen to lead the Sioux attack, while Two Moons would command the Cheyenne. By early June, this large gathering of Natives, united by a single cause, made their way towards the valley of the Greasy Grass, or the Little Bighorn River, as the whites knew it. They made camp near the Rosebud River just east of the Little Bighorn and prepared for battle. Sitting Bull walked through the camps and sang his new war song.

"You tribes, what are you saying? I have been a war chief. All the same, I'm still living." Men and women took heart.

Jumping Bull was busy with his arrows when his adopted brother Sitting Bull arrived at his lodge. One glance at the older man caused Jumping Bull to drop what he was doing and stand. Sitting Bull's hair fell loosely about his shoulders, his two tight braids undone and his eagle feather headband discarded. The red paint that he usually wore on his face was washed off.

"Jumping Bull, gather White Bull and the son of Black Moon and come with me," he directed.

Jumping Bull did as ordered and the four men rode south. Although curious about Sitting Bull's intent, the men held their tongues. Within a few hours, they had reached the top of a butte, the highest land within view. Below, the fork of the Yellowstone and the Rosebud rivers was visible. Once there, Sitting Bull revealed his purpose.

"My brothers, I bring you here so that I may renew my vow to Wakan Tanka before witnesses."

He retrieved his pipe from a pouch and held it so that its stem pointed at the sun. His companions saw it was wrapped in sage, a sacred plant to the Sioux. He then began to sing for mercy. After a few moments, his singing stopped and he offered a prayer.

"Wakan Tanka, save me. Bring the wild animals near so that my people will not go hungry when the snow falls. Let those with good hearts have more power, so that my people can get along with them and be happy. Do this, and I will dance the Sun Dance. From me you will have a red blanket and a buffalo."

Sitting Bull sat down.

"Smoke with me, my brothers." The pipe was lit and passed around. The smoke rose to Wakan Tanka. He would see it and know their honesty. When the tobacco stopped burning, Sitting Bull unwrapped the sage from the pipe stem and wiped it over his face.

"Let us return," he said simply.

They were not long in camp when Sitting Bull called White Bull to join him on a hunt. Success came quickly and the pair soon had three buffalo at their feet.

"This one is the fattest," determined Sitting Bull, pointing at the cow. "Help me roll it onto its stomach." Once so positioned, Sitting Bull splayed the animal's legs and ensured that its head lay flat on its chin.

"Wakan Tanka, here is the buffalo I promised you. In three days, I will dance before the sun and you will have your red blanket." He needed time to prepare for the important ceremony. It would honor Wakan Tanka as always, but would also serve to unify the Sioux and their Cheyenne allies, and give them direction in their dealings with the Long Knives. Sitting Bull wanted it to be perfect.

Three tipis were built near the circle where the dance was to be performed. One tipi was for the singers, one for the council and one served as a medicine lodge. Their entrances faced east, to greet the rising sun. The dance circle was about 60 feet in diameter and would be centered with the Sun Dance pole. Gravel was sprinkled liberally on the ground where the dance would be performed, to increase the pain of the bare-footed dancer.

In the council tipi gathered the Sioux elders, there to tell the stories of their coups. With 10 Sioux tribes and some

Cheyenne camped on the west bank of the Rosebud River, many tales were told, although some chose only to watch and listen and not actively participate in the ritual. While their stories unfolded, the singers readied themselves in their tipi. In the medicine lodge, objects to be used during the dance were prepared. Of particular importance were the unblemished buffalo skull, its red cloth altar, the awl to cut Sitting Bull's flesh and the white loin cloth and rabbit-skin anklets that would serve as his only coverings.

The evening before the dance, the singers performed. First was the song of the buffalo, a song for plenty. Then came the song of the people, a song for long and good life. Finally came the song of the dance, one for good weather so that the dance might proceed uninterrupted. The chanting and drumming, the beating heart of the community, pulsed through the night.

Early the next morning, a young 15-year-old girl of irreproachable character, who had been selected to be the White Buffalo Maiden of the Sun Dance, chose the tree that would serve as the Sun Dance pole. Once cut, the chiefs carried it back to the camp on poles. While the ceremony song was sung, the pole was dedicated and placed in the dance circle, colorfully decorated with eagle feathers, sage and other symbols and offerings.

As the preparations were made and the rituals undertaken, Sitting Bull was purifying himself in a sweat lodge. Already, he had long fasted. The warmth of the heated stones found no escape from the airtight structure of willow and buffalo robes. He found temporary relief by chewing sage and spitting on his burning flesh, but it was fleeting at best. Sitting Bull smoked his sacred pipe and contemplated what was to come. Finally satisfied, he stepped from the lodge and made his way to the dance circle. All was ready. The buffalo skull sat atop the red blanket and the Sun Dance pole was mounted securely. As he performed the pipe ceremony, the onlookers stood silent, their eyes lost as they traced the many scars on his body, evidence of his past dances. Eventually, he stopped and sat at the base of the pole.

Jumping Bull made his way over to his brother and knelt beside him. He took Sitting Bull's left arm in his hand and, starting near the hand, inserted the awl beneath his skin, removing a piece of flesh about the size of a match head. He punctured and tore until he reached Sitting Bull's shoulder, leaving 50 marks on his arm. Then, he repeated the ritual on the other side. All the while, Sitting Bull's arms remained relaxed, his only words a mournful prayer to Wakan Tanka. The exercise lasted half an hour, but once completed, Wakan Tanka had his red blanket.

Unfazed, Sitting Bull rose and began to dance. Blood flowed freely down his arms and dripped from his fingers, leaving a red trail as he hopped and shuffled around the Sun Dance pole. All the while he stared straight at the sun, until it slipped below the horizon. He continued dancing through the night and greeted the rising sun the following day. His arms were swelling under the pressure of the congealed blood; his raw feet continued to darken the red circle of his dance. About noon he stopped, his eyes riveted to the sun.

Black Moon ran to him and lowered his exhausted body to the ground. He listened to Sitting Bull's raspy whispers. When others hurried to tend to their chief, Black Moon spoke.

"My brothers, Sitting Bull has had a vision. Wakan Tanka has answered his prayers!" he shouted. "Sitting Bull wishes me to tell you that he heard a voice commanding him to look below the sun. As he did he saw many soldiers falling to the ground in our camp, their heads below their feet. Under them were some Natives, also upside down. Again, the voice spoke to him. 'These Long Knives do not have ears. They will die, but do not take their belongings.'"

The words of Black Moon were met with great enthusiasm, for all knew what Sitting Bull's vision meant. The Long Knives would not give the Sioux peace. They would attack and the Natives would kill them. Victory would be theirs; Wakan Tanka had said so.

The valley of the Greasy Grass was alive with the colors of spring. Trees bloomed, their branches speckled with birds, and wildflowers were sprinkled across the grass like cunningly threaded beadwork. The valley was a fitting backdrop for the six camp circles of the gathered Natives. The Sioux and Cheyenne were in the midst of an ongoing celebration. They had good cause. Days earlier, they had met the Long Knives at the Rosebud River and won.

Sitting Bull, Crazy Horse and White Bull removed themselves from the celebrations. Experienced warriors, they knew victory in the Battle of the Rosebud would not vanquish their enemy.

"Our new strategy worked," said Crazy Horse. "Holding back so many of the braves allowed for a strong and tireless assault."

"Three Stars believed that those few who attacked him were all the warriors we had. Those in the rear were well concealed and the bluff and rocks were used effectively as barriers. They were not easy to kill," agreed White Bull.

"There is no honor in counting coup against the Long Knives. The young braves do not yet see this. They are determined to ride the daring line. But it is better to hide and shoot than it is to be shot," said Sitting Bull. "And we were so close, so close to trapping them in Dead Canyon. We would have left a tribute well suited for its name."

"It was disappointing when they retreated back up the ravine," conceded Crazy Horse.

"We will fight again," consoled White Bull. "To hunt buffalo, we need to travel to the plains where the sun sets. The Long Knives will try to stop us. Those battles will result in the death of many soldiers, as Sitting Bull has seen. There will be no escape for the Long Knives. With each passing of the sun, more Natives arrive. Nearly 1000 lodges."

"Which means thousands of warriors," added Sitting Bull. "We will have to plan carefully now. They are aware of our numbers. They know we will not fight carelessly. They know they have chosen to fight against true warriors. Like the birds, we will protect our nests," concluded Sitting Bull, his dark eyes fixed on the future.

His pronouncement was met with agreement.

It was the greatest victory yet enjoyed by the Sioux and their allies. General Crook had been caught totally unaware when his troops reached the headwaters of the Rosebud River. His Crow and American scouts had greatly underestimated the numbers of Sioux and Cheyenne. Figuring they numbered a few hundred, Crook was unprepared for 1500 warriors. Their mistake was understandable. Never had so many of the "hostiles" gathered as a fighting force. Never had they fought with such a coordinated plan of attack.

Crook's troops outnumbered their enemy and used 25,000 rounds of ammunition to kill just 20 Sioux and Cheyenne. In addition to 90 injuries, nine soldiers and one Crow were killed. The casualties would have been much greater had Crook not called a retreat just prior to entering Dead Canyon, not because he suspected a trap, but because his men were four days out of their base camp and low on rations. Surprised at the strong defensive,

Crook was unwilling to re-engage until reinforcements arrived. By then, the Sioux had enjoyed a victory that was both colossal and, up to that point, inconceivable.

In early June 1876, some weeks after the Battle of Rosebud, General Custer sat in his tent, reading a directive from his commander, General Alfred Terry. He threw the paper down with a sigh of disapproval. Terry had outlined a plan to trap the Sioux. The general wanted Custer to proceed with the Seventh Calvary west to the Rosebud River. Additional troops, from the west under the command of General Gibbon and from the south under General Crook's command, would close in, effectively snaring the Sioux. In total, 2500 soldiers were mobilized for the offensive, considered more than enough to conquer the hostiles. Strategically, the plan was sound, but to Custer, it was riddled with shortcomings, not the least of which was the matter of timing. The attack was set for the morning of June 26 and Custer was concerned that the Sioux might well be gone by then.

"Sir, the Ree scouts are here as you requested," interrupted his orderly.

"Send them in."

As the two Ree stood before him, Custer revealed his deepest secret.

"You're aware that we will soon commence our attack on the hostile Sioux. It is an important battle. I am counting on your assistance. Should I win, I will soon be the Great Father," confided Custer, "and your people will be greatly rewarded."

Custer was only too aware of the American tradition of elevating its war heroes to the presidency. Despite certain blemishes, his record as a soldier was enviable. He was certain that one great victory over the Sioux, perhaps coupled with the capture or death of Sitting Bull, would vault him into the office, especially with the election only months away.

"The Seventh Calvary will march on the Sioux and, with your support, victory will be mine."

"General, there are too many Sioux and Cheyenne in the valley of the Greasy Grass. Too many for the Seventh Cavalry alone," countered one of the scouts.

"You boys always exaggerate the enemies' numbers," replied Custer. "The Seventh is the greatest force of Indian fighters in the West. We'll have no problems." Even if the hostiles were met in unexpected numbers, the general was sure he could depend on Custer's Luck.

"Remember now, I'm counting on you," said Custer as they left. Glory and its rewards would be his.

On May 17, Custer led his regiment out of Fort Abraham Lincoln. When he arrived at the Little Bighorn River, he divided his force of 750 men into three battalions. He would retain command of one, while Major Frederick Benteen and Major Marcus Reno would each have command of the remaining two.

"Reno, your three companies will attack the southern end of the camp. While you have the Sioux engaged, I'll lead my five companies in an assault against the northern end of the village. Benteen, take your three companies and scout the hills to the west for more Indians. If you find none, come back and provide support for Reno. There's no hurry. We want to lull the Indians into a false sense of security," directed Custer. "We'll reconnoiter and attack tomorrow." It was an odd strategy; usually, there would be more reconnaissance prior to an attack, but Custer was not inclined to delay. And if the officers were aware that the date of Custer's offensive was before that planned by General Terry, they held their tongues anyway.

As Custer made his plans, Sitting Bull was alone on a bluff overlooking the valley of the Greasy Grass. He was there to speak with Wakan Tanka, to plead for his people. He knew that, sooner or later, an attack would come. After smoking his pipe, he stood and raised his pipe to the sky.

"Wakan Tanka, take pity on me. In the name of the Sioux and their allies, I offer you this pipe. Where there is the sun, moon, four winds, there are you also. Wakan Tanka, save my people, I beg you. We wish to live. Guard us against misfortune and calamity. Take pity on us." His prayer completed, he returned to his camp.

As fate would have it, Reno's battalion of 175 men attacked the Hunkpapa encampment. They rode hard into the camp, guns blazing. Against the dust-clouded backdrop of shredded tipis, the mournful wails of old women singing the death song for the warriors and the urgent calls of old men giving advice, the women and children were shuttled off to safety. Quickly, the initial confusion dissipated. Under the direction of Gall and Sitting Bull, who had delayed only long enough to retrieve his war shield, bow and arrows and to ensure his mother was directed to safety, the Hunkpapa mounted a counterattack. When the Natives stood their ground, the soldiers were surprised. They fully expected the Natives to fall back. As the Hunkpapa were joined by increasingly large numbers of Sioux, the confidence of Reno's men melted away. In the face of upwards of 1000 warriors, his men dismounted and scrambled for the trees. All Reno could do was wait for Benteen's reinforcements.

With Reno's soldiers pinned down, Gall was able to divert a few hundred warriors to repel Custer's attack near the center of the encampment. As Gall kept the battalion occupied from the front, Crazy Horse and his Oglalas attacked Custer's flank, while Two Moons and his Cheyenne assaulted the rear of the column. For a while, Custer's men pressed the advantage of their superior firepower. Eventually, however, as the number of soldiers killed and wounded increased and ammunition ran low, the tide turned. The remaining soldiers were forced to fight hand-to-hand, and they didn't have a chance against the more experienced Natives. Before sundown, Custer and his 225 men were dead. Only 30 Natives died.

With Custer's force decimated, the Natives turned back on Reno's battalion, which had finally been joined by Benteen. When it got too dark, the Natives halted their attack. At sunrise, they began again with renewed vigor. Before the offensive ended, Reno and Benteen had lost some 50 men. More might have died had Sitting Bull not called an end to the fighting. There had been enough bloodshed.

Sitting Bull remained near Reno's battalion for the duration of the encounter. He thought Reno's flight into the woods a defensive action designed to save time until reinforcements arrived and he directed some of the braves to keep watch with him. His suspicions proved correct. As a result, neither Reno nor Benteen were able to lend support to Custer.

For the most part, the Hunkpapa chief fought from behind the cover of trees, firing the occasional shot with a repeating rifle One Bull had given him in exchange for Sitting Bull's shield. Like so many of the young braves, One Bull had been anxious to prove his courage in hand-to-hand combat, where his rifle was of no use. Sitting Bull's position during the fight went without comment by his people. He had little reason to expose himself. The Natives were brave that day.

When the battle was over, Sitting Bull rode through the valley, surveying the damage. He counted more than 30 dead Sioux and Cheyenne. The number of Long Knives who died was less important to him, though he could see there were many (in fact, over half of Custer's regiment—five companies—was killed). He could not be sure whether Long Hair, as the Sioux called Custer, was among them, for no soldier had the telltale flowing reddish-yellow locks. Unknown to the Sioux, Custer had shorn them prior to leaving Fort Lincoln.

Although many Americans soon branded Sitting Bull as the mastermind of the Seventh Cavalry massacre, it was clear that he was little more than a minor participant in the battle. Americans had a narrow concept of warfare— they believed everyone fought as they did. But there was no place for a general in the Native scheme of warfare. A chief might give the call to fight, but warriors engaged in battle because they wanted to; each man fought in the way he believed could best demonstrate his bravery. Still, there was not a Sioux who failed to realize the importance of the Hunkpapa chief. Sitting Bull had emerged as the one Native who could unite such an imposing force of Sioux and their allies under a single purpose: to protect the lands they had called home against white encroachment. They had acted on his vision, strengthened by his determination. When Americans held Sitting Bull responsible, they had stumbled onto the truth.

The victory celebrations began on the fourth day after the fight, following a suitable period of mourning. There was great reason to rejoice, because the Long Knives had been soundly defeated. But victory brought little joy to Sitting Bull. The losses of his people weighed heavily on his heart. So did those of the soldiers. The war was necessary, but the casualties were no less lamentable. One Bull questioned him on his reluctance to participate in the celebrations.

"The young braves have taken the spoils of victory," he replied. "They have taken the Long Knives' guns, clothing, horses. From this time on, they will covet his goods. They will be at his mercy; they will starve at his hands. The soldiers will crush them."

The outcome had been foretold by his vision. The truth of it would soon enough be evident in the response of the Long Knives, who would be all too anxious to satisfy American demands for revenge and an end to the Sioux problem.

Sitting Bull walked into White Bull's tipi and squatted next to his nephew. White Bull was nursing his left arm, which had been shattered above the elbow by an army bullet. The day before, while searching for buffalo north of the Yellowstone River, the Hunkpapa had discovered a westward-bound wagon train. It was a considerable size, nearly 90 wagons and a guard of some 200 soldiers. Their presence did not deter the Sioux. They were determined to take what supplies they could and send the train back.

Though they harassed the soldiers and set fire to the prairie, the Sioux were unsuccessful. The soldiers had long-range infantry rifles and the warriors could not get close enough to the train to do any damage. The firepower of the Long Knives didn't prevent their trying, though. White Bull and other courageous braves pressed hard against the slow-moving column in search of an opening. It was during one such run that he caught a bullet.

The young man looked up at Sitting Bull. His face was gaunt and bloodless.

"You have earned your red feather and Wakan Tanka will be pleased at the sight of your red blanket," he comforted.

"Without the Sun Dance, will Wakan Tanka care?"

"Wakan Tanka sees all acts of bravery, all deeds of sacrifice," replied Sitting Bull, smiling. "Perhaps it is not where
that is important, but that it is evident."

White Bull nodded.

"The chiefs have just met," he continued. "We have
decided to make peace with the soldier chief. Big Leggings,
the interpreter from Standing Rock, put my words on
paper for him to see. The message was simple; I spoke what
was in my heart. 'I want to know what you are doing traveling on this road. You scare away all the buffalo. I want to
hunt on the place. I want you to turn back from here. If
you don't, I will fight you again. I want you to leave what
you have got here and turn back.' I said that what I wanted
them to leave was all their rations and some of their powder. I also told them that I was their friend."

"You think they will listen?"

"It is true, they have poor ears. Many times I have told
them I do not wish to fight. I can only hope they will
finally hear," replied Sitting Bull.

The troops, under the command of Lieutenant Colonel
Elwell Otis, weren't in much of a mood to listen. Since the
overwhelming and surprising defeat at the Battle of Little
Bighorn, Washington had adopted a new Native policy:
drive them into submission by whatever means necessary.
They forced the Natives to abandon the Black Hills and all
unceded territory outlined in the Laramie Treaty of '68.
The government declared that the Natives had gone to war
against the United States and, in so doing, had relinquished
any right to the region.

A commission was sent west to ensure the concessions.
The Natives pointed out that any modification of the treaty
required the signatures of three-quarters of the male population. The commission countered that it required only
three-quarters of the friendly Natives; those not on the

reservation, including about half of the warrior population who traveled with Sitting Bull and Crazy Horse, were hostiles whose agreement was unnecessary. When some of the Natives continued to resist, they were told there would be no more rations until they capitulated. It wasn't difficult to convince an agency Native, and all present soon signed.

In the eyes of the government, those on the reservations were now prisoners of war. To ensure they would no longer be a threat, they were forced to surrender their arms, ammunition and horses. Here was only the first part of the government's strategy to deal with the Sioux. Responding to increasingly vocal public pressures, the government pledged to wage an all-out attack on the hostile Natives. By the fall of 1876, nearly half of the American army was mobilized on the northwestern plains. Despite Sitting Bull's wishes, they were not there to listen.

The great Sioux force that participated in the Battle of Little Bighorn dispersed in the months that followed. Feeding such a large group proved impossible and bands broke off in search of buffalo. As their numbers dwindled, Generals Terry and Crook finally felt confident enough to begin their pursuit. In early September, Crook managed to engage some of the remaining bands at Slim Buttes, near the mouth of the Moreau River. Having marched for the better part of a month, however, his troops were tired and the battle was short-lived. Unknown to Sitting Bull, who joined in the Sioux defensive, Crook's attack would be only the first of many in the government's new long-range policy. The following spring, reinforcements would be sent to the Yellowstone region, where a new fort was to be constructed. Until then, troops were ordered into the buffalo country to interfere with the Sioux hunt. The tactic was an extension of the policy to starve the Natives into submission.

Watching Otis' wagon train, the chiefs sent two Sioux, under the protection of a white flag, to the column. When they returned, they informed the Native chiefs that the chief of the Long Knives would talk. Sitting Bull accompanied the Sioux delegation, but said little. He mourned the death of his son, recently killed when kicked by a horse. When the two parties stood face to face, the Sioux went on the offensive.

"Why do you drive off the buffalo. We are hungry. We have little ammunition to hunt. We are tired of fighting and wish for peace."

"For a peaceful people, you've sure got a funny way of showing it," replied Otis. "And as for ammunition, well, you've fired enough at us to take you through half a dozen buffalo hunts."

His reflections went without response, so he continued.

"I can't negotiate peace. I'm not authorized to do that. And I'll be damned if I'll give you any food," he concluded, well aware of the army's new position.

"We are hungry and your presence has scared away the buffalo," asserted the chiefs. "Without food, we will continue to fire on the wagons."

"I don't enjoy being threatened," he snarled. Still, as Otis looked at the body of Sioux warriors in the distance, he thought it might be advisable to bend army policy, just this once. "Corporal," he barked, "bring over here 150 pounds of hard bread and a couple of sides of bacon." When the supplies were placed on the ground, the wagon train moved on. The Sioux took the food and disappeared.

Sioux harassment of the wagon train had slowed its progress considerably, so Colonel Nelson A. Miles was worried. He was waiting for its arrival near the mouth of the Tongue River, where his Fifth Infantry was camped for the winter. His patience expired, he led the soldiers east in search of Otis. On finding them, he was hastily informed

General Nelson (Bear Coat) Miles (1839–1925),
colonel of the Fifth Infantry, age 37, taken in 1876

of the reason for their delay and immediately set out to trail
the Sioux. He caught up with them on October 20, near
Cedar Creek, midway between the Yellowstone and the
Missouri. Sitting Bull was one of a handful of Sioux who
watched from a ridge as the Long Knives settled into attack
formation. In response to their preparations, Sitting Bull
decided to send two men to arrange a parley. Miles agreed.

They met in the shelter of a hill. Sitting Bull and the other chiefs arrived with open hands, though a mounted band of armed warriors was not far behind. A column and a cannon perched on an adjacent hilltop were support for Miles and his staff.

Dismounting, the two parties warily approached one another. Sitting Bull, dressed in buckskin and cloaked with a buffalo robe, led his party, while Miles wore a long coat trimmed with bear fur. The Sioux came to call him "Bear Coat." The Hunkpapa chief spread a buffalo robe on the ground and invited Miles to sit. He declined at first, but eventually knelt. They shared the smoking of the pipe. It did not add to the civility of the meeting.

"Sitting Bull, you have long been an enemy of the whites," began Miles.

"No, I am not against the white man, though I admit I am not for him," replied Sitting Bull.

"You are ready to fight the white man. You do it all the time. You like to."

"Your words are not true! I do not wish to fight. I only fight when I have to. I want to be friendly. I like the traders."

"There are no traders here," countered Miles. "They are at the reservation. Why are you not there?"

"I look out for my people and find meat for them. We search for buffalo. You try to stop us."

"It was you, Sitting Bull, who attacked our wagon train. Where are the mules that you stole?"

"Where are the buffalo that you have scared away?" responded Sitting Bull.

Miles had had about enough of talking. Sitting Bull was evasive and clearly a liar.

"There will be no more buffalo, Sitting Bull. You and your people are to surrender unconditionally. You will accompany me to the Tongue River post, where we will await further instructions from the Great Father," proclaimed Miles.

"No," countered Sitting Bull. "You will withdraw your soldiers from the Yellowstone, and close the post at Tongue River and the fort at Buford. That will allow the buffalo to return, and my people may hunt them in peace as we have always done."

Miles abruptly stood. "This is going nowhere. We should think through the night and talk again tomorrow."

Sitting Bull agreed and the two parties left.

The meeting on the following day was even more rancorous. Miles believed that he had the upper hand. Intelligence reports revealed that the Miniconjou and the Sans Arc in Sitting Bull's party did not wish to fight and were willing to return to the reserve. However, Miles had overestimated their influence; the Hunkpapa chief's position did not waver. Before long, the yelling of both parties betrayed their anger and impatience. Finally, Miles issued his ultimatum again.

"The Great Father demands that you surrender immediately and unconditionally. Fail to do so and we will attack."

When he fell silent, White Bull made his way to Sitting Bull.

"Uncle, I have come from near the soldier's camp. They prepare for battle."

Sitting Bull rose.

"Your soldiers prepare to fight. You are losing your temper. We will stop talking before someone does something regretful."

The Battle of Cedar Creek was another of the many inconclusive fights between the two opposing forces. One Sioux died and two soldiers were injured. The Sioux retreated toward the Yellowstone, with Miles in close pursuit. Sitting Bull and his Hunkpapa followers separated from the dissident Sioux, who were soon overtaken. They agreed to report to the Cheyenne River Agency and surrender. Sitting Bull's nephew, White Bull, was among them.

Throughout the winter, Sitting Bull kept his small band on the move, traveling between the Powder River and the Bighorn Mountains, well aware that a moving target was difficult to hit. They did encounter the Long Knives on two occasions, but suffered no losses. Desperately he sought food but found few animals in the uncommonly cold winter. He also looked for his close friend Crazy Horse, who had gone south after the Battle of Little Bighorn. He had no luck with that search.

Throughout the long winter nights, Sitting Bull gave great consideration to his position, praying often to Wakan Tanka. His band numbered about 135 lodges. They were hungry and tired. He could not ensure their survival if they continued to live as they had. He took no responsibility more seriously and knew a radical solution was required. Finally, he settled on a new strategy, the only one that seemed to offer any hope to his beleaguered people.

With the arrival of spring, he led his ragged band north across the Medicine Line, to the land of the Great White Mother.

CHAPTER FOUR

The Canadian Connection

Prime Minister John A. Macdonald and a confidant sat at an isolated table in a popular eating establishment in the Canadian capital. Their meal just completed, they turned to a discussion of matters of national interest.

"I'll be damned, but Rupert's Land came with quite a kick. I wonder if we weren't snookered by the Hudson's Bay Company," mumbled the prime minister's companion. "Do you suppose that they suspected the problems the Dominion government would face once we took ownership of the territory? Perhaps they sold it a little abruptly to avoid the headaches?"

"Certainly they knew the West better than anyone else," Macdonald replied. "But I'm not convinced that they so willingly gave up the territory."

"Well…perhaps you're right. They did drive a hard bargain. But I can't help but think they were aware of the problems with the half-breeds and the Indians. They haven't been small obstacles and, certainly, they had the potential to throw our plans for the West…and for Canada…into total disarray."

John A. Macdonald (1815–1891), the prime minister
of Canada who was instrumental in forming
the North-West Mounted Police

"They still might," suggested Macdonald. "If past events
are any indication, it will take precious little to cause that
pot to boil over again." He lifted a tumbler of gin to his
mouth, took a generous swallow and fell silent for a
moment. "We need a strong lid. We should give a closer
look at the idea of the mounted rifles."

The plans in question were truly monumental. They were designed to forge a nation in the northern half of North America that could survive in a continent increasingly dominated by the United States. The first step had been the creation of the Dominion of Canada in July 1867. During the nation building conferences of the mid-1860s, Macdonald had worked tirelessly, handling the negotiations until four of the eastern colonies of British North America were finally comfortable enough to unite as a single nation.

The second step had been to gain control over Rupert's Land, the immense territory owned by the Hudson's Bay Company. In the late 17th century, The Company of Adventurers Trading into the Hudson Bay were granted a charter by the English king, Charles II, giving them exclusive trading rights to the lands that drained into the northern bay. No one could have guessed that the grant would include millions of square miles extending west to the Rocky Mountains and south into present-day United States. The dealings were protracted and difficult, but by late 1869, the Hudson's Bay Company and the Canadian government reached an agreement securing Rupert's Land for Canada.

In Macdonald's eyes, the purchase was critical. Although the pivotal role of the West in what he would call his National Policy would not crystallize for another decade, the seeds of that vision were undoubtedly planted in his first term as prime minister. Rupert's Land, re-christened the North-West Territories upon purchase, would be thrown open for settlement. Eastern industries would grow strong, providing the new arrivals expected to pour into the country with the supplies necessary to carve out a life. The Canadian economy would boom. The new nation would emerge as a crown jewel in the British Empire and perhaps, some dared to dream, might even supplant Britain's position as leader. Macdonald would have a legacy with a brilliant luster.

As a vision, it seemed perfect. But when the Dominion government attempted to put it into action, the flaws became apparent. They neglected to consider the people who called the West home. Most of the tens of thousands who lived in the North-West Territories were Native. However, a handful were the mixed-blood offspring of European traders (generally French, English and Scottish) and their Native partners. There was also a scattering of English and Scottish. Many of these three peoples lived in Red River, a settlement in the south-east corner of the territory (present-day Manitoba). To varying degrees, they had lived in the region for generations. The Métis, in particular, had strong links with the land. Their culture had matured over the past century and they had fought many battles to ensure that their rights would be recognized by others and thus protected.

Objections to the sale of Rupert's Land caught the government off guard. Western support for some form of self-governance had been simmering for some time, and the government's self-centered action brought it to a full boil. Under the leadership of Louis Riel, the Métis resisted transfer of land. In October 1869, Dominion government land surveyors were forced to abandon their efforts in the area. Soon, the newly appointed and recently arrived lieutenant-governor, William McDougall, was forced to retreat across the border to Pembina. The first campaign of the Red River Rebellion came in early November, when the Métis seized Upper Fort Garry. With control of Red River securely in his hands, Riel called for a convention to establish a provisional government. Its proclamation was accompanied by a declaration of Métis rights. The winter months

Louis Riel (1844–1885), who asked Sitting Bull
to join him in his fight against Canada
to preserve Métis and Native culture

were interspersed with talks designed to defuse the situation, but tempers flared again when the provisional government asserted its supremacy with the execution of a bigoted Orangeman named Thomas Scott.

Despite cries from Ontario demanding blood for Scott, the Dominion government could do nothing but negotiate with the community's leaders. It had no effective military presence in Red River and no way of transporting troops there during the winter months. Macdonald's hand was forced, and in the spring, representatives from Red River were invited to Ottawa to discuss terms to end the rebellion. As a result, the new province of Manitoba came into existence on July 15, 1870 and its enacting legislation protected Métis cultural and linguistic rights.

Macdonald was enough of a pragmatist to realize that he had to bend to bring closure to the Red River affair. However, he was unyielding when it came to his vision. He knew well that the Métis resistance had the potential to interfere with his plans for the Dominion, especially if such resistance was repeated elsewhere in the West. He also had an even greater concern. What if the Métis fomented unrest among the Native population? The Dominion government simply could not afford costly Native warfare. To deal with its western Natives, the United States government spent an annual amount equivalent to Canada's national expenditure. A similar use of funds would bankrupt the new nation and leave Macdonald with a legacy of a much different sort.

The possibility of Native warfare was all too real. For the better part of a decade, the American Midwest had run red with the blood of conflict, as single-minded armies sought to reign in uncooperative, angry Natives. Macdonald could only hope that Canada's Natives would not look south for either example or inspiration. Even without violence between government forces and Plains Natives, Canadian officials still had cause for concern. The Natives had a nasty habit of fighting one another, and while cynics suggested that alone would soon end any potential Native problem, such warfare created its own set of problems. Settlers would not emigrate to the West if there was violence.

And there was violence. The fall of 1870 witnessed a particularly nasty affair, the Battle of the Oldman River, near the junction of the Oldman and St. Mary's Rivers. The Assiniboine and Cree were on one side and the Blood and Blackfoot were on the other. Uncharacteristically—intertribal warfare was more often concerned with displays of bravery that did not always require the death of an opponent—some 300 were killed, most of them Cree. In the spring, the Cree sent tobacco to the Blackfoot. Once accepted, peace was formalized. Large-scale Native warfare never again set the North-West Territories ablaze, but it remained a looming possibility in the eyes of the whites. Efforts were required to ensure peace.

Ironically, the spark that might well have engulfed the West in new flames was struck by white men. Throughout the late 1860s and into the 1870s, American whisky traders began crossing the Canadian border to sell their rotgut to the Natives. It was a powerful mixture, usually combining iodine, Tabasco sauce, gunpowder, water and just enough alcohol to pass the fire test—a match thrown on the liquid would send up a blue flame. Although alcohol was foreign to the Natives, they took to the swill like a fish to water. Some say they were attracted to the booze because it fit well into the spiritual aspect of their culture; if they drank enough of it, they had the visions that were so important to them. Whatever the reason, the well-prepared trader could unburden himself in a matter of hours and fleece the inebriated Natives while doing it. The Natives were usually shrewd traders, but when the liquor took hold, they were easy marks.

It didn't take long for the whisky traders to realize there were great profits to be made. To ensure continued and ready access to the Natives, they established trading posts in the southwestern corner of the North-West Territories. The region became known as Whoop-Up country. Supplied by merchants in Fort Benton, Montana, the most famous of these trading posts was Fort Whoop-Up, located close

A hunter's cabin (1870s) in the Cypress Hills,
shown with a practical mode of transportation for the day:
a Red River cart

to the site of the Battle of the Oldman River. Selling
whisky to the Natives was illegal, but there was no law
enforcement in the deep West or any part of the West
beyond the Manitoba border. As a result, both the trade and
the Native violence that inevitably followed went
unchecked.

Throughout the early part of the 1870s, Macdonald
turned a blind eye to the illegal activities in Whoop-Up
country. Money the government could afford to spend on the
maintenance of law in the West was better spent in Manitoba,
where the presence of a militia might deter further Métis
uprisings and soothe the concerns of anxious white settlers.
He was forced to change his plans in the spring of 1873,
when news of the Cypress Hills Massacre filtered east.

The Cypress Hills are a mountainous plateau of about 200 square miles between the Missouri and South Saskatchewan Rivers. Green with vegetation and abundant with wildlife, many Native tribes frequented the region. It was only natural that traders smelling money would set up posts in the area.

In May, a gang of wolfers, considered by Natives and whites alike to be the lowest form of life on the prairies, made their way north from Fort Benton. Known as the Green River Renegades, these folks made their living by poisoning wolves (and anything else unfortunate enough to eat the strychnine-coated buffalo used as bait). Even sober, these were ornery folk. On this occasion, they were on the trail of thieves who had stolen their horses. The trail went cold long before the Cypress Hills, but since it seemed to lead in that direction, the wolfers figured that the culprits must have made their way there.

Upon their arrival, they confronted a local proprietor, Abe Farwell. Although they had no reason to believe that the thieves were Native, they told Farwell that such was the case. Farwell informed them that the only Natives nearby were some Assiniboine from up north, who had wintered near the place. In his opinion, there was no way they were involved with the theft. Angry, the Green River Renegades hit the kegs. They drank into the next day. And when a fellow imbiber casually remarked that one of the Natives had stolen his horse, the wolfers had all the proof they needed. They rode into the Assiniboine camp and when they left, they carried one wolfer back with them (in addition to a half dozen Native women whom they abused throughout the night). There were some 30 Assiniboine dead.

News of the atrocity offended even eastern sensibilities. "Old Tomorrow," as Macdonald was called, knew that any further delay in establishing a western presence of law and order could only be done at the risk of further violence. In the fall of 1874, the Dominion government issued an order-in-council that put into motion previously passed legislation, allowing for the creation and training of a police force for the North-West Territories. Some 300 men would be responsible for ensuring that western violence would be a thing of the past, thereby guaranteeing Macdonald's vision for the future.

The graduating ceremony for Kingston's School of Cavalry was completed and the celebrations had played themselves out. James Walsh threw open the door of the pub that had witnessed the unrestrained joy of the graduates and stepped into the moonless night. The stale air behind him, he took a great deep breath and began the walk back to his lodgings. There was a lightness to his step, reflecting his especially good mood. He smiled broadly as he thought of his certificate. He unrolled it and read it yet again. The words of the cavalry commandant were barely legible in the dark...no matter, they were already etched deep in his mind.

"He is the smartest and most efficient officer that has yet passed through the Cavalry School. He is a good rider and particularly quick and confident at drill. I thoroughly recommend him to the notice of the Adjutant General."

Gently nodding, he declared to any who might hear, "Finally, I have discovered my destiny." With that, his face broke into a great grin.

James Morrow Walsh was born on May 22, 1840, in Prescott, Upper Canada. Son of Lewis Walsh, a ship's carpenter, and Elizabeth Morrow Walsh, he was the oldest of nine children. There was nothing to distinguish him in academics; Walsh would have been the first to admit that he was much more comfortable outside the classroom. Whether using his fists in a scuffle or his feet on the soccer pitch, he commanded attention in a world unhampered by walls. He was a leader even then and his companions acceded readily to him. When the boys played Native war games, "Bub" Walsh was the general or the chief. In his late teens, he was captain of the Prescott Lacrosse team, then recognized as the world champions. When only 20, he found himself in charge of the Prescott Volunteer Fire Brigade.

The transition from the carefree days of youth to the obligations of manhood proved to be a real challenge for Walsh. Try as he might, he could not find a suitable occupation. Initially, he was employed as a clerk at a dry-goods store. He went on to try his hand at a machine shop. Employment as an engineer in training on the railway was no more useful at scratching his itchy feet, and he was ready to abandon yet another potential career when fate finally intervened.

On this occasion, fate spoke with an Irish accent and was called Fenian. The Fenians were a secret Irish revolutionary movement. Located in the United States, their mission was to overthrow British rule in Ireland. In 1866, they began raiding from across the American border into the British colonies. When Walsh heard of the need for volunteers to repel the invaders, he'd readily signed up. While his parents may have wondered whether his choice was merely another fleeting interest, they were hardly surprised by it. Not so very long ago, his Irish ancestors had fought with the Duke of Wellington in the Napoleonic War. Military service was in his blood.

James Morrow Walsh (1840–1905), shown here with rank
of inspector in the North-West Mounted Police

When he volunteered, Walsh was enrolled at the Royal
Military College in Kingston. Graduating at age 24, he was
commissioned as a lieutenant and posted immediately to
the 156th Grenville Regiment (Lisgar Rifles). His efforts
against the Fenians attracted notice and soon drew praise
from his superiors. Especially noted was his ability to gain
the respect of his men. Undoubtedly, it was an ability linked

to the direct manner in which he commanded and carried himself. Before long, he was promoted to the rank of captain. Increasingly convinced that the army lifestyle was for him, he continued his military education at the Kingston School of Cavalry. The glowing evaluation of the school's commander suggested it was the right decision. On the basis of the cavalry commandant's assessment, Walsh was accepted into the Militia School of Gunnery in Toronto, where he proved that his performance at the Kingston School of Cavalry had been no accident. Upon graduation, he obtained a first-class certificate.

It was an exciting time to be in the military, because opportunities for engagement abounded. In August 1870, the Red River Expedition of Colonel Garnet Wolseley caught Walsh's eye. Wolseley led a force of nearly 1300 men (450 British regulars and 800 Canadian militia) west to Red River. Since it had no active force in the region, the hastily organized Wolseley expedition represented the Dominion government's tardy effort to impose order on the region.

As it turned out, Walsh did not march West with Wolseley. Some weeks before the force departed, Walsh resigned his position as ensign and acting adjutant. He had fallen in love. In the early spring of 1870, he married Elizabeth Mowat of Brockville. Unwilling to leave his young wife, Walsh settled into family life in Prescott, where he became the manager of the North American Hotel. Soon, the couple was blessed with a daughter, Cora, who would be their only child. Walsh, however, did not totally sever his link with the military. The bug had bitten him too deeply. He organized the volunteer Prescott Calvary Troop, which he commanded. His efforts with the troop won praise from no less an esteemed individual than Lord Dufferin, the governor general.

Walsh enjoyed success as the hotel's manager, but the sedentary life of a small-town businessman left him unfulfilled. The part-time command of the local militia only served to remind him of how much he enjoyed the military lifestyle. In the summer of 1873, when word arrived that the Canadian government was establishing a new force to bring law and order to the North-West Territories, Walsh informed officials in Ottawa that he was willing to serve. The summer months were anxious ones for Walsh, because Prime Minister Macdonald procrastinated on the matter. When his hand was forced in early fall, an order-in-council was finally passed, authorizing the formation of a "Police Force for the North-West Territories" (commonly, and in 1879 officially, known as the North-West Mounted Police). Walsh surely exhaled a great sigh of relief when, on September 25, he was appointed one of the first nine officers of the new force at an annual salary of $1000.

Walsh met the requirements of employment as set out by the act: of sound constitution, able to ride, active and able-bodied, of good character, between 18 and 40, with sufficient education to read and write in either English or French. Although the force wasn't truly a military body, since it was assigned civilian duties dealing with the administration of justice in the West, military experience in potential recruits was a definite asset, even more for the officer corp. Walsh's military record, though brief, was enviable, and the high praise he had won from prominent individuals strengthened his standing.

The first challenge of the force was to recruit the 300 men authorized by the legislation (initially the quota was reduced to 150). Walsh was responsible for efforts in eastern Ontario, around Ottawa and along the St. Lawrence Valley to Kingston. Recruitment proved easy enough because there was no shortage of volunteers. But the process was hurried as mounting political pressure necessitated that the recruits make their way to Lower Fort Garry in Manitoba before winter freeze-up. The recruiters had little more than a week to make their selections. Under such conditions, it wasn't possible to check references and to verify claims. The result was that unqualified recruits slipped into the ranks.

By October 1, Walsh had selected 32 men. On that evening, A Troop, as it was dubbed, boarded a train in Ottawa and set out for adventure in Canada's new West. The sun hadn't even greeted them on the following day when the force had its first casualty: Walsh had to discharge T. O'Neill, a trumpeter, for being drunk and disorderly and making a disturbance. Walsh was a man well acquainted with the bottle and was hardly concerned if his men were as well. But he drew the line when drinking interfered with a recruit's ability to do his job. That included proper conduct. As law enforcers, their behavior needed to be of a better quality than the lawless element they were charged with restraining.

The trip to Lower Fort Garry was fraught with delays and hostile weather. Upon arriving at Collingwood, at the eastern end of Lake Superior, it was discovered that their transport vessel, the *Cumberland*, would be 24 hours late. Walsh issued a notice to the men to refrain from drinking too freely, reminding them that their behavior would justify the trust placed in them. On October 8, the *Cumberland* steamed into Port Arthur's Landing, where the troop made its way to the long and exhausting Dawson route. The only mark in favor of the route was that it was solely in Canadian territory. On a stretch of waterways connected by portages of corduroy road (roads too muddy to travel on without the use of uncut logs as a surface), travel was a trying experience, even when conditions were ideal. On this occasion, they were far from it.

By the time the troops reached Fort Frances, the weather had turned bitterly cold. As the steamer made for the North-West Angle, the next stop on the journey, sleet and harsh northerly winds added to the men's discomfort. Sight of the port brought some relief, but it was short-lived. The water around the North-West Angle was too shallow for the steamer to make port, so the men were forced to disembark onto barges to be pulled ashore by a tug. The tug made it to shore easily enough, but the barges drifted. Only when the wind and the waves grounded the vessels were the men were able to disembark. A seething Walsh made his way directly to George Dixon, the tug's engineer.

"Goddammit man! What the hell was that about!?" he roared. "I had sick men aboard those barges. Cripes, even the healthy ones were at risk of exposure."

"Now listen…," began Dixon.

"Listen nothing! You're a goddamn black-hearted villain, one step away from being a murderer! Leaving us out there in this kind of weather."

"I don't have to take…,"

"You'll take what I give you and a hell of a lot more if I had my way," interrupted Walsh. "Where I come from, we'd shoot a man like you and not give it a second thought!"

Walsh berated the engineer for the better part of half an hour, in an energetic and colorful barrage of the most metaphorical language. Finally, Dixon escaped and filed a report on being treated in such a vile manner. It was no matter to Walsh, but it certainly had an impact on his men. When they finally arrived at Fort Garry on October 21, they knew that Walsh was a man who stood for no non-sense, who was quick to act in the most determined of ways and who would stand up willingly for his men. They were characteristics that would define his years of employment with the Mounted Police.

September had arrived and, by then, the men of the North-West Mounted Police had been marching west for the better part of two months. No one, from Commissioner George French to the Métis scouts on whom he was forced to depend, could hazard even a good guess as to exactly how close they were to their destination, Fort Whoop-Up. In the face of such uncertainty, frustrations mounted to a breaking point. The men had signed on in search of adventure. All they had so far were sore feet, sun-burned skin, empty bellies and ongoing cases of prairie cholera—diarrhea. Faced with yet another day of the same monotonous marching, more than a few wished wistfully that they had joined the dozens of troopers who had deserted back in Fort Garry. Some would have split that very day...if there had been anywhere to go.

With great effort, James Walsh sat ramrod straight on his wagon, his forearms resting on his thighs, the reins of his horse limp between his fingers. Despite the sheer physical challenge of the march, Walsh's determination to set an example for the men was enough motivation for him to overcome his exhaustion. Then, with a sudden jerk, he reached to his side and scratched vigorously. Damn lice! For the better part of four weeks now, ever since they'd camped at that cursed Old Wives Lake, the lice had been their constant companions. It was just another miserable thing to endure.

"That's just what this bloody march is," Walsh mumbled to himself, "an endurance contest." Whether the plains or the troopers would win still remained in doubt.

As he rode along attempting desperately to ignore the jarring of the wagon and the hellish noise of its wheels as they ground against the axle, Walsh must have wondered

A drawing by Henri Julien for the *Canadian Illustrated News* of the NWMP crossing the Dirt Hills in the North-West Territories (Saskatchewan)

how matters had deteriorated so. The march had begun on a high note, both for the force and himself. Prior to setting out for Whoop-Up country, the Dominion government had agreed with Commander George French's assessment that the original recruitment of some 150 men was inadequate for the task at hand. As a result, the force had been doubled. The increased number of troopers had translated into a promotion for Walsh. During the first months of training, he was acting adjutant, acting veterinary surgeon and riding master. Before the force began its march west, he was elevated to the rank of inspector, in charge of B Troop, one of the six troops into which the men had been divided.

Reflecting as he bumped along, Walsh considered that had he been a superstitious man, he would have seen the events of June 21 as a harbinger of what was to come. It seemed like an eternity ago, but on that night, a thunderstorm with a ferocity unknown even to locals, cracked the night air and sent the horses into a tearing panic. They broke through their makeshift corrals, overturning wagons and equipment and shredding tents in their single-minded determination to flee. Walsh led a party south into the United States in an effort to recover the horses. As he rode in search of the animals, he found that it wasn't difficult to reach the conclusion reached by so many of the men. French had chosen eastern horses as the mounts for the march simply because they were more majestic than their smaller, shaggy western cousin, the mustang. But the eastern horses weren't used to western conditions and the choice had been a poor one. Appearances meant a great deal to French; he held dearly to the old axiom that men were governed by their eyes. Usually, Walsh was inclined to agree with the sentiment, as long as it was seasoned with a dose of practicality.

Now it was September and here they were, the better part of 700 miles out of Fort Garry. The consequences of the commissioner's decision were all too clear. The horses were exhausted, that is, those that weren't dead. Their distended bellies and protruding ribs were evidence enough that they couldn't adjust to prairie grass. They had to be fed oats, which were too often in short supply. Walsh was one of many who considered the force fortunate not to have encountered hostile Natives on the western journey. Rumors of wandering Sioux were plentiful, and had they attacked, the men, without usable mounts, would have been sitting ducks on the flat prairie.

The troop had, however, encountered a party of Santee Sioux a few weeks back. For all that the men had heard about the ferocity of these people, the meeting was both a disappointment and a relief. The band bore the merciless marks of poverty. Long displaced from their homeland by a determined American army, their clothing was ragged, they needed food and many of them were disease-ridden. It was a pitiful and sobering sight, one etched in Walsh's memory.

Walsh allowed his eyes to drift away from the marching column. It was hardly worth the effort. Since they had left Old Wives Creek, the landscape remained the same, day after day of flat, rolling land. As his eyes scanned the horizon, in a desperate search for a hill or a tree or anything that might bring a little variety to the draining dreariness, he spotted something strangely out of place. A little darker than the surrounding prairie…and moving!

"Hey, Pierre," he called to one of the Métis cart drivers. "What do you make of that?" he asked, pointing to the odd sight.

"Ahh, my friend, that can only be one thing!" came the excited reply. "Buffalo!"

The word was hardly out of the Métis' mouth when Walsh broke from the column and towards the herd. He leaned forward in anticipation as he lashed his horse in an effort to speed his progress.

"Yee-haw!" came his cry of delight. He was followed by a handful of others, including Commissioner French. Even those who were holding to the column were excited. A scout had killed a buffalo a few days before, but it had been a tough, gamey old bull. Here was their first real encounter with the great buffalo herds they had all heard so much about. Walsh was unsuccessful, but others were able to bring down the huge animals and the men ate their fill of fresh meat that night. It was a welcome change from the pemmican and hard biscuits on which they had come to depend (though, as an officer, Walsh had his rations supplemented). Walsh wasn't overly disappointed because the Métis assured him that there would be many more herds.

They were right. By the time the force camped at the South Saskatchewan River a few weeks later, Walsh had opportunity enough to become well-practiced at buffalo hunting. However, he soon discovered it was a skill for which he'd no longer have much use.

"Orderly," called Commissioner French. "Get Inspector Walsh in here."

It had taken French some time to get use to Walsh. The man had an independent streak that just didn't sit well with the commissioner. There were occasions when he couldn't tell whether Walsh was going to answer an order with a "Yes sir," a "Go to hell" or, even worse, an insolent chuckle. Still, French couldn't deny that the man had done a fine job with his men on the march. He obviously enjoyed the respect of B Troop.

"Sir," barked Walsh as he entered French's tent.

"Ahh, yes Walsh. I've decided that it's time to further divide the force," the commissioner declared. In late July, most of A Troop, along with some of the weakest animals and excess supplies, had been dispatched to Fort Edmonton in an effort to relieve some of the pressures of the march. "Take your own B Troop and what's left of A Troop to the north bank of the Saskatchewan River. When you receive my further instruction, you'll go to Fort Edmonton and join up with Inspector Jarvis and the rest of A Troop."

"Yes, sir."

"Prepare to move out immediately."

Walsh never received those instructions. Reports from a scout indicated that the terrain north to Fort Edmonton was far too dense with brush and trees to allow for the passage of the exhausted animals. Walsh remained with the main body of the force and was there on October 9 when they finally stumbled on Fort Whoop-Up.

Truth be told, the Mounted Police might have been searching for the elusive site for a lot longer were it not for the timely hiring of Jerry Potts. He was a Blood Native who knew the territory more intimately than most men knew their wives. The force had hired him on the recommendation of the Conrad Brothers, the proprietors of the I.G. Baker Company, a prominent trading firm in Fort Benton. Commissioner French and a few of his men had arrived in the northern Montana town in late September, eager to purchase supplies, to communicate with superiors in Ottawa and to gather intelligence on the traders. With the three tasks completed, French returned to Manitoba never to reach Fort Whoop-Up. James Macleod, the assistant commissioner of the force, was left to ensure that the American traders were routed. To assist him, he hired Potts, and Macleod likely never made a better command decision. Potts led the Mounted Police straight to Fort Whoop-Up.

It was an imposing enough structure, oddly out of place on the barren plains. Palisaded, the corner bastions were loopholed to allow for the use of rifles in defense. A crudely made American flag fluttered in the breeze, offending Canadian sensibilities.

"I don't see any movement," said Macleod.

"But there's smoke," replied Potts, pointing to a wisp of gray that trailed skywards.

James Macleod (1836–1894), assistant commissioner of the vanguard NWMP force who marched west to put the Fort Whoop-Up whisky traders out of business

"We'll take no chances. Winder, prepare the nine-pounder for firing. Walsh, organize a scouting party to check those ridges. We don't want to be surprised."

The two inspectors carried out their duties. Soon, Walsh came back to report that he had found nothing suspicious.

"That's good enough then. Let's get to it," concluded Macleod.

Jerry Potts (center), interpreter and guide, hired by James
Macleod to lead them to Fort Whoop-Up from Fort Benton

Macleod strode to the fort's great wooden door and
banged on it. After a few moments, an eye-high opening
swung ajar. A old creased face with a bushy gray beard and
eyebrows to match met Macleod.

"Yes?"

"I'm Assistant Commissioner James Macleod of the
North-West Mounted Police," he replied. "We understand
that this location is used by traders. Trading liquor to the
Indians is against the law. If it's done here, we mean to put
a stop to it."

"Don't know where ya heard that. Ain't no one here but
me and a few squaws."

"Then you won't mind then if we take a look around."

"No, sir." The door creaked open.

"Dave Akers at yer service. Welcome to Fort Whoop-Up," said the old man, swinging his arm before the buildings that lay inside.

"Walsh, have B and F Troops inspect the fort."

"Yes, sir."

A thorough inspection turned up nothing in the way of booze.

"Don't want to sound rude, but I told you so," commented Akers. "But listen, I don't want you to go way mad. How's about a feed of buff and beans?"

Macleod agreed, and while they were eating, he made Akers an offer of his own.

"On behalf of the Canadian government, I'm prepared to pay you 10,000 dollars for this fort."

A gristly piece of buffalo fell from Akers' mouth and he coughed in surprise. Recovering, but still beet red, he mumbled, "10,000…?"

"You heard me right."

After a moment of silence, Akers finally replied. "Well, ahh, can't say as I can do that. It's not my place to sell."

"In that case, you tell your employers that the Mounted Police are here to stay. Traders who deal illegally with the Indians will be dealt with to the fullest extent of the law. And remember, we're the law in these parts now."

With that, Macleod led his men out of the fort and a new chapter in the history of the Canadian West had been opened. James Walsh would play a prominent part.

Louis Léveillé took one look at the Marias River, shook his head and rode back to the small party of Mounted Police. He was the scout on an ill-considered late fall journey from

Fort Walsh to Helena, Montana. When he reached the group, he made straight for Superintendent Walsh (an inspector, Walsh actually preferred to be called Major, his rank in the militia).

"Ain't going to be easy to cross the Marias, Major. The river she is frozen on both sides, with an open channel of water in between," he explained. "No trouble in getting the wagons into the river, but getting them out will be a whole other problem."

Walsh scanned the horizon. Imposing snowdrifts covered what had been, only a handful of days before, hard barren ground. They were only just out of Helena when winter's first storm struck. With Fort Benton behind them, blizzards still raged and the temperature was fixed at −20°. Even under ideal conditions, they had at least a week of travel before they reached Fort Walsh. The delays caused by the weather could easily double that time. Walsh sighed. Well, at least they had incentive to move quickly.

"No sense in sitting here stewing about it," Walsh finally said. "Let's make for the river and see what we can do."

Walsh bristled with irritation as he rode. Only the mistake of some unknown bureaucrat had caused them to be in Helena in the first place. The blunder was a financial one, the worst kind possible since it resulted in insufficient funds to pay the men. Assistant Commissioner Macleod had ordered Walsh to travel to Helena to retrieve the necessary funds and also to bring back some horses and equipment. Fortunately, among the equipment was winter wear. The fur mittens and buffalo moccasins were put to good use immediately.

Upon reaching the Marias River, Walsh realized that Léveillé had not understated the problem. The horses would not be able to drag the wagons onto the jagged ice that extended from the far side of the river. Someone was going to have to take on the elements.

"Sub-constable Fullwood!"

"Sir."

"Boy, I wouldn't ask you to do this if it wasn't absolutely necessary. You're going to have to wade across the river and chop a passageway through the ice to the shore."

"Sir?" replied Fullwood as his jaw dropped.

"It's either that or we stay here until the river freezes over. And we're sure as hell not going to do that!" barked Walsh.

"Yes, sir."

Fullwood set out on the unenviable task. In a few hours, they had forded the river. The party continued on, their frozen clothes taking the worst of the bite out of the cold wind. Regularly they were forced to shovel out a wagon that had become lodged in a snow bank. As their task preoccupied them, the new horses always scattered and the men had to struggle through deepening snow to retrieve them. Perhaps it was for the best, since the exercise kept them warm, as did the steady stream of curses that tumbled from their mouths.

Finally, Walsh called to set up camp. There was nothing to commend the spot at which they anchored for the night, neither fuel nor water. The men had simply expended all their energy. As they gnawed on hardtack and chewed on cold sowbelly, one of the party broke into song.

"The priest of the parish and his caravan, came over the mountain to visit Suzanne."

It was an odd sight indeed, a handful of men veiled by clouds of frosty breath, sheltered in a snow bank and kept warm only by the flapping of their arms and the stamping of their feet. Perhaps the crazed singing was an indication of the onset of hysteria. If so, it was a shared hysteria. They all joined in, all that is, save one.

"Where's Major Walsh?"

"Can't you hear him?" replied Fullwood. "He's cursing things out over in the wagon."

"Best to steer clear."

"Yup," came a chorus of agreement.

After the better part of two years with Walsh, the men knew when it was best to leave him alone. The storm eventually blew itself out and the party made it back to Fort Walsh without further trouble.

When they first arrived in Whoop-Up country, Walsh and B Troop wintered at Fort Macleod with the rest of the force. During that time, there were troubling rumors about the persistence of traders in the Cypress Hills. Reports suggested that those who operated Fort Whoop-Up had simply pulled up stakes and moved east into that region. And, because the Cypress Hills was the location of the Green River Renegade's massacre of the Assiniboine a few years earlier, officials believed that there might be some truth in the rumors. To address the problem, Macleod directed Walsh to take the 30 men under his command, move into the region and set up a post. It was an ideal location. Not only were they able to tackle the problem, but they were also in a position to keep their eyes on the border country to the south.

There's no denying that Walsh was pleased to have his own command. He hardly expected, however, that he would be given command over a post named in his honor. Assistant Commissioner Macleod apparently knew how to motivate men. The location of the fort, chosen by Walsh, was in a valley near Abe Farwell's old trading post, about 160 miles east of Fort Macleod. Legend has it that the location of the fort had less to do with access to the American border and its booze peddlers than it did with a nearby resident, one Mr. McKay. The homesteader had several attractive daughters and, when the scouts saw them, they figured their work best be brought to a close. B Troop hobbled their horses on June 7, 1875 and immediately began on the fort's construction. Just as quickly, they had their first encounter with hostile Natives.

As he often did, James Walsh stood at a table marked by a lazily floating Union Jack. He was lost in plans for the fort when one of the men shouted.

"Indians!"

Walsh looked up in surprise and discovered that a large band of Natives were already in the camp. He called to Louis Léveillé, who trotted over to his side.

"Sioux, Major," he whispered.

These were not anything like the ragged bands of Sioux that the force had encountered on their march west. They were warriors, their bronze and painted skin pulled tight over their muscular bodies.

"Ask them what they want."

Léveillé translated the question and waited for an answer.

"They were pursued by the Long Knives. The Americans gave up when the Sioux crossed the Medicine Line into the land of the Great White Mother."

"Tell them that we are Mounties and that they are safe here as long as they break no laws."

As Léveillé translated the message, there were grunts of approval and much nodding of heads among the Natives. Suddenly, one of them shouted.

"What the hell is he on about, Léveillé?" asked Walsh.

"He says that the white chief lies, that you are Long Knives. He says that the two men over there are proof of your lie."

Walsh looked to where Léveillé pointed. There, he saw two sub-constables partially clad in American military garb.

Save for official occasions, the Mounties never wore their dress uniforms. Walsh himself preferred a fringed buckskin jacket and a slouch hat, as popularized by Custer.

"Goddamn it," muttered Walsh. His eyes back on the Sioux, he watched as they raised their rifles. The troopers had stacked their own weapons in a pile while they were engaged in constructing the fort. No one was near them.

A Native barked out what even Walsh could tell was a threat.

"He says they're going to clean out the camp."

The Sioux began to press in when Walsh held up his hand.

"If you fire upon us, many Sioux will also be killed. Soon, there will be more Red Coats, many more than the buffalo. They will hunt you down and not one of you will live."

As Léveillé translated, Walsh watched as the gaze of the Sioux was drawn to the east. Suspecting it might be a trick to break his attention, Walsh held his eyes on them. One of the Sioux shouted a command and, as suddenly as they'd arrived, they were gone.

"What the hell happened?" asked Walsh.

Léveillé pointed to the ridge behind them.

"Cree," he answered.

It was a large party and thankfully so. The Sioux and the Cree were long-time enemies and obviously the Sioux, tired after their flight, weren't interested in fighting an enthusiastic opponent.

"Sergeant," barked Walsh. "Make sure that from now on the men keep their rifles with them. And post a double sentry tonight."

"Yes, sir!"

The construction of the fort continued without further incident. When completed, it was palisaded with logs that

North-West Mounted Police camp at Fort Walsh
near the Alberta and U.S. borders,
named for James Morrow Walsh

extended about 12 feet from the ground. Inside were
housed the quarters (four in total: one for Walsh, one for
the officers, one for the noncommissioned officers and one
for the men), a powder magazine, a blacksmith shop, a carpenter shop, a kitchen, a bakery, a guardhouse and a stable
for about 30 horses. There wasn't much to differentiate the
buildings; they were all constructed of whipsawed lumber
and chinked with mud. Expert axemen from eastern
Canada ensured they were well-built and Walsh made sure
they looked good too. He issued orders to ensure that the

buildings were whitewashed regularly. The fort had two entrances. The main gate faced the trail towards Fort Benton. Near it, a Union Jack stood as a high sentry. A second gate faced Battle Creek on the west. The gates were open from reveille till sundown, at which time visiting Natives were ejected.

It's unlikely any such Natives were well received by those in the small community that sprang up around the fort. The agents of I.G. Baker and T.C. Power, merchants out of Fort Benton, were particularly prominent. A billiard hall, a stopping place billing itself as a hotel, a restaurant, a barber's shop and a photographer's studio soon joined 40 or so other buildings, and gave some validity to the claim that Fort Walsh was the busiest town west of Manitoba. Buffalo hunters, traveling Métis and freighters regularly called on the town. There was a mail route to Fort Benton, about 275 miles to the southwest, and northern-bound bull and mule trains passed through the community.

As was the case in Whoop-Up country, the mere arrival of the Mounted Police effectively ended most of the illegal operations in the Cypress Hills region. Walsh put the nail in the coffin of the trade by establishing a detachment at Kennedy's Crossing, named after an American who traded there, close to the international boundary where the Benton trail and the Milk River intersected. Patrols were regularly sent out to hunt for traders who might try to slip by Kennedy's Crossing. It wasn't long before the illegal trade was no longer a problem. By then, Walsh had bigger fish to fry.

CHAPTER FIVE

Red Coats and Refugees

James Walsh relaxed in the natural spring water of the health spa at Hot Springs, Arkansas. Bathing in the sulfurous waters had done wonders to ease the pain of his erysipelas, a skin disease also known as St. Anthony's Fire. It had flared up again in the fall of 1875, and his sympathetic superiors had seen fit to allow him some time to recover.

"Can I get you anything, sir?" asked the attendant.

James Walsh's eyes fluttered open and they fell upon the man, his white outfit seeming to glow against the deep blue sky.

"No thanks, I'm fine," he replied.

He was feeling pretty good, all things considered. Not only had two weeks at Hot Springs reduced both the swelling and the temperature that accompanied his erysipelactic outbreaks, but he had also filled the emotional void of his domestic situation. Part of the leave had been spent in Brockville, visiting his wife and daughter, neither of whom he had seen for about two years. Following the family reunion, he went to Hot Springs. For the first time in months, he was not feeling on edge.

He closed his eyes and his thoughts drifted back to his daughter. Such a pretty young girl. It had been difficult to leave her yet again, but Fort Walsh was hardly the appropriate place for a bud to flower. Still, it was changing quickly. Perhaps it might soon shed its raw frontier character and mature into a proper town. If that happened, well, they could be a family again.

"Begging your pardon, sir."

"Yes man," sighed Walsh.

"Sorry to disturb you, but a telegram has arrived and I was told to inform you that it was urgent."

Walsh reached for a towel and, once his hands were dry, he took the paper from the attendant.

"Thank you."

He unfolded it. With each word read, his pulse quickened. The Sioux had wiped out Custer and his Seventh Cavalry on June 25. Everything pointed to the Natives fleeing north, where they could escape the pursuing American army. Walsh's superiors determined it imperative that he return to Fort Walsh, because intelligence suggested that the Mounted Police post was nearest to the anticipated point of entry for the Sioux. Walsh leaped from the pool and made his way quickly to his room. There was no time to lose. Already, it was well into July.

Walsh boarded the first train north and arrived in Ottawa in a matter of days. Once there, he met with R. W. Scott, the Dominion government secretary of state. Scott filled him in on the details at which the telegram only hinted.

"It's not good, Inspector," began Scott, who moved from behind his desk and motioned to Walsh to sit down. "The specifics of Custer's defeat are as yet contradictory and uncertain, but they're hardly relevant to our predicament in any case. It's enough that his men suffered a terrible loss and that the U.S. army is intent on avenging its losses."

"I've heard that the Sioux were led by Sitting Bull."

"None other. By God, if they were mad at him before, surely he's not seen anything of their anger yet. It was a humiliating defeat, one the Americans will not take lightly," continued Scott. "Thus Sitting Bull's desire to flee north. Presumably he's aware that the American army cannot follow him here."

"The Natives refer to the border as the Medicine Line," offered Walsh. "They've learned that once they cross it, they're safe from their American enemies."

"At which point they become our problem. And it seems that they might become quite a problem, Inspector Walsh."

"They might continue their aggressions here? One would hope that they're smart enough to realize that doing so would deprive them of any possible shelter," suggested Walsh.

"Far be it from me to comment on the intellect of the red men," said Scott, shaking his head, "but it seems that may be just the case. And the Sioux may not be our only problem."

"Our own Indians…?"

"Yes. Recently Commissioner Macleod forwarded a most disturbing report to the government." Scott retrieved a page and read the notes from it. "Sub-Inspector Cecil Denny was on patrol in search of a suspected murderer. In the vicinity of the Red Deer Valley, he came into contact with Chief Crowfoot's band of Blackfoot. Apparently, they were most interested in talking to him and arranged a council to that effect," explained Scott. "During the council, one of the chiefs revealed that the Blackfoot Confederacy had received a twist of tobacco as a peace offering from the Montana Sioux, allegedly sent by Sitting Bull."

Walsh thought as he listened. There was little reason for the Blackfoot and the Sioux to join under any peace agreement. Their territories were far apart and they had little cause to come into contact. Unless the Sioux had a reason to seek their cooperation.

"An alliance to fight the white man," guessed Walsh.

"Exactly. The Sioux wanted the Blackfoot to smoke the tobacco and join with them in an attack on the Americans. Denny's report on this matter is confirmed by confidential information obtained from the Americans in late May. Officials there were convinced that their own hostile Indians would cross the international border and, while using Canada as a safe haven, continue their depredations in the south," explained Scott. "You can imagine the diplomatic problems that would cause."

Walsh nodded.

"And that may not be the worst of it," continued Scott. "Once they had destroyed their enemy, the Sioux pledged to ride north and assist the Blackfoot in the destruction of a Canadian presence in the West. Apparently, the Sioux feel that the presence of the Mounted Police is no obstacle to the success of their proposed northerly enterprise. The Sioux sweetened their case with offers of horses taken from the Americans in battle, and also of white women. Barbaric," spat Scott as he shook his head.

"And the Blackfoot reply?" asked Walsh.

"Thankfully, they rejected the overture. Evidently, Chief Crowfoot made it clear that he did not want peace on such terms. He emphasized that the Mounted Police were his friends and that they had already done much to prove their friendship by ridding the region of whisky traders. In fact, he spoke very highly of the Mounted Police, asserting that they are white men who treat the red man fairly."

"A solid fellow, Crowfoot. His response bodes well for treaty negotiations."

"Indeed. Efforts are already underway to obtain a medal for him, something flashy to commend his loyalty. Unfortunately, the story doesn't end there. The Sioux had not anticipated Crowfoot's answer. Rebuffed and angry, the Sioux claimed that after they had dealt with the Americans, they would ride north and attack the Blackfoot," explained Scott.

"It sounds like so much bluster. Despite their numbers, the Sioux are hardly in a position to defeat the American army," stated Walsh. "Scattered victories, yes, but anything more is unrealistic."

"We know that, but the Blackfoot were nonetheless concerned. Crowfoot wanted to know if the Blackfoot could count on the support of the Mounted Police if the Sioux tried to make good on their threat. Denny assured them that, as subjects of the Queen, they would be well protected."

"Certainly."

"Certainly, hell! If the Sioux assemble en masse in the West and are intent on fomenting violence, there'll be damn little a few hundred Mounted Police can do about it."

"Perhaps you're right sir. I agree that if they decide to come north, there'll be nothing we can do to stop them. We can, however, work to ensure that their presence is a peaceful one."

"If their presence doesn't enrage our own Natives. Crowfoot offered 2000 braves to fight with the Mounted Police should the Sioux cross the border."

"Indeed!"

"Denny thanked him for the offer, but made it clear that it was the desire of the Canadian government that the Blackfoot remain peaceful. Can you imagine the atrocities should 2000 Blackfoot engage just as many and more Sioux on the western plains? We can forget about settlement, I can assure you. And the transcontinental railroad that was promised to British Columbia as a term of confederation will surely go unfulfilled."

That was all politics to Walsh, who was more inclined to get to the nuts and bolts of the situation.

"Where are the Sioux currently?" asked Walsh.

"All reports still have them in Montana, in the vicinity of the Yellowstone River. Already, however, the American government has redoubled its efforts to bring them under control. If the past behavior of the Sioux is any indication, their willing agreement is not likely forthcoming. Intelligence points to their coming north instead. That's why it's imperative you return to Fort Walsh and make efforts to ensure that matters do not explode."

"I leave immediately, sir."

Walsh got up to leave and, as he grasped the doorknob, the secretary of state called to him.

"Remember, Inspector. Should Sitting Bull and the Sioux arrive, the very last thing we want is an Indian war."

"Yes, sir."

Walsh's departure to the post near the Cypress Hills was delayed only by a brief visit to his wife and daughter. With his goodbyes said, he made his way to Bismarck, Dakota Territory, by train and to Fort Benton, Montana, by sternwheeler. He completed the journey by horse and arrived in Fort Walsh in August. By December, the Sioux had become his problem.

Rumors had it that a band of Natives were moving up from the south. They were close to the Canadian border, not far from the Cypress Hills. Although the rumors weren't clear on the matter of tribal identity, Walsh had every reason to believe that the band was the first of the Sioux refugees. He had sent Sub-Inspector Edmund Frechette to investigate. Out for some days, the patrol was now long overdue. Walsh looked out the window at the blowing snow. An early winter blizzard assaulted the post. He wasn't one given to either undue concern or second guessing, but with every passing hour, both troubled him. Certainly the weather could have delayed the patrol, but what if the Natives had been hostile? Should he have led the patrol?

Walsh directed Sergeant-Major Joseph Francis to prepare a second patrol.

"I want a sergeant and 11 men. Sufficient rations for ten days. And tell them to dress warmly. This'll be no picnic. Send Léveillé in here."

"Yes, sir."

Soon Louis Léveillé arrived. Walsh thought highly of the Métis guide, whom he had first met on the Mounties' march west. The man was in his sixties, but like a bull buffalo, he only got tougher with age. Most importantly, he could speak Sioux.

"Léveillé, I'm leading a patrol south to Wood Mountain in search of the Frechette patrol. They should have returned by now."

"I'll pack."

"You're sure you want to go? In these conditions, it won't be the easiest patrol you've assisted."

"I'll pack," he repeated.

"Glad to have you aboard, Louis," smiled Walsh.

As the patrol rode southwest to the Cypress Hills, there was little to suggest they were Mounted Police. Riding boots and spurs were abandoned in favor of moccasins and woolen socks, both for comfort and practicality. The latter kept feet warmer and the former froze too readily to the stirrups. Fur caps were pulled tightly over their heads, but offered only limited protection from the sharp wind. A small opening exposed their eyes and noses to the merciless elements and the resulting deep redness was the only grim indication that these were the men in scarlet.

Five days out and about halfway to Wood Mountain near the White Mud River, the patrol sighted a band of horsemen struggling through the deep snow. As they got closer, a much relieved Walsh determined they were Frechette's patrol.

"Cripes, Frechette!" exclaimed Walsh. "Where the hell were you?"

"The snow, sir. It's made travel damn near impossible. We've had to make our way through drifts that literally swallowed the horses. On more than one occasion we couldn't move," he replied.

"Did you find the Natives?"

"Oh, yes, sir. Some 50 lodges, camped about 10 miles north of the boundary. They're Sioux. Claimed they didn't fight against Custer, but they had U.S. army Springfield rifles and horses with the army brand. They say there's plenty more coming."

"Let's make camp and get these men warmed up," barked Walsh. *So it's finally begun,* he thought to himself.

Jean Louis Legare heaved a great sigh, his expanding cheeks lost beneath a full, bushy beard. Reluctantly, he took out his ledger to begin the tiring task of taking inventory at his trading post. December was a good time to do it since business had fallen off dramatically. The hunters had long since arrived to trade for the goods they'd need for the winter. It would be spring before they were back with their thick furs, one of the few benefits of the cold, snowy season to come. A cursory glance at his shelves suggested that his supply was not terribly wanting. He had taken advantage of a late arriving bull train from

Fort Benton to stock up on most of what would be needed. From experience, he knew that by late winter the community's needs would be considerable. With or without money or trade goods, they'd come to his post. He always helped them if he could.

Legare was from Quebec, and through hard work and good luck had become the chief trader at Wood Mountain. There was only one other trader in the community, and Legare ensured that he made an adequate living. Both the Métis who wintered there and the Natives who traveled through or camped nearby thought highly of him. Legare was a rare commodity, an honest trader, one for whom profits did not fix the bottom line. He flipped through the pages of his ledger. There was as much red ink there as black and, more often than not, red numbers once penned were rarely removed to the black column. It was the price of compassion, one that he was willing enough to pay.

The door of his trading post flew open, and a man so tightly bundled that it was difficult to identify him blew in with the gust of cold wind.

"Jean Louis!" he called, as he pulled the fur cap from his head.

"Inspector Walsh, mon ami!" replied Legare, as he walked over and took Walsh's hand in his own. "It is good to see you and surprising too, with this weather."

"Yes, well we were out in search of a delayed patrol. But only the most serious of business encouraged me to continue onto Wood Mountain in these conditions."

"Ahh," replied Legare, "the Sioux."

"So you've seen them?"

"Mais oui. Two days ago a dozen Sioux come to the post. They do some trading. Their pack mules have American army brands."

"Our reports have it that about 50 lodges have recently crossed the boundary into Canada. Is that what you have heard?"

"Fifty!" Legare shook his head. "With these Sioux came maybe 400 lodges. Many different Sioux—Hunkpapa, Minniconjou, Sans Arc, Blackfoot, Oglala, Two Kettles. They are camped not four miles to the east with White Feather's band of Sisseton Sioux."

"And, if I'm not mistaken, White Feather has 150 lodges."

"That would be about right."

"Damn," muttered Walsh, "that makes for about 4000 Sioux."

Legare nodded. Both knew that a Sioux lodge might have as many as seven or eight inhabitants.

"Any sign of Sitting Bull?"

"I don't think that he is with them. Their leader is Black Moon, a Hunkpapa. I have been told that he is the hereditary chief of all the Sioux. An important leader."

"I guess I best pay him a visit then," concluded Walsh as he left the post. But first he'd visit White Feather.

Walsh and the small patrol he had with him made their way directly to the Santee camp. In less than an hour, he could see the wisps of smoke trailing skyward from their tipis. The wind had died down and the thin, light gray lines might have been drawn with a ruler. Soon enough, the tipis were in sight. Judging by those he could see, Walsh figured that the camp had at least doubled in size since his last visit. How many more lodges were lost among the trees or behind snow drifts? The Inspector made his way directly to White Feather's tipi. Before he arrived, the chief was informed of his presence and was ready to greet him.

"Ahh, Shagalasha, it is good to see you," began White Feather, as he embraced the inspector. The Canadian Natives commonly called Walsh "White Forehead," because the brim of his hat protecting his forehead against the sun had left a white patch against an otherwise darkened face. "I have been worried."

"And what worries you, my friend?" asked Walsh.

"You know that my people are peaceful. We obey the laws of the Great White Mother."

"And the Great White Mother has been pleased," replied Walsh.

"Now, our brothers and sisters have arrived from the south. They do not know the laws of the Great White Mother. They do not know what they must do to remain above the Medicine Line. I believe that if they knew such things they would obey. They wish to stay here and live in peace."

"I hope so. In any case, it's best that I explain those laws to them. That way there can be no misunderstandings."

White Feather gave a visible sigh of relief.

"I will call a council for this very night," offered the chief.

Walsh nodded his agreement.

The large lodge used for the council was well attended that night, and the warmth of the small fire in its center was hardly necessary. Powerful Sioux chiefs who had fought against Custer, including Black Moon, Little Knife, Spotted Eagle and Long Dog, sat on buffalo robes. Lesser chiefs and warriors were arranged behind them. Walsh, along with Léveillé who was there to translate, stood before the chiefs. A handful of Mounted Police stood nearby.

Walsh opened the council.

"I have little to say, but what I say is important and must be agreed upon," he began. "I will ask you some questions. The answers you give will be relayed to the Queen's Great Chief in this country." Walsh referred to Commissioner Macleod. "Then I will tell you the laws that govern all men in this country, red and white men alike. They must be obeyed."

"Do you know that you are in the Great White Mother's country?" asked Walsh.

"Yes," replied Black Moon, who spoke for his people.

"Why have you come here?"

"We have been driven from our homes by the Long Knives. We have come seeking peace. Our grandfathers have told us that we would find peace in the land of the Great White Mother. They told us of times past when they fought for her father," explained Black Moon. "Our brothers and sisters, the Sisseton, found peace here. We are tired. We want a place where we can lie down and sleep."

"Do you intend on remaining peaceful for the cold months of winter, only to return to the United States when the snow melts to fight the Long Knives?"

"No." Black Moon was emphatic. "We wish to remain here for good. We ask the Great White Mother to have pity on us."

"The laws of the Great White Mother are few, but they are important," continued Walsh. "You must not kill. You must not steal the belongings of another, including their guns or their horses. Above all, you must protect women and children. And, most importantly, you will not be allowed to make war on the Americans and then return to Canada for shelter. If that is your intent, leave now and do not return."

"We do not wish to fight. We never wanted to fight the Long Knives. They made treaty and then broke treaty. They brought the fight to us. But we will fight no more. We will obey the laws of the Great White Mother," concluded Black Moon to a chorus of murmuring agreement from those assembled.

Once Black Moon was finished, each of the chiefs stood and gave a speech echoing his sentiments. Finally, Walsh spoke again.

"I am pleased by what I have heard here tonight. I will tell the Great White Chief what you have said. Remain true to those words and you will be safe here."

The lodge erupted in exclamations of praise and thanks. Walsh left the council and, with his men, bedded down in the Native community for the night. The following morning as he prepared to leave, he was met by a delegation of the chiefs. White Feather spoke for them.

"White Forehead, we are hungry. Our women and children starve and their cries of suffering echo through the night. We have no ammunition to kill the buffalo. We hunt them with lances and lassoes and bows and arrows, but that is hard on our horses. They are nearly used up," explained White Feather. "Without ammunition we will truly starve."

Walsh was silent for a moment as he considered the request. Although he had their word that the Sioux would obey the Queen's laws, the evidence of their recent southern aggressions was all too overwhelming. And beyond their commitment, there was little to suggest that those violent ways had been abandoned. Still, he didn't want them to have to resort to theft and there was no reason to make winter any more insufferable than it had to be.

"The Great White Mother does not wish any people in her country to starve. I could give you some ammunition if I knew that it was to be used only for hunting. I know that the Santee will use it for that purpose. They have been peaceful since their arrival. But how do I know that the rest of the Sioux will not use the ammunition to fight the Americans?" asked Walsh.

"Again, they say they do not wish to fight the Long Knives," assured White Feather.

"I will trust them. I will meet with Mr. Legare, the trader in Wood Mountain. I will tell him to trade 2000 rounds of ammunition, and some powder and ball. It is to be used for hunting purposes only," he restated.

It was little enough, less than three rounds per family, and certainly insufficient to do much damage if used in an aggressive fashion. But what it did for the morale of the Sioux was not so insignificant. They were considerably relieved. In fact, they had much to consider. The white chief had told them that they would be treated the same as all others. He had given them ammunition. The white men who invaded their homelands had never treated them so. Crossing the Medicine Line was truly magical.

James Walsh gave the mid-section of his horse an easy squeeze with his legs and the animal broke into a slow trot. He and the three guides who accompanied him rode south along the White Mud River. It was early spring, and while coulees and ravines continued to give shelter to scattered patches of snow, the prairies were already alive with color and sound. The grass was green and reaching, with red-winged blackbirds and yellow-rumped warblers singing as they perched on the strongest of the blades. The buds of the first of spring's flowers were beginning to open and to decorate the riversides.

Walsh might have paid more attention to the natural beauty of the place had he not more important matters on his mind. Only three days before, scouts had ridden into Fort Walsh and reported that a large band of Sioux was just south of the border and moving rapidly north. The scouts couldn't say for certain whether or not Sitting Bull rode with the band, but Walsh wasn't taking any chances. Rumors abounded about the Sioux chief, none of them speaking well of either his character or his intentions. Walsh considered it essential to be present when the Sioux chief crossed the border, for he believed that a true measure of the man could only be gained by looking him in the eyes. It was also the only way to ensure that there would be no misunderstandings about the law and the necessity of obeying it.

After two days of riding, the party had found no sign of the Sioux. Perhaps they weren't as eager to arrive as he had been led to believe. Walsh looked to the south. In the near distance was a stone cairn recently built by the Boundary Commission to mark the invisible line that separated Canada and the United States. When they reached it, Walsh drew his horse to a halt. He scanned the southern horizon. Not a Sioux in sight.

"Boys, if the scouts were right, the Sioux must have crossed the line by now. Let's spread out," directed Walsh. "Louis, you and Daniels head east. Cajou and I'll go west. Scout for about 15 miles and then make your way back here. We'll meet up before nightfall."

Léveillé and Daniels splashed across the river while Walsh and Morin made their way through the prairie grass. As they rode, Morin's eyes were fixed on the ground, searching for any sign of recent activity. He finally shouted that he saw tracks. Even a tenderfoot couldn't have missed them. The ground was marked with an uncountable number of pony tracks, long deep lines of travois poles and the occasional dog print. The evidence suggested that here was a large band.

"How long since they crossed, Cajou?"

"Them tracks are real fresh. Not more than a couple of hours, boss."

"Let's follow them."

The trail continued north until it reached the White Mud River, after which it followed the direction cut by the flowing waters. They rode in silence, each aware that they were only two and that the Sioux undoubtedly numbered in the hundreds. Visions of what might transpire colored their imaginations blood red. But Walsh was nothing if not sure of himself and his mission. Sitting Bull and the stories of his savagery be damned. Walsh had a job to do.

They weren't riding too long when Cajou broke the silence.

"There, Major, up on the bluff. Two Indians."

"I see them Cajou. Keep riding. A nice, easy pace."

As the pair drew closer, more and more braves appeared and soon their presence blocked the rays of the low sun and cast a jagged black shadow on the river valley. Sitting astride their cayuses, with rifles across their laps, they were an imposing sight. A lesser man might have turned tail.

"We must be nearing the main camp," suggested Walsh.

The words weren't out of his mouth when they went around a bend in the river and came upon women and children busy setting up camp. Chaos ensued. The women screamed and, clutching their infants, ran from the approaching men. Those children old enough to scurry away on their own weren't far behind and dogs barked wildly at their heels. As quickly as they had appeared, the Sioux braves swept down from the hills and formed a barrier on the river, preventing Walsh and Morin from crossing it. The Sioux waved their rifles and started shouting at the pair.

"What the hell are they saying, Cajou?"

"They say we are scouts for the Long Knives," replied Cajou. "They say that many more are sure to follow."

"Tell them they are in the Queen's country and that we are her representatives! And, for God's sakes, tell them to lower their rifles!" barked Walsh.

The translation fell on deaf ears. As the two groups continued their uneasy standoff, Léveillé and Daniels barreled in under a cloud of dust. Their appearance did nothing to reduce the fear of the Sioux, who simply saw them as more American soldiers.

"Bloody great timing," muttered Walsh.

"I see that you have found them, boss," said Léveillé.

Walsh looked at the old scout and couldn't help but chuckle.

"I've always held that your powers of observation are remarkable, Louis. Cajou, tell them again who we are. Then tell them that we want to cross the river to meet with their chief," directed Walsh.

"I think that me saying it and them doing it are two different things, boss."

Nevertheless, Morin translated. After a few moments, the Sioux fell back and a narrow passageway into their camp emerged. With hundreds of rifles trained on them, the four rode carefully through the lines of tense braves.

"Steady, boys. And show no fear," encouraged Walsh.

As they rode into the camp, Walsh took note of the number of lodges. He guessed that there were about 60. When they reached the center of the camp, they were greeted by a handful of Sioux. For the most part, they were younger men, but one was noticeably older. He stepped forward. Walsh and Morin dismounted and walked towards him.

"I am Inspector James Walsh of the Mounted Police. You are in the Queen's country and we are the law here," explained Walsh.

"I am Four Horns," translated Morin as the elder spoke. "And this is my band of Teton Sioux. We are happy to be in the land of the Great White Mother. Our fathers fought with her father. We are glad to return."

"Is Sitting Bull with you?" asked Walsh.

"Sitting Bull is my adopted son," replied Four Horns. "He is still south of the Medicine Line."

"Four Horns, please call a council of your chiefs and leaders," requested Walsh. "I wish to address them."

Four Horns agreed and informed Walsh that a council would gather later in the day. Meanwhile, Walsh was directed to the lodge of Little Saulteaux. He was taken by the cleanliness of it. The tipi was constructed of newly tanned buffalo hides and made comfortable by plush buffalo robes laid on the ground. A most pleasing atmosphere was provided, one made all the more so by the presence of some Native women busily engaged in domestic activities. An older one cooked, while two others beaded moccasins. Little Saulteaux introduced them as his wife and daughters. Walsh's eyes then fell on a fourth young woman. Little Saulteaux said that she was his niece. Walsh later revealed that she was the most beautiful woman of any race that he had ever seen. All stood straight and wore well-kept clothes. It was not what he expected.

"Use my lodge as if it were your own," offered Little Saulteaux.

Walsh took the offer to heart and soon was asleep on one of the robes. An amazed Little Saulteaux left and told Four Horns.

"He is either very tired or very brave," suggested Little Saulteaux.

"Or perhaps both," replied Four Horns.

Too soon for Walsh's liking, Daniels rustled him from his slumber.

"What?" he grumbled.

"The Sioux are ready to hear what you have to say, Major."

Walsh stepped from the lodge into the twilight. Before him were assembled what he guessed to be the whole band. They were silent and solemn. Even the children were quiet, their desire to play lost, apparently during the flight north.

Walsh began to speak and Léveillé translated his words dutifully.

"Do you know that you have left your own country and entered into the Queen's territory?"

"We do," replied Four Horns.

"Do you know that there are laws here that all men, regardless of color, must obey?"

"We are new to this land," replied Four Horns, "and do not know of the laws that all must obey. Tell us of them."

Walsh repeated the directives that he had recently given to Black Moon.

"Do not disobey the laws if you want the Red Coats to defend you. And we *will* defend you. Your people may sleep soundly. You will be as safe as if protected by 10,000 Red Coats. But if you disobey our laws, you will not be permitted to live on British soil," concluded Walsh.

"We are tired and wish to sleep well," replied Four Horns. "We want peace. We want to hunt the buffalo. We will hold the words of the British chief close to our hearts."

"Hold the laws there too," advised Walsh.

Suddenly, a Native rider burst onto the scene. He leapt from his horse and made his way to the center of the council. Once there, he shook hands with the Sioux and planted himself firmly in front of Walsh and his men.

"Is it Sitting Bull?" Morin asked Léveillé, who shrugged in response.

"Mebbe."

The newcomer stared straight at Walsh and began to speak. Walsh listened for Léveillé's translation.

"The first time I met you was at Fort Buford. The last time was at the camp of Bear Coat. You tell these people that you are a Red Coat, but you are a Long Knife," he snarled.

He turned to the assembled Sioux.

"Do not listen to this man. He tells lies. He is no Red Coat, but a spy for the Long Knives," accused the Native. "As sure as the grass is green, he will kill you as you sleep. Do not let him go until you are sure that no other Long Knives follow."

When he fell silent, all eyes fell on Walsh. It was a pivotal moment. The Mountie seized the moment.

"I have spoken and what I say is true. Who is this man? Do you know him? Can you trust him? Can you be sure he is a friend and not a traitor?" he asked the onlookers.

Then, turning to the stranger, he continued his questions. "Why do you lie to these people? What is your purpose? Do you want them to break the law? Look at them," implored Walsh. "They are your blood. If you are not a devil, pity them. They are not my people and yet I pity them. And I will protect them as if they were my people. You are mistaken, man. You think I am someone else."

"It was you I saw on the Yellowstone," asserted the Native.

"You are a liar and a traitor! You are an enemy to these people!" exploded Walsh. He put his hand on Léveillé's arm as he saw the scout begin to bring up his rifle. Then he turned to Four Horns.

"I know not who this man is. But he is your enemy and I advise you to keep a close watch on him."

"We wished to sleep soundly," replied Four Horns, "but now our hearts again beat quickly with fear. I wish you to remain in camp until tomorrow."

"This will ease your fear?"

"It will."

Walsh fell silent as he considered the chief's request. He couldn't leave the Sioux uncertain about either his identity or intent.

"I will, but with two conditions," agreed Walsh. "Hold the newcomer, and send two men to Burnt Timber. There they may meet with Chiefs Medicine Bear and Black Horn of the Yankton Sioux. Tell them that Chief White Forehead is being held by Four Horns."

"No, we do not hold you!" objected Four Horns.

"If I tried to leave, you would stop me. I am being held," retorted Walsh. "But do as I ask and you will soon be shown a rascal."

Walsh slept soundly that night in the lodge of Little Saulteaux. He awoke to what he could only describe as an idyllic scene. Hundreds of horses grazed quietly on the spring grass. The outlines of restful warriors could be seen on the hilltops. Those who had long since seen their last battle relaxed in the shade. The lodges were animated by the activities of graceful women and children who remembered a little of how to be carefree in the light of day. The picturesque scene was shattered by war whoops traveling along the river. Within moments, a band of 200 braves exploded into the camp. At their lead were Medicine Bear and Black Horn. All wore the feathers and war paint.

Immediately, Black Horn recognized Walsh and rode to him. He dismounted and embraced the inspector. Then he turned to the Teton.

"Where is the man who says that White Forehead is one of the Long Knives? Bring him to me!" he demanded.

Four Horns called to have the command obeyed. Soon, a brave stood before him and, with his head low, spoke quietly. When he finished, Four Horns yelled at the man and finally turned to Black Horn and Walsh.

"The impostor has escaped."

"It is just as well," replied Black Horn. He put his hand on Walsh's shoulder. "Four Horns, this is my friend, White Forehead, chief of the land north of the Medicine Line.

You are fortunate that no hair on his head has been harmed. Had it been so, your camp would not be standing now. His tongue is not forked. No man who is in the land above the Medicine Line can disobey the laws. Should he, he will be punished."

Walsh was disappointed that the troublemaker had escaped. But as he prepared to return to Fort Walsh, he informed Four Horns that he was willing to forget about the unfortunate incident. For his part, Walsh was content to let the camp think about Black Horn's words. They had been well spoken.

Walsh and his party returned to their post after the encounter with Four Horns, but they hardly had time for a decent cup of tea when they were forced to ride out again. Word came from the south that a new band of Sioux was about to cross the boundary into Canada. The scouts who made the report were certain that Sitting Bull was among their number. In May 1877, Walsh set out with four troopers and two guides, one of whom was his trusted companion, Louis Léveillé. On this occasion, Walsh had abandoned his buckskin garb in favor of his official dress. The last thing he wanted was a misunderstanding with Sitting Bull.

The party made for Pinto Horse Butte, near the lower reaches of the White Mud River, which marked the western edge of the Wood Mountains. Walsh's goal was to arrive before the Sioux, camp and wait for them. In late spring, travel was easy and in two days, the party reached their destination.

"They already been here, Major," said Léveillé.

Walsh nodded as his eyes scanned the terrain. From fire pits to trampled grass, there were plenty of signs to suggest that a large gathering had recently camped in the area.

"Over here!" called Gabriel Solomon, the other scout.

As the men rode towards Solomon, the reason for his summons became apparent. On a wooden platform supported by four stripped saplings rested a body wrapped in a blanket. It was a traditional burial practice for many Plains Natives.

"Sioux. Bullets did him in," said Solomon in a matter of fact tone.

"Recent wounds?" asked Walsh.

"Non. They festered and ugly colors."

Walsh nodded. "Let's follow the trail," he directed. "Maybe we can catch up with them before dark."

That was not to be. Nightfall forced Walsh to make camp. Early the next morning they were off again and, within a few hours, they spotted Natives in the distance.

"Let's keep moving, men. Nice and easy, nothing surprising," ordered Walsh.

As the party progressed through the increasingly hilly terrain, what had been a handful of observing Natives multiplied into dozens. The braves held their positions, content to watch the Red Coats.

Soon, the camp came into view. The Mounties dismounted and began to walk towards the tipis. Their arrival was not greeted with the same surprise and chaos as when they entered Four Horns' camp. The Sioux scouts who watched their approach had given ample warning to their band. The Mounties hadn't walked far when a party of Sioux emerged from the interior of the camp. At the lead was one dressed in fine regalia of beaded leather and fur trimmings. A feathered headdress and stout wooden shaft embedded with three steel blades suggested he was of some importance. As he strode closer, Walsh recognized him.

"Spotted Eagle, it is good to see you again," said a smiling superintendent.

The chief nodded, extending his hand to Walsh.

"You are in the camp of Sitting Bull, White Forehead. You should know that no white man has so casually ridden into the camp of the great Sioux chief," informed Spotted Eagle.

"Those who obey the law in the land of the Great White Mother have nothing to fear," replied Walsh. "You will tell Chief Sitting Bull that White Forehead wishes to speak to him?"

"Sitting Bull wishes to hear what you have to say," answered Spotted Eagle. "Come."

The Mounted Police were led into the center of the camp. Gathered around a large lodge were several headmen, all donned in ceremonial garb. As the party approached, the seated men stood. One who was clearly the shortest limped towards the white men. In greeting, he grabbed the hand of Sergeant Bob McCutcheon, who was at the head of the party.

"I am Sitting Bull. Welcome to my camp."

"Uhh, thank you," blurted McCutcheon, likely aware of the historical nature of the episode. He was the first white man to greet Sitting Bull in Canada.

Sitting Bull made his way through the party. His broad face was alight, his great smile disarming the newcomers.

"It is good to be back in the land where my grandfathers fought," said Sitting Bull as he shook hands with the Mounties. "Truly, I feel as if I am home."

Walsh ignored the comment and instead directly broached the reason for his visit.

"I speak for the Great White Mother," he began.

"Then speak," said Sitting Bull. "I wish to hear what the Great White Mother has to say."

Walsh repeated the speech he had given to Black Moon and Four Horns while Léveillé translated. He outlined the laws that guided the conduct of all the Queen's subjects, and Walsh again emphasized that the Sioux under no circumstances would be allowed to use Canada as a base for warfare against the Americans.

"Do you agree with what I say?" asked Walsh of Sitting Bull.

"In the land below the Medicine Line, I fought only because I had too. I had no wish to fight," stated Sitting Bull. "But my wishes were as smoke in the wind. I tell you now that I have crossed the Medicine Line and my weapons are buried."

"That is good to hear," replied Walsh.

"Look around you," said Sitting Bull, as his arm made a great arc towards the lodges. "My people are tired and hungry. We have no bullets left to shoot the buffalo. Our horses have not the strength to chase the great herds. Can the Great White Mother give us ammunition?"

"You will be given enough to provide meat for your families. None of the ammunition must go south or be used to fight the Americans."

"My heart is full with feeling for the Red Coats," replied Sitting Bull, his fist on his chest. "I will do no wrong in the land of the Great White Mother. If I go south to fight the Long Knives, I will not return to her land. White Forehead, know that my heart is good...except when I come into contact with the Long Knives."

"That won't be a problem as long as you remain in the land of the Great White Mother. The Americans will not come here. Obey her laws and you will be treated as any other who lives in her territory."

Sitting Bull, 43 years old

"This is the greatest experience of my life," declared
Sitting Bull. "Truly a change has come over me. This is
a world different from the one I have left. The white men
are brave and fearless. Chief White Forehead walks into my
camp and takes my hand in friendship and peace. He treats
me as a man, not as an enemy to hunt. Have I fallen? Is this
the end, my brothers?"

Walsh didn't know quite what to make of the chief's praise and eloquence. Certainly, he spoke in a manner that demonstrated great oratorical skill. Whether there was truth in what he had said was another matter. Sitting Bull then fell silent and the other chiefs spoke. They made pledges similar to that of Sitting Bull, and with those words of commitment, the meeting came to an end.

As Walsh and his men made their way to their horses, Sitting Bull came to him.

"The sun will soon set. You will spend the night with us?"

"We gratefully accept the offer," replied Walsh.

Soon, the small party was alone, resting on comfortable buffalo robes in one of the tipis. As the men drifted off to sleep, Walsh whispered to Léveillé, "What do you make of him, Louis?"

"He does not look the part of the great warrior."

"We've both seen enough of this world to know that looks can be deceiving."

"True. There is no doubt that he has the respect of his chiefs and braves."

"What do you make of what he had to say?"

"Who knows the truth of what a red man says. Though he says it good."

"He speaks of his affection for us, but I look in his eyes and see revenge in his heart. If he is given the chance, he will go south to fight the Americans. He will have to be closely watched."

"Uh-huh," grunted Léveillé.

The next morning the party prepared to leave when three Natives rode into camp, leading five horses. Walsh paid them little mind until Solomon came over with some unsettling news.

"Them Injuns are Assiniboine from down Missouri way. Three of their horses belong to Father De Corby," he confided. De Corby was a Roman Catholic priest, lately working in the Cypress Hills.

"You're sure?"

"Pretty sure."

"Léveillé," called Walsh. "Head over to the horses those three Assiniboine just brought in. Solomon thinks they're stolen from Father De Corby. See if he's right. And don't be too obvious."

Léveillé did as asked and returned a few moments later.

"Oui, they are De Corby's."

Walsh reflected for a moment. Here was a good opportunity to demonstrate to Sitting Bull and his followers the law and his determination to enforce it. But was it foolhardy to attempt an arrest with a half dozen Mounties right in the heart of Sitting Bull's camp? It was no more than a fleeting concern. Walsh knew what he had to do and circumstances would not deter him from doing it.

"Sergeant McCutcheon!"

"Sir."

"Arrest the three recently arrived Indians for horse theft."

"Yes, sir."

Without a moment's hesitation, McCutcheon, with two constables and an interpreter, made his way to the three men. They were surrounded by some 50 Sioux, lost in conversations describing their recent trip. The Mounties weren't even noticed until they stood before the suspects.

"Your name?" asked McCutcheon, through the interpreter, of the man who appeared to be the leader of the trio.

"White Dog," he snarled.

"White Dog, you and your two companions are under arrest."

"Under arrest!" he laughed. "What for?"

McCutcheon explained the charges.

"The horses are mine. I will not give them to you. I will not be placed under arrest," he stated firmly, his cold eyes challenging the Mountie.

Walsh had been watching the event and, sensing that the dispute might not be put to rest quickly, walked over to take control.

"You think you can arrest me? A handful of white men in a camp of many braves. You are wrong. I am White Dog. I fear no white man. Feel my bite if you dare."

Walsh restated the charge and placed his hand on the shoulder of White Dog.

"You are under arrest for theft. Sergeant, disarm the men." The Mounties carried out their orders so quickly that they were completed before the observing Sioux had a chance to act. One of the constables held a pair of leg irons before White Dog.

"White Dog, you best tell me where you got these horses and what you're doing with them. Otherwise, you'll be placed in these leg irons and taken to Fort Walsh to stand trial."

White Dog looked to the Sioux who surrounded him. There were suddenly many more than there had been. It was clear that they would do nothing to support him. His eyes fell to the device. As he looked at it, he spoke.

"I found the horses wandering in the Cypress Hills. There was no one around, so I took them. It is the custom south of the Medicine Line."

"It is not the custom in the land of the Great White Mother," replied Walsh. "It is theft." Walsh fell silent. He didn't believe White Dog's explanation, but he suspected that his point had been made. "I will take the horses and return them to their rightful owner. You may go, but if this happens again, you will be arrested."

White Dog turned to leave. Disgraced, he had lost face among the Sioux. He was determined to regain some of it.

He muttered something and, even though Walsh could not understand it, he knew it to be a threat.

"What did he say, Léveillé?"

"I shall meet you again."

"White Dog!" shouted Walsh. "Repeat those words!"

White Dog turned and looked at him with defiance in his eyes. But he remained silent.

"Withdraw what you just said," ordered Walsh, "or you will return to Fort Walsh in leg irons."

"I did not mean what I said as a threat," replied an apparently chastened White Dog.

Walsh looked at the man and knew that he was clearly lying.

"Good. I want no misunderstanding. You may go."

With his chin low, White Dog left the gathering. Walsh and his men soon followed, with the horses in tow. Their departure was observed by Sitting Bull and Spotted Eagle from a nearby hilltop.

"It seems White Dog is not the warrior we were led to believe. Perhaps it is just as well he refused your offer of last summer to fight with you against the Long Knives," said Spotted Eagle.

Sitting Bull grunted in agreement.

"These Red Coats are strange men," continued Spotted Eagle.

"Yes, but clearly they are men to be reckoned with," replied Sitting Bull.

CHAPTER SIX

In the Medicine House

It was a hot summer day in 1877, and only the dependable westerly winds brought relief to the men stationed at Fort Macleod. Commissioner James Macleod was seated in his office. Resigned to the heat, he used a handkerchief to wipe the beads of perspiration from his face. At Macleod's insistence, the southwestern fort had recently been made the headquarters for the Mounted Police force. While the weather presented certain challenges to comfort, the new commissioner considered it a much more practical location than the northeasterly, isolated Swan River Barracks that had served as the command center under Commissioner French. On this day, however, such bureaucratic matters were far from his thoughts, which were instead dominated by a consideration of the Sioux situation.

Macleod had not met the refugee Sioux, but he had received detailed, firsthand reports from both Assistant Commissioner A.G. Irvine and Superintendent James Walsh. Based on those, he was confident in his understanding of the situation. The commissioner was both reassured and troubled by what he read in the officers' reports. Certainly, it was a relief to be informed that all the refugees, including Sitting Bull, had pledged to obey the Queen's law. Of course, neither Macleod nor the men who served under him were green enough to believe that such pledges meant much of anything. Only time would tell whether the Sioux planned to live by their commitments. From Walsh's observations about Sitting Bull's revengeful disposition, their continued peaceful demeanor was anything but assured.

Even if they did not harass Americans across the border, odds were good that there would be problems with the Cree and Blackfoot, long-time enemies of the Sioux. A recent report from Walsh gave evidence that suggested intertribal enmity might well erupt into large-scale prairie warfare. The superintendent had outlined the events of a troubling episode between some 30 British Saulteaux and 200 American Assiniboine. As Macleod again reflected on the confrontation and the manner in which Walsh had addressed it, he had to agree that the officer had carried out his duties most effectively.

Crow's Dance, the Assiniboine chief, had led his band from south of the border into the Saulteaux camp, where he demanded the immediate allegiance of Little Child and his band. Crow's Dance had emphasized his wishes by stating that he was an ally of the great Sioux war chief, Sitting Bull. The information was clearly meant to intimidate the Saulteaux. Little Child replied that he was a British Indian on British soil, that he listened only to the Red Coats, and that he would not bend to Crow's Dance's will. The Assiniboine chief had spat out his threat that he would eat the heart of any Red Coat who dared to step into his camp. Crow's Dance followed the threat by clubbing Little Child's head with the stock of his rifle. When the Assiniboine departed, the Saulteaux camp was in ruins.

After retrieving the horses scattered in the attack, Little Child went directly to Fort Walsh. The Saulteaux chief reminded Walsh of the promise made to him by the Red Coats: if he obeyed the laws of the Great White Mother, he would be protected. Incensed, Walsh led a party of 14 men in search of Crow's Dance and the outlaw Assiniboine. Macleod knew it was the correct decision. Not only did it enforce the rule of law and reassure friendly Natives of the honesty of the Mounted Police, but also it sent a message to Sitting Bull and his associates that violence would not be tolerated north of the border.

Within a few days, Walsh found the Assiniboine camp, only to discover that instead of 200 braves, as originally estimated, there were closer to 400. Macleod smiled to himself as he recalled the details of Walsh's arrest of the criminals. With the first rays of dawn catching the dew on the grass, the superintendent led his men quietly into the sleepy camp. They made straight for the largest of the tipis, believed to be the war lodge. They pulled the pegs from the ground and the Mounties slipped into the dwelling. Their assumption had proven correct; the tipi sheltered a dozen sleeping braves, each with faces painted in the dark colors of war. Little Child, who had accompanied the party so as to identify those who had attacked his band, pointed out Crow's Dance immediately. Walsh stepped over the sleeping bodies, grabbed the suspect's upper arm, dragged him outside and had him handcuffed. Within minutes, some 20 Assiniboine, all singled out by Little Child, stood shackled in the center of camp. Before the wakening camp could organize a response, Walsh and his men had retreated to a nearby butte with their captives. Even Macleod had to admit that the man had gall!

As the Mounties relaxed and enjoyed a leisurely breakfast, the scouts informed them of an approaching Assiniboine party. They rode under cover of a white truce flag and indicated that they wanted to discuss the capture of their chief and headmen. Walsh agreed to meet with them, but only after he had finished eating his breakfast. When they finally stood before him, Walsh lectured the group on the need to obey the Queen's law while in British territory. Then, he allowed the Assiniboine to take half of the captives back with them. They were young braves who had only followed the command of Crow's Dance. As for the chief and the older warriors, Walsh was determined to take them back to Fort Walsh to stand trial. He informed the Assiniboine that the captives would either walk or ride back to the fort; the choice was theirs. The Assiniboine left, only to return shortly with cayuses for the captives. Assistant Commissioner Irvine later sat in judgement of the culprits. Crow's Dance was sentenced to six months' hard labor, the others to lesser terms.

Macleod gave a silent nod of approval for his agreement with Walsh's performance. Undoubtedly, the moccasin wireless had spread the message that neither the law nor the Mounties were to be trifled with. Surely, the word strengthened Native respect for both. Macleod was less certain of the appropriateness of R. W. Scott's (the secretary of state) decision to send a personal note to Walsh to underscore the Dominion government's appreciation for his courage and determination in carrying out the arrest. After all, the officer was merely doing his job.

As he reflected further upon the Sioux presence, Macleod realized that there was more to consider than the possibility of increased intertribal warfare. Of even greater concern was the Sioux insistence that they were British Indians. They claimed the Great White Father (King George III of England at the time) had promised their grandfathers that in fighting for him against the Americans, they could return north and live again on British soil. Walsh himself reported having seen medallions struck with the image of George III in the possession of Sitting Bull and other Sioux. The claim was all the more troublesome given the American assertion that the Sioux, having crossed into Canada, had become a Canadian problem. Officials from the south insisted that the Dominion government establish a reserve for the Sioux and keep them there, far away from the border. Ironically, Sioux wishes and American demands seemed to dovetail on the matter.

Macleod believed simply that such a consequence would not do. To that end, he had already suggested to his superiors in Ottawa that the Sioux problem be dealt with quickly and firmly. Months prior to Sitting Bull's arrival, he had advocated their expulsion from British soil before they were too strong to remove easily. No action had been taken.

Throughout the summer, following the appearance of the great Sioux chief, Macleod had continued to strike at the same vein, suggesting that communication be opened with the United States government to determine the terms under which the Sioux might be permitted to return to their homeland. Macleod had pointed out that the limited resources of the Mounted Police could not restrain the Sioux presence effectively. The Sioux outnumbered the Red Coats by 15 or 20 to one. To keep the peace in the West successfully would depend a great deal on the cooperation of the newcomers, which could not be taken for granted. The financial position of the Dominion government could not easily support thousands of Sioux over the long term. Currently, it was easy enough to provide them with limited rounds of ammunition to shoot buffalo. Macleod had supported Walsh's decision in that matter. Clearly, it was cheaper than providing rations, even if it did strengthen the Sioux. But the great herds of buffalo that roamed the prairies were disappearing and the day was coming when they would no longer provide for the needs of the Plains Natives.

From whatever angle Macleod studied the problem, the only practical solution he could reach was to return the Sioux to the United States, and soon. The commissioner dipped his pen in his inkwell and once more outlined his thoughts on the matter to Secretary of State Scott. Then, he turned to the matter of Treaty Number 7, which was to preoccupy him through the late summer of 1877.

In the days following Walsh's departure from Sitting Bull's camp, the Hunkpapa chief devoted much time to considering what had transpired. Truly, the Red Coats seemed different than the Long Knives. Rather than use words to mask their intentions and then fire bullets to get their way, the officers above the Medicine Line actually did what they said they would. And they showed courage that would have been honored even among his own people. To arrest the Assiniboine in such a manner demonstrated a courage like that of braves who ran the daring line. The Red Coat Walsh, or "Long Lance" as the Sioux had come to call him (in recognition of the lances that flew the red and white pennons when the Mounties were on parade), seemed especially fearless.

Seeing white men behave in such a fashion was a new experience for Sitting Bull and it was puzzling. Perhaps the land of the Great White Mother was the Medicine House, the place where his people would be protected against harm. Other bands of Sioux had sought the safety of the land above the Medicine Line and had been treated well.

But, it was just as possible that the Red Coats were not what they seemed. Sitting Bull and his followers had no reason to trust any white man, and doubts about the Red Coats' trustworthiness nagged at him. The Hunkpapa chief shouldered a great responsibility for the welfare of his people and the past months had been difficult ones. Often, he wondered whether he was still fit to be their chief. Much depended on his decision to flee north. What he needed was some way to test the Red Coats further. Fortunately, just such an opportunity was about to present itself.

"Uncle!" called One Bull from outside Sitting Bull's tent. "Uncle!"

Sitting Bull stepped from his lodge.

"What is it, One Bull?"

"Three Long Knives have come to our camp. They claim to have messages from important people," explained One Bull.

"The Long Knives have nothing to say that I wish to hear," replied Sitting Bull as he turned to go back in his tipi.

"Uncle, one of the men is a Black Robe. The other two are known to ride for Bear Coat." One Bull spat the name given to the hated Native fighter, General Miles. "Should they be killed?"

At the mention of the name of Bear Coat, Sitting Bull stood still. He was silent for a moment before he spoke.

"There was a time when the presence of the Long Knives would surely have meant their death. But we have made a promise to Long Lance. We will not hurt the intruders, but we will keep them here. The Black Robe will be well treated. Take five braves and ride to Fort Walsh. Tell Long Lance of the Long Knives. Ask him what we should do," directed Sitting Bull. In dispatching One Bull for advice, Sitting Bull had kept his word to the Red Coat. He was eager to discover how the lawmen of the Great White Mother would respond.

Upon hearing of the presence and detainment of the Americans, Superintendent Walsh quickly assembled a party and made for Pinto Horse Butte. With him was Assistant Commissioner A.G. Irvine, who was at Fort Walsh at the direction of Commissioner Macleod. Irvine had moved rapidly through the ranks of the Mounties. He had been in the militia prior to the Red River Rebellion and had gone west with the Wolseley expedition. Later, he commanded the military garrison at Fort Garry. He joined the Mounted Police force as an inspector in the spring of 1875, and in little more than half a year, had been promoted to the position of assistant commissioner. Macleod wanted Irvine at Fort Walsh to oversee the handling of the Sioux. Walsh may have bristled at the presence of his superior and what it might suggest about his abilities, but he was likely satisfied that Irvine saw his decisions to be nothing but commendable.

The Mounted Police set out on May 31, arriving at Sitting Bull's camp in a place known locally as the Holes on June 2. There were some 150 lodges in the camp, and a Yankton camp with another 100 lodges was situated nearby. As they entered the Hunkpapa enclave, they were greeted by Sitting Bull and his headmen. The Mounties were informed that a council lodge was being constructed and that they would meet there shortly. Soon, four Red Coats—Irvine, Walsh and Sub-Inspectors Clark and Allen—stood in the lodge before Sitting Bull. Scouts were also present. Some half dozen lesser chiefs and a much larger body of braves starkly clad only in breech cloth were arranged around Sitting Bull. Men, women and children took up the space left in the council lodge. Walsh began the meeting, his words translated by one of the scouts.

"When One Bull came to Fort Walsh with news of the Americans, I was glad. I knew then that Sitting Bull is true to his word. I have come with Lieutenant Colonel Irvine, who is the highest chief of the Great White Mother in these parts," he informed Sitting Bull. "We wish to know why the Americans have come here."

"The Long Knives will not stay," Sitting Bull stated calmly.

"The chief will speak on that matter later," replied Walsh.

At that point, Chief Pretty Bear opened the meeting officially with a prayer to Wakan Tanka. As he spoke, he began the pipe ceremony.

"Look on me my grandfather. Have pity on me. You raised me to eat buffalo meat, to be strong. I am nothing now." Pretty Bear took the pipe and lifted it to the four cardinal points, giving praise to each as he did so. "My mother, take the pipe," he continued. "We are going to be raised in this land. My mother wants us all to smoke this pipe. My mother, make this land plentiful and full of peace."

Pretty Bear lit the pipe with a glowing buffalo chip. He gave it to Sitting Bull who again pointed it to the four cardinal points, eventually passing it to Irvine. "Grandfather, have pity on me. We are going to be raised by a new people." All then smoked the pipe, and in so doing, shared the strongest oath of the Sioux.

With the ceremony completed, Sitting Bull was the first to speak. He talked of the choice his people had made to cross the Medicine Line, of their decision to raise their children in a new land.

"Today, I come to speak what is in my heart. I shake hands with the British." He did so as he spoke. "I have shaken hands with the Long Knives since I was in my mother's womb. We were raised strong, with good hearts. The Long Knives chased us and we went north. They gave us flour. I said we want buffalo meat. They would not give us ammunition. If we had done what the Long Knives wanted, we would be nothing today," he explained. "My grandfather's spirit told us to come to this side of the Medicine Line."

"You told me that if anyone came into camp to let you know. These Long Knives arrived. They asked me for my gun and my horse. I was raised on a horse. Once we had plenty of them, but the Long Knives wanted them all, just as they want everything. They said they will take care of us. I told them that Wakan Tanka did not tell me to give our horses, our guns or our land away. I let the Great White Mother know. I am through," he concluded.

Other chiefs then spoke. They accused the Americans of dishonesty, describing their efforts to interfere with Sioux ways, especially the buffalo hunt. Each man held that any badness in the hearts of the Natives existed only because of the Long Knives. All were quick to add that such badness had been left behind at the Medicine Line. While the chiefs would shake hands with the Red Coats, and did, they would not with the visiting Americans. The Americans were ignored.

Assistant Commissioner Irvine responded to the words of the Sioux chiefs. He began by reminding them of the previously outlined laws that they must not wage war on the Americans across the border. He reassured them that if they obeyed those laws, there would be nothing to fear.

"In the land of the Great White Mother, we live as one family. If any man does wrong, whether white or Indian, he will be punished. I am glad to hear that you desire peace. It is good that you did as Major Walsh requested and sent for assistance from Fort Walsh when these Americans arrived. When word came, we left quickly, so that I might shake hands with you. Do not be afraid of the Americans, for they will not cross the border after you. Your families may sleep soundly."

"We are tired and wish to sleep," replied Sitting Bull. He then told the Mounties what the priest had said to him. The American suggested that the Canadians might not have the Sioux in their land. Even if they so agreed, the priest described an unpleasant future for the Sioux, one that would see them live poorly and dwindle in numbers. And if they remained in Canada, they would lose their land on the other side of the border. The priest asked Sitting Bull to surrender his arms and return to America with his people. He promised that American hearts would be glad. To protect Sitting Bull and the Sioux from bad men, he gave the chief a Roman Catholic medal. Sitting Bull held it high for all to see.

"Why should I return?" asked Sitting Bull. "For Long Knives to again chase me? Wakan Tanka will provide for me. I have only two friends," he confided, "the English and the Spaniards. I am glad you came, for had you not been here, I would not have known what to do."

"I have told our young warriors to put down their weapons," added Pretty Bear. "The only blood I wish to see spilled is that of the buffalo. If you send the Long Knives away, the buffalo will come and I will be glad. If the Long Knives would come as friends, I would be glad."

"If that is all you wish to say, I will meet with the Americans and determine their purpose for being here," said Irvine. With that, the council broke up. Later that day, after the Assistant Commissioner had interviewed the Americans, the council reconvened.

"The priest comes with letters of encouragement from the Commissioner of Indian Affairs and the Bureau of Catholic Indian Missions. They represent important officials. I believe his intent to be good. He has come to discover your intentions, whether you plan on remaining here or returning to America," Irvine informed the gathering.

"I was brought up here," claimed Sitting Bull, "and it is the reason I came back. Wakan Tanka brought food for me here. He will provide for my children here." Then he turned to the priest. "Listen to me. Look into my eyes. Wakan Tanka sent you to me. Can you tell me that what you say is what will happen? Do you know why we fought? You ask me if I will go back to your county. It is impossible. Once my heart was strong. Now it is weak and the Long Knives wish to lick my blood. Why do the Long Knives drive me? Because they want the land for themselves. Wakan Tanka did not tell me to fight the Long Knives and that is why I left. Wakan Tanka told me that if I did anything wrong, my people would be destroyed. So I came here. I followed the buffalo."

You say that you are a messenger from God, but what you tell me is not good for my people. I don't believe that the Long Knives ever saw God and that is why they try to fight me. I told the Long Knives to keep off my land. You ask me if I will throw my land away? I never will." Sitting Bull was emphatic. "I will trade. I was raised on horseback. I am made poor when my horses are taken. I will make treaty if we can keep our horses.

"I never did anything wrong to the white men. My body is clean," asserted Sitting Bull. "The Long Knives tried to cut me. Use your influence with the Great Father to send the bad men away. Then there will be peace."

"I have no influence to use," replied the priest. "Remain here if you wish. If you return, you will have to give up your horses."

"What you say is not what you told me yesterday," replied Sitting Bull.

"I do not want you to come back. But know that if you do, I would do all in my power to protect you," answered Father Martin. "But, after hearing what you and these British officers have to say, perhaps you are better off here."

"Have the Long Knives sent you here?" asked one of the chiefs.

"I am not an agent of the government, but I promise that my words are true," assured the priest. "Do you intend on returning or staying?"

"If I remain here, will you protect me?" Sitting Bull asked Irvine.

"I told you that the Great White Mother will protect you as long as you behave yourself," Irvine replied.

"Why would I return? To have my guns and horses taken? What can the Long Knives give me? The land they have taken is mine. I will remain with the Great White Mother's children," concluded Sitting Bull.

With that, the meeting ended. The Mounties were invited to stay the night in camp and they accepted. Following supper, the Red Coats walked freely through the camp, readily, if not quite comfortably, intermingling with the Sioux. Initially, the Mounties felt some surprise at the joyous atmosphere of the camp. On reflection, however, the dancing and singing were quite understandable, because for the first time in many months the Sioux were not worried their sleep might be interrupted by an assault of the American cavalry.

Before Irvine went to sleep, he received a surprise visit from Sitting Bull. The Hunkpapa chief described the Sioux encounter with General Custer. The assistant commissioner had noted previously the many trophies taken from the Seventh Cavalry, from animals to ammunition pouches to rifles. Sitting Bull's position was more understandable after he outlined his many grievances with the Americans. When the impromptu meeting ended, Sitting Bull gave Irvine a pair of his beaded moccasins.

As Irvine reclined on the soft buffalo robe, he reflected on the man with the terrible reputation. The stories preceding him seemed difficult to believe, unreasonable even. In fact, Irvine had formed a very favorable opinion of the man. Sitting Bull was amiable, his smile warming. His people were clearly in need and it seemed as if the chief was acting in their best interests. He had obeyed the directives of Major Walsh. Irvine could only conclude that the meeting would bode well for Sitting Bull's future conduct in Canada.

Prime Minister Alexander Mackenzie and Governor General Dufferin were seated in the prime minister's office in the parliament buildings. For the better part of the morning, they had been discussing the recently arrived Sioux. The two men shared a certain resentment at having to devote so much energy to the Natives, but both were well aware that the situation could all too easily develop into a problem of considerable magnitude. The prime minister was outlining his position on the matter.

"It is true that the Sioux who fled from Minnesota in the early 1860s were granted a reservation in Canada. However, the continued presence of the current wave of Sioux refugees in Canada is not a possibility," he emphasized. "I've talked with cabinet ministers and I've read reports from a variety of western officials. From whatever position their presence is examined, it heralds difficulties for the Dominion."

The governor general remained silent.

"If they remain, they will have to obtain a livelihood," he continued. "Their options are limited. They might raid our settlements in the West. Such an eventuality might well destroy our police force, for the Sioux greatly outnumber it.

You are aware that I've harbored doubts about the ability of the Mounties to perform the tasks for which the organization was created. This may well be their Waterloo. And, if by some chance the Sioux remain passive, the government will be forced to feed them, at what will be an enormous expense."

Mackenzie stood and stepped from behind his desk. He walked over to the window, which gave an unobstructed view of the Rideau Canal.

"Lord Dufferin, I am not a callous man. But surely the government's course of action on this matter is dictated to us."

"Indeed, it would seem to be," replied Lord Dufferin. As the governor general, Lord Dufferin was involved intimately in the Sitting Bull affair. At this point in Canada's history, Britain represented the country in all matters of external affairs and the governor general was the Queen's representative in Canada. As such, he exercised considerable influence, though generally in a most cautious manner. Over the past few years, he had provided delicate direction to Mackenzie's foreign policy, especially when it involved the Dominion's western expanse and her southern neighbor.

"Even their temporary presence is likely to cause problems," added Mackenzie. "Macleod has informed me that the location of the Sioux camp is in the heart of buffalo country. He warns that our own Indians—Cree, Assiniboine, Blackfoot, what have you—will hunt in the area for their own sustenance. Apparently, none of these tribes are friendly with the Sioux. To bring them together in a relatively small geographic area and then have them vie for an increasingly limited resource is in no one's best interest. While the Dominion government will not be providing rations under such circumstances, we will likely be witness to the rather undesirable sight of bloodshed. Macleod, for one, seems convinced that violence is imminent."

"The commissioner's observations are well reasoned. I agree that they should form the foundation for the Dominion's policy on the Sioux matter. They are American Indians and should return there. The challenge will be to avoid an international incident over Sitting Bull and his kin," concluded Dufferin.

The governor general got to work on avoiding just such an outcome. With the aid of the British foreign secretary, Macleod's proposal was forwarded to the American Secretary of State William Evarts, via the British charges d'affaires in Washington. Evarts received the proposal in mid-June 1877. He did not respond to it until late July and even then, his answer came only after the careful prodding of the charges d'affaires.

Evarts agreed that it was a sticky situation, one without a ready solution. His tentative conclusion was rooted in the American government's position that it was in no way prepared to make any concessions for the return of the Sioux. And why should it? Americans were quite happy to see the backs of the whole nasty lot of them! Furthermore, he did not see the Sioux as criminals subject to extradition, but rather as political offenders who had sought asylum in Canada. As such, he contended that their return could not be sought legally by the American government.

Evarts' position was unacceptable to Mackenzie, who was determined to have Sitting Bull and the Sioux removed from Canadian territory. Bypassing the British Foreign Office and attempting to do the same with obstructive American cabinet officials, the prime minister dispatched David Mills, the Minister of the Interior, to Washington. Mills was instructed to meet with President Rutherford B. Hayes and to urge him to organize a commission to see Sitting Bull and his followers. The commission's objective would be to induce them to return to their own country.

Fortunately for Mackenzie, all American government offi-cials did not share Evarts' view. General William Tecumseh Sherman, the commander of America's western forces, was of much the same mind as Macleod. If the British did not want to adopt the refugee Sioux as their own (unlike Macleod, however, Sherman would not have rejected this outcome), immediate action should be taken to force them back to America, before they recovered in strength and posed a renewed threat to the United States.

The American cabinet approved the proposed commis-sion on August 10, likely because it trusted Sherman's advice and it did not want to insult the British. It did alter its objectives slightly. Rather than focus on the return of the Sioux, the commission would investigate the best manner by which to avoid a hostile Sioux incursion into the United States. It's not clear that either the Canadians or the British were aware of this subtle change.

President Hayes' first choice to lead the commission had not been General Alfred Terry; however, if honest negotiations with the refugees were truly the intent of the American government, Terry was a strange choice indeed. The Seventh Cavalry had been under Terry's command during the Battle of Little Bighorn and he had been charged with punishing the Sioux following Custer's defeat, an assignment that he had performed enthusiastically.

On September 14, Terry, along with General A.G. Lawrence and Lieutenant H.C. Corbin (the commission's secretary), set out from St. Paul, Minnesota for the Canadian border. They were delayed by events that nearly saw the commission's collapse before it reached its destina-tion. American forces were engaged in yet another hostile action against resisting Natives and the commission's escort was called to aid in the fight.

Throughout much of the summer of 1877, the cavalry was preoccupied with its attempts to force the 800-large band of Nez Perces onto a reservation in Idaho. The Natives had resisted and, led by the savvy Chief Joseph, they had out-maneuvered the Long Knives successfully for some time. The army had chased the Nez Perces through the Rocky Mountains and onto the Montana plains. As the Natives con-tinued to ride north, it was clear that they sought the Medicine Line and the sanctuary enjoyed by the Sioux. On September 30, 40 miles from Canada, perhaps a ride of a few days, Bear Coat Miles met them at Bear Paw Mountain.

Desperate, the Nez Perces sent word to the Sioux and implored them to ride south and assist them in their flight. Though traditional enemies of the Nez Perces, the Sioux did consider the request. However, mindful of their prom-ises to both Walsh and Irvine, the Sioux decided not to par-ticipate.

James Walsh wasn't aware of either the Nez Perces' over-ture or the Sioux rejection of it. But he was certain that the army's pursuit of the Nez Perces wouldn't make the job of convincing Sitting Bull to meet with the commissioners any easier. Walsh wasn't against negotiations designed to return Sitting Bull and the Sioux to America. In fact, he believed that to be the most desirable outcome to the whole affair. But given the stand of the Hunkpapa chief, it seemed an uphill battle, one getting steeper by the day. He had left Fort Walsh on October 1 to carry out his charge of bringing Sitting Bull to the post. Upon his arrival on October 7, the Sioux chiefs had met in council to dis-cuss the proposal. Their words of opposition still rang in the Mountie's ears.

"Long Knives lie. The commissioners will lie. Meeting with them will make our hearts feel bad. There is nothing they can say that will make us return."

Later, Walsh met personally with Sitting Bull to try to change the council's decision. It was an effective strategy. Sitting Bull agreed to meet with the commissioners, but only because his good friend Long Lance and the Great White Mother wished it.

Sitting Bull and his headmen made preparations to go and, on October 8, they were ready to depart when Sioux scouts roared into camp with word that many people were approaching from the south. Immediately, rumors spread that the Long Knives rode to attack. Nothing Walsh said could convince them otherwise. They had good reason to believe confrontation was imminent. As the day progressed, upwards of 200 Nez Perces refugees who had escaped Miles' clutches filtered into the Sioux camp. Wounded, bloody and exhausted, they collapsed at the feet of the bewildered and worried Sioux.

"Chief Joseph surrendered three days ago," explained White Bird, their leader. "The Long Knives wanted us to give up our cayuses and rifles. Otherwise, they wanted us dead."

As the Sioux listened to the dire warnings of the scouts and the bleak descriptions of the new arrivals, they began to wonder whether they had made the right decision in opting not to aid the Nez Perces. They also began to question the words of the Red Coats. Perhaps the Medicine Line was not strong enough to stop the Long Knives. The Sioux held another council to contemplate the matter further. Walsh was invited to attend.

"Tell us, Long Lance, why do you wish us to meet with the men who kill Indians? You see the Nez Perces wounded. The blood of their women and children stains the ground of the Great White Mother. We cannot talk with the men who have such blood on their hands."

How could he disagree with their argument? Walsh had witnessed the plight of the Nez Perces for himself. He felt

A drawing of Sitting Bull's traveling outfit during the
Terry Commission; Red River carts shown beside the tipi

for their position, yet he was professional enough to realize
that he had a duty to fulfil. Throughout the day and into
the next morning the Mountie explained, argued and
debated, until finally the Sioux agreed to travel with him to
Fort Walsh and meet with the commissioners.

They set out quickly, Walsh trying to get the Sioux en
route before they changed their minds again. As the
Mounties and the 20 Natives rode west, they met up with
Commissioner Macleod, who had wrapped up Treaty
Number 7 with the Blackfoot and was heading to the border to greet General Terry. Upon discovering who he was,
the Sioux insisted on having another council meeting.

"Our hearts beat with fear," began Sitting Bull. "For many nights we have slept well in the land of the Great White Mother. Now we see our brothers and sisters, the Nez Perces, wounded and bloody. We are again afraid to sleep. The Long Knives will cross the Medicine Line and attack us."

"Nonsense," countered Macleod. "When you crossed the border, a wall was raised up behind you that your enemies dare not breech. So long as you behave yourselves, you will be protected by the Red Coats."

"There is no sense talking to the Long Knives," added Sitting Bull on a familiar note. "They are liars. We cannot believe what they say. We cannot accept any terms they offer because we have no faith in their promises."

In spite of his continuing doubts, the council ended with Sitting Bull agreeing to continue on to Fort Walsh, where they arrived in mid-October. It was slow going as the Sioux demanded regular stops to smoke their pipes and further consider meeting with the commission. Even when they set up their tipis around the palisades of the fort, they remained uncertain that they should be there.

The American commissioners were a day's march from Kennedy's Crossing, where arrangements had been made to meet with their Mounted Police escort. On this last night before they reached the border, Generals Terry and Lawrence were finalizing their strategy. Once again, they both read the missive sent by the secretaries of war and of the interior outlining their commission. Its objectives were twofold. First, they were to determine the danger of hostile incursions by Sitting Bull and his followers into America.

Second, they were to make the necessary arrangements to avoid such danger and to ensure that they were acceptable to the Canadian government.

"We're agreed, then. We'll make no concessions to Sitting Bull and his Sioux," said Lawrence, as he tossed the directive onto the table.

"It's enough that we've convinced the secretary of war to allow the Indians to keep their horses until they are safely on their reserves. It would have been a challenge to have them march such distances. Not that they don't deserve some punishment," added Terry, the decimation of the men under his command at Little Bighorn a constant thorn in his side.

"Clearly, the strength of our position rests in our government's desire to maintain much of the status quo," observed Lawrence.

"Yes, and it provides us with a 'no lose' situation. If we insist that the Sioux relinquish their arms and horses and cease their hostile operations, they will be easy enough to manage should they choose to return to their reservations. If they object to such terms and continue to live in Canada, we can at least say we made an effort to encourage their return. It must not be forgotten that the raison d'être of the commission is political," reflected Terry. "The Canadian and British governments contend that the Sioux remain American Indians while our superiors mostly hold otherwise. The meeting is designed as much to neutralize their complaints as it is to have the Sioux return."

"And should the Sioux choose to remain, and truthfully, I believe that there is little doubt of this," said Lawrence, "we can insist rightfully that the British and Canadian governments take action to ensure that the Sioux do not continue to be a hostile threat on our border."

"We'll make the case that they should be given a reserve far to the north. International law dictates such a course of action. Insurgent bodies driven by force across the boundary of a neutral state must be interned far enough away from the state from which they've come so that they can longer pose a threat to it. With any luck, this will be the last time we'll have to deal with Sitting Bull."

After a moment's silence, Terry continued.

"A rather unfortunate outcome. The bastard should pay for what he did to the Seventh Cavalry."

By the middle of the next day, the advance scouts of the commission's wagon train reported that the Mounties were waiting for them at the Canadian border. Terry, flanked by two captains, rode to meet the escort. Commissioner Macleod greeted them. He was splendidly dressed in his official scarlet uniform. Terry saluted him and the men dismounted to shake hands.

"Commissioner Macleod, your reputation precedes you," said Terry.

"Well, despite that, I trust you and your men will feel comfortable traveling with us to Fort Walsh," replied Macleod.

"We could ask for no better escort," chuckled Terry. "So, it is Fort Walsh where we will meet with Sitting Bull, then." The initial arrangement had the commission meeting with the Sioux at their encampment near Pinto Horse Butte. The commissioners requested the meeting be moved to Fort Walsh to save travel time.

"It was a challenge, but Major Walsh convinced Sitting Bull to come to the fort. However, the chief was none too enthusiastic about it. In fact, when he arrived, it took further words of encouragement to even get him to enter the fort," replied Macleod.

"The man is suspicious to the end."

"Perhaps with some reason," proposed Macleod. Terry's face darkened noticeably upon hearing the observation and the commissioner quickly changed tack.

"I see that you have quite a contingent with you, General."

"Three companies," replied Terry. "But I am well aware of the dictates of international law. The soldiers have been ordered to make camp in American territory and wait for our return. I would, however, request that the infantry company in charge of the wagon train be permitted to accompany us. I regard them as servants rather than soldiers."

"Certainly," replied Macleod, who was more concerned about the practical impact of three cavalry units on the Sioux than he was about the vagaries of international law. "And please, General, be so good as to accept our hospitality at Fort Walsh. No need for tents and cots where there are walls and beds."

"Thank you, sir."

The formalities complete, the commission advanced before a line of scarlet-clad Mounties, their red and white pennons fixed atop lances presented in honor of the visitors. That night they camped about 40 miles south of Fort Walsh. Moving quickly, the determined party reached their destination on the evening of October 16. The infantry pitched their tents at the south end of the fort, well away from Sitting Bull and the visiting Sioux, who were at the north end. Natives and soldiers alike passed a tense night, neither quite certain about their safety. The following day, the conference began.

Generals Terry and Lawrence were seated at a table, with their staff recorders and three accompanying press representatives seated at an adjacent one. Across the room that normally served as the officers' mess (chosen for the occasion because it was the largest room in the fort), a collection of buffalo robes were laid on the floor.

Sitting Bull led the Native delegation. The braids of his long, black hair fell from beneath a wolf-skin cap. He wore a black shirt decorated with large, white dots and a blanket covered his lower torso. Ornately beaded moccasins completed his outfit. Sitting Bull made himself comfortable on a robe, took out his pipe, filled it and began to smoke. As he sat there, content to watch the bluish clouds of smoke rise from his pipe and to ignore the Americans, his fellow Sioux entered the room. There were 10 chiefs in all and one woman, but none was as imposing as the leader of the Sans Arc, Spotted Eagle.

All eyes were drawn to the young chief as he made his way next to Sitting Bull. Spotted Eagle's naked, muscular upper body was decorated with figures drawn in white paint. Across his chest a rifle cartridge belt was strapped. From his neck dangled a charm of colorful feathers, a marked contrast to the single eagle feather that reached high from his head. His dress was completed by a buffalo robe wrapped around his waist. But the eyes of the Americans were drawn to his war weapon, a thick stick several feet long, from one end of which protruded three honed blades of steel. Spotted Eagle held its business end close to his heart.

Just before 3 PM, the designated time for the opening of the conference, the Mounties entered the room. Macleod and Walsh led a handful of officers. Sitting Bull and his fellow Sioux warmly welcomed them and each rose to shake hands with the Mounties. No similar greeting had been offered to the Americans. In fact, the first indication that the Sioux were even aware of the blue coats' presence was when Sitting Bull demanded their tables be removed so that he could see the Long Knives. Once some were, the conference began.

"For the record," began General Terry, "Baptiste Shane will translate. Two others translators are also present to verify what he says."

"We are a commission of the president of the United States, at the request of the Government of the Dominion of Canada, dispatched to meet you. The president wishes to make a lasting peace with the Sioux. He wants to end all hostilities, so that all of the people of the United States might live in harmony. He wishes this for both the whites and the Sioux," explained Terry.

"The president makes an offer to you. Should you return to your country and hereafter refrain from hostility against its government and people, you will be granted a full pardon for all acts previously committed. Let me be clear: you will not be punished for any such acts. They will be forgotten. You shall be received with the same friendly spirit that has welcomed other surrendered Indians. As the last band of Indians yet to surrender, you should look to your red brothers," advised Terry. "Like them, you will not want for either food or clothes as long as you remain peaceably at your agencies."

"It is true that those Indians who have surrendered were required to give up their horses and arms. But most of those goods have been sold to aid them. The money so obtained has been used to buy cows and farming equipment, so that they may make an easy transition to an agricultural lifestyle. Eventually, the proceeds of all such goods will serve that purpose," assured Terry. The offer made no visible impact on the Sioux.

"Under no circumstances will the president allow you to return to the United States mounted, armed and ready to fight. The violence of years past is not an option.

"There should be no more bloodshed," declared Terry. "The president has asked us to travel many hundreds of

A drawing from the *New York Graphic* of Sitting Bull and Commissioners Terry and Lawrence during the Terry Commission at Fort Walsh in October 1877

miles to deliver this message of peace. Let me conclude by emphasizing that under no circumstances will you be allowed to return to the United States unless you accept the proposals as laid out here today. Should you attempt to return with arms in your hands, you will be treated as enemies of the United States. Please consider the propositions made here today. We are ready to listen when you have arrived at an answer."

Sitting Bull had no need to talk matters over with his fellow Sioux. Instead, he embarked on a verbal reprimand of the Long Knives, one well practiced over many moons of flight.

"For 64 years, you have kept me and my people and treated us bad. What have we done that you should want us to stop living as we do? We have done nothing. Long Knives have committed the hostile acts. We had nowhere to go but to the land of the Great White Mother. We did not give you the country," Sitting Bull emphatically stated. "You followed us all over, so we came to this country. We learned to shoot in this country. I was raised hand in hand with the Red River half-breeds."

Sitting Bull rose from his seated position and walked to the Mounties. He shook hands with each of them, then continued to speak.

"You have ears and you have eyes and you see how I live with these people. Here I am! If you think me a fool you are a bigger fool than me." Sitting Bull watched as Terry's jaws clenched in anger. "This is a Medicine House," he continued. "You come here with lies, lies to tell in the Great White Mother's House! I do not wish to hear them. Go back to where you came from. This country is mine, and I intend on staying and raising my people here. We were raised with these British," restated Sitting Bull, again shaking hands with the officers. "That is enough. No more," he concluded.

Sitting Bull invited other Sioux to speak. Each chief in turn emphasized the points made by the Hunkpapa chief. In their greedy pursuit to own all the Sioux territory, the Long Knives had stolen their land and had chased them without mercy. Any action taken by the fleeing Sioux was in response to the depredations of the Long Knives, who were always the initiators. Forced to abandon their home-land, they chose to cross the Medicine Line to be with those whom they had known since childhood and could consider friends. A few Santee Sioux spoke of how well they were treated in the Medicine House. All the speakers took time to shake hands with the Mounties; all ignored the commissioners.

One of the last to speak was the lone Native woman attending. The presence of The-One-That-Speaks-Once was surprising. Sioux women generally played no role in such formal discussions. Her presence was meant as much a slight to the commissioners, a mark of Sioux disrespect, as it was designed to engender sympathy.

"I was in the land of the Long Knives. I wanted to raise my children over there," she explained, "but you did not give me time. I came here to raise my children and to have peace." She too shook hands with the Red Coats. "You go back. I will stay here and raise my children with these people."

As a group, the Sioux rose and prepared to leave the room. "Am I to understand that you have refused the offer of the president?" asked Terry, anxious for a response before he was presented with their backs.

"I could tell you more. If I did, you would pay no attention to it," replied a calm Sitting Bull. "This part of the country does not belong to you. You belong on the other side; this side belongs to us."

Crow, one of the Sioux chiefs, walked over to Commissioner Macleod and embraced him.

"This is the way I live in this part of the country. This is the way I like them," he declared as he opened his arms in a gesture of embrace.

"Go back to where you were born and stay there," he demanded of the commissioners.

"Is there anything more that the Long Knives wish to say?" asked Sitting Bull.

"No," came the terse reply. The conference was over; neither the words spoken nor the result were unexpected by any of its participants.

James Macleod heaved a great sigh of resignation as he left the conference room. He didn't enjoy being in Fort Walsh, and the failure to reach an agreement meant he would have to spend much more time at the post. In an effort to bring a resolution to the crisis, he decided to meet once again with the Sioux in a final attempt to change their minds. He asked Walsh to join him in the Superintendent's office, where he informed his subordinate of his intentions.

"This will not do," stated Macleod. "The permanent presence of Sitting Bull and his Sioux in Canada is not an option."

"And yet it would seem that our hands are tied in the matter," replied Walsh. "Both parties are equally stubborn. Perhaps with good reason."

"Reasons have become irrelevant. We have to make further efforts to ensure that Sitting Bull is aware that he must return to America."

"I'll organize another meeting."

"Inform Sitting Bull that only the Sioux and the Mounties will be present. Perhaps he will be more flexible in such company."

In the late evening hours of October 17, the meeting took place. Commissioner Macleod opened the discussions.

"You were asked to come and meet with the American commissioners and to listen to what they had to say. You were told that no force or influence would be used to interfere with the answer you chose to give them. Your answer is of the greatest importance to you and I hope that you have thought it through well."

"You must know that the Queen recognizes you as American Indians who have come into her territory for protection," reminded Macleod. "Your answer prevents you from ever returning to the United States with either arms or ammunition. Should you attempt it, you will also be our enemies."

"As long as you behave yourselves, you will not be driven from here. You will have to live by the buffalo that roam on this side of the line, a fact that presents its own problems. Surely you know that the buffalo will not last forever. Soon, they will all be killed. When that day comes, you will have to seek some other means of support. It will not be provided by the government of Canada," asserted Macleod. "Think not only of yourselves as you make your decision, but also of your women and children."

"I will communicate to the government what transpired here today. When they respond, I will give you their answer. I also wish to tell them of the grievances that you have suffered while in America. I can then tell the government what caused you to leave your country," explained Macleod.

Sitting Bull rose and shook hands with Macleod and Walsh. He needed no more urging to detail American depredations against his people.

"You know well how the Long Knives have treated us. They took me for their son, they came behind me with their guns. I have been in misery since the English taught us to shoot our meat with guns," lamented the Hunkpapa chief.

"I will speak the truth. Since I was raised, I have done nothing bad. Wakan Tanka and the Great White Mother know I have done nothing wrong. The Long Knives learned that our country, the Black Hills, was full of gold. I told them not to go there, but they wanted our country. I did not give them the land. Now in my country, my people suffer terribly. The Long Knives kill 10 or 20 of us every day for no reason," asserted Sitting Bull. "I wish to see my children alive and come to this country to be strong and live well and happy.

"Wakan Tanka gave us the buffalo to keep us strong. There will be plenty of buffalo for a long time. And there are other animals here. On the other side is only blood," he sadly reflected.

"I do not believe that you will help the Long Knives do me harm. Today you heard their sweet talk. I hope they do not come a second time. On the other side, we asked for traders, we got fired balls. The Long Knives robbed, cheated and laughed at us. I could never live there again. They never tell the truth. They told me that they did not wish to fight, yet they started it," contended Sitting Bull.

"I am glad we came here. You heard our woman talk today. We want to raise our children. We want to be friends with all who are here, white and Indian. None need fear," concluded Sitting Bull.

Macleod continued to listen in silence as the other chiefs added to the points Sitting Bull had made. They described treachery and lies, the deceit of open arms and concealed weapons. Their anger was well summed up in the honest words of Spotted Eagle.

"I wanted to trade, but the Long Knives fight. They break their word and I fight them. The Long Knives took our land. We did not take annuities from them. They say they treat their prisoners well. This is a lie. They kill plenty of us; I kill plenty of them," he proudly revealed. "I am glad we came here; all on this side of the line seem to have the one heart."

"So am I to understand that you have been driven out of your country?" asked Macleod after Sitting Bull had finished speaking.

The agreement of the chiefs was unanimous. Macleod looked into the eyes of Sitting Bull and after a moment's silence again spoke.

"I believe that you will do as you have promised. Go to your camps and tell your braves of the words spoken here today. If they misbehave, it may involve the lot of you in trouble," warned Macleod. "If trouble comes once, there is no telling where it may end."

"Major Walsh will return with you to your camp. You will be given provisions for the journey. You will also be provided with powder and ball to shoot the buffalo, some tobacco and a blanket for each. I give you these to show that I am pleased with your willingness to meet with the commissioners. And if you wish to trade, there are no restrictions save on the amount of ammunition you may receive. You may go where you like as long as you obey the laws. You know that you can trust us. The Mounted Police will always be your friends," concluded Macleod.

Sitting Bull and his Sioux left Fort Walsh pleased with the unfolding of events. The Mounted Police had been true to their word. The Sioux were allowed to state their case and had not been forced to return with the Long Knives. When the white chiefs in the east heard of their plight, they might be more willing to give the Sioux a reservation. And despite the commissioner's position that no goods would be distributed to them, he had given them provisions on their departure. Perhaps more would be forthcoming. Still, that was no great concern. They could live well off the buffalo, as they always had. Wakan Tanka would not abandon them.

Before the American commissioners left Fort Walsh, they were informed of the results of Commissioner Macleod's impromptu meeting with the Sioux. By the 18th, they were in possession of his hastily written report.

"Macleod thinks that the Sioux will not cross the line for some time to come. He contends we need not be anxious about that," suggested Lawrence.

"Anxiety is the least of my concerns," snorted Terry. "But I agree with the assessment. The last thing the Sioux want is to be further pursued by General Miles. And Macleod was clear and forthright in his government's position that a choice to return and fight will result in them losing their safe haven. One gets the sense that their hostility to us seems to dictate an opposing course of action."

"Perhaps they also believe that Canadian authorities will ultimately relent and give them a reservation as was done for the Sioux who fled after the Minnesota massacres," observed Lawrence.

"An unobjectionable outcome, as long as the reserve is not near the border where it might pose a threat to American security. Already Sitting Bull attracts disaffected Indians. We have to look no farther than the Nez Perces. Even if the Sioux did not venture across the border, their influence on our northern tribes would surely be an evil one. One can imagine the acts of hostility that they would counsel," suggested Terry as he stroked his goatee.

"It is not within our mandate to suggest measures that our government may take on this matter, but it seems appropriate to offer some recommendations."

"Get Corbin in here. We'll not waste any time in writing this up."

Upon its departure, the Terry Commission had sketched out the details of its report to the president. As they had long anticipated, central to their recommendations was the position that it was time to demand that the Canadian government provide some sort of reservation for the Sioux far from the American border. It was an option that clearly opposed the position held by Canadian authorities. As the American delegation rode south, the Sioux situation was no closer to being resolved than it had been before its arrival to Fort Walsh.

CHAPTER SEVEN

Sitting Bull's Boss

James Walsh felt the movement of the train slowing and he opened his eyes. Gone were the open vistas that he'd seen before drifting off to sleep. The train was passing through the outskirts of Chicago and would soon pull into the main station near the stockyards. With any luck, he'd be greeted there by a strong gale and be upwind of its stench. He rolled his shoulders, rubbed his face and stretched his arms as he tried to work out the effects of the nap on the awkward seat. He then reflected on the past few months.

Early in 1878, Walsh had been called to Ottawa to discuss the Sioux situation with Secretary of State Scott. While in the capital, he was also to recruit a new crop of Mounties. The trip required him to travel through the United States and Walsh still remembered his surprise when he found himself swamped with questions from reporters at each stop along the way. Every town wanted a first-hand account of Sitting Bull. Walsh got over his surprise quickly and soon came to look forward to the interviews. He was more than willing to give his "expert" opinion, which invariably ended up filling more than a few columns in local papers.

During the interviews, Walsh discovered that he enjoyed being the center of attention. He also learned that rarely did the reporters have their facts right. Walsh still shook his head in disbelief at some of the stories he'd heard. The most ludicrous was the assertion that the Natives north of the border were uniting in a great alliance to confront and crush the whites. Walsh had to stifle a chuckle when he'd first been asked about it. He was aware of the rumors suggesting some disaffected Cree were gathering around the renegade Chief Big Bear, but he knew that nothing had been proven. He wasn't surprised when his contacts informed him later that Inspector Crozier, who had been placed in charge of Fort Walsh during his absence, had investigated the reports only to discover that they consisted mostly of hot air. But American newsmen were convinced that the alliance was a reality and that, somehow, Sitting Bull figured prominently in it.

"No," Walsh declared. "Sitting Bull is not part of any such plan. Fact is, there's no truth to the alliance whatsoever. Likely, it was dreamed up by someone looking to play a joke or to curry favor with anxious American cavalry officials."

"So the Sioux pose no problem?"

"They're obeying the laws of the Dominion of Canada and as long as they do, there'll be no trouble," Walsh assured the reporter. "The problem is that the cavalry under Miles too readily accepts the word of traders and half-breeds who see the Sioux hunting buffalo and believe they're on the warpath. For my money, more than one of Miles' expeditions has been dispatched on the say of those unreliable jokers.

James Morrow Walsh—Sitting Bull's Boss—
in the Custer-inspired "uniform" he often wore
during his tenure with the NWMP in the West

"Now, I'm not going to suggest that there *might not be* problems with the Sioux," Walsh continued. "But if there is, it'll more than likely be a result of agency frauds in the States than of any action Sitting Bull might take."

"Pardon me sir, but isn't the Canadian government arming Sitting Bull and his men? Isn't that a little like putting the keg of gunpowder too close to the fire?"

Walsh bristled at the question.

"They are provided with ammunition to hunt. The officers of the Mounted Police carefully investigate each request and authorize traders to sell a limited amount of ammunition. We aren't about to let them starve, sir."

And on it went as he traveled through Montana, Utah, Illinois and Michigan. Americans proved hungry for information on the Hunkpapa chief, and Walsh fed their appetites enthusiastically. His fervor was somewhat dampened following a chance meeting en route with Commissioner Macleod, who was traveling west to the prairies.

"The newspapers are writing about a fellow named Sitting Bull's Boss," Macleod observed.

"I've seen it. I didn't choose the name, sir," Walsh replied.

"It's bad enough reporters use it to describe you, Walsh. You're far too liberal with your commentary on the Sioux situation. We're not likely to get them to return to the States any faster if you continue to criticize the American army and government—whether they deserve it or not. Use good judgement," Macleod advised. "You're an officer, man."

How many times had Walsh reminded his men of their position and the responsibility that accompanied it? Suitably humbled, he'd agreed to be more circumspect in his comments.

When Walsh later met Secretary of State Scott, however, he discovered that the last thing the minister wanted was a restrained view of events around Fort Walsh. He demanded a frank assessment of the conditions in the region.

"I'm afraid that the Sioux position seems to be solidifying," Walsh declared. "After the Terry Commission concluded, I rode back to Pinto Horse Butte with the delegation of Sioux. Never have I witnessed that kind of joy. The Sioux took the return of Sitting Bull and the chiefs to mean that they would not be forced to return to America. They had thought the meeting was a trap. Most were certain they'd never see their chief again—certainly not in Canada. Honest to God, there were tears of relief. At least the episode served to demonstrate that the Mounties are true to their word."

"Then it does not appear as if their return is imminent?"

"My feeling is that they'll return, but not in the near future. Last winter was a good one, with plenty of buffalo. But, if anything, the numbers of American Indians are increasing. The Nez Perces arrived before the conference. In the fall, the first of Crazy Horse's band arrived. You might recall that he was killed by the cavalry in September. Apparently his dying wish was that his people follow his spirit to the land of the Great White Mother," Walsh explained. "More are expected this spring—Oglala, Miniconjou, Sans Arc. Some are joining with Sitting Bull, others with Spotted Eagle. Whatever chief they chose to follow, it doesn't change the fact that there are some 800 lodges representing 5000 people. That translates into as many as 1500 warriors, about 500 more braves than were in the unceded territory around the Great Sioux Reservation before 1876."

The secretary of state was not pleased with the news.

"Five thousand! Can you imagine the cost of feeding them?"

"That might just be our ace in the hole," Walsh suggested. "The mildness of the winter past was unusual. If they are cold and without buffalo, they'll be miserable and more likely to return."

"So Commissioner Macleod assures me. But if the American public gets its way, we may well be filling pots left empty by the buffalo's demise. Their newspapers are full of accounts that suggest that the failure of the Terry Commission means that Sioux have become Canadian Indians. American government officials have not yet reached that conclusion, but they are pressing for us to intern the red devils. The presence of the Sioux is already taking on too much of a permanent character. If we were to grant such a request, we'd never be rid of them," Scott asserted. "We've let the appropriate American officials know that we continue to stand by our position. They are refugees seeking temporary asylum and we anticipate that arrangements will soon be made to return them to their homeland."

"A greater challenge might be to get Sitting Bull to accept such conditions. He has little faith in American promises."

"Convincing him is your job, superintendent."

The meeting concluded after Walsh had assured Scott that there was no truth to the rumors of a Native alliance. He went on to complete the task of recruiting. It was well into spring before Walsh was finally able to take a westward-bound train. As the stockyards came into view and the train rolled to a stop, Walsh decided to take time to stretch his legs. There'd be a delay before he continued on to Corrine, Utah. As he stepped onto the platform, a man ran up to him. His rumpled jacket, eager eyes and notepad identified him as a reporter even before he spoke.

"Inspector Walsh! Inspector Walsh! I'm with the *Chicago Times*. Might I have some of your time to discuss Sitting Bull and the Sioux?"

While he was down east, Walsh had continued to keep himself abreast of happenings around Wood Mountain, so he knew he could give an accurate assessment of the situation. He also knew that he'd been asked to hold his tongue on the matter. But surely a few words wouldn't offend any-one. Truth be known, he enjoyed the spotlight. Sitting Bull's Boss! It brought a measure of satisfaction. He glanced at his watch.

"A few minutes."

"Do you think the Indians will return to the United States? Will they consent to being disarmed?"

"I believe they can be induced to return. But it will not be a speedy process. Any proposals must be made before each band's council of chiefs. There it would have to be debated. Any objections made to it would have to be satis-factorily explained before agreement is secured. It is slow work and it might take as much as a year. But I do have faith that such a proposal will ultimately succeed.

"There is a reality that is rarely appreciated but that must be accepted if there is to be any understanding of the Indian situation," explained Walsh. "Indians are independent of each other. They don't readily follow their leaders as might be expected. They don't govern as we do. Suppose that Sitting Bull had returned to his people after agreeing with General Terry to return to America. His people likely would have replied, 'Fine, you go back.' Then they would have watched him leave."

"Sitting Bull's influence among the Sioux has diminished and his decision is not likely to carry great weight. Spotted Eagle grows in power." Even as he said this, Walsh knew it to be doubtful. The Sioux were likely to follow Sitting Bull's word, but it was best not to add to the concern.

The reporter scratched his notes eagerly and Walsh waited for a moment.

"Should they return," he finally continued, "it will be as a series of small rolling waves and not one great surge. A few families will cross the border as 'feelers.' Those remaining behind will wait to see how they are treated."

"Let me be clear," stated Walsh. "If the return of the Sioux can be accomplished, it will be a blessing for them and agreeable for those on the frontier. It would certainly be a happy result for both Canada and the United States since it would terminate the hostile question. Should they return, they would necessarily be disarmed and dismounted and thus conquered."

"Canada does not want the Sioux," he assured the reporter. "The proper place for them is on an American reservation."

"What of the possibility of a confederation of the Indians north of the border?" The damned question would not disappear.

"It is not natural to assume that the Sioux and Blackfoot would become allies," sighed Walsh. "They have been enemies far too long. We need have little concern about that possibility."

"The rumors to that effect..."

"...are exaggerated. I expect there to be little trouble when I return."

With that, Walsh went for a walk. Wood Mountain was suddenly on his mind. It didn't have great appeal. But he had little choice about where he was stationed. The Wood Mountain post had been established after the arrival of Black Moon and the first wave of Sioux refugees. In December 1876, Macleod had instructed him to remain there until the Sioux situation had been resolved. It didn't appear that would happen anytime soon, and Walsh resigned himself to spending considerably more time in the small, sod-roofed log dwelling.

Apparently, James Walsh didn't know as much about the Sioux and their activities among the Canadian Natives as he thought he did. In fact, Sitting Bull had been using his diplomatic skills in an effort to build an Indian confederacy. Walsh would have been very much surprised to learn that Sitting Bull had made overtures to the Blackfoot as early as 1876. However, Walsh was correct in claiming that long-standing animosities would present obstacles for Sitting Bull.

The Blackfoot and the Sioux actually had much in common. The Blackfoot were the strongest Native tribe on the southern Canadian prairies. They resisted assimilation to white ways. The buffalo was central to their way of life, figuring prominently both spiritually and physically. But, as Walsh had noted, the two tribes were also traditional enemies. Under normal circumstances, to have the two meet would be to see coup sticks lifted. But these were not normal circumstances.

Sitting Bull always gave careful consideration to the choices he made. And he always tried to plan ahead. He was astute enough to know that, if hostilities erupted between the Sioux and other Canadian Natives, he would be forced to return to America and live either by the rule of the Long Knives or die fighting it. His followers were weak after their northern flight, and Sitting Bull knew they could offer little resistance to the determined, unbending cavalry. To avoid surrender and its attendant humiliation, he sent tobacco to Crowfoot, the powerful Blackfoot leader. Why he did so is not clear. He may have sought to ensure the Blackfoot's active support in his anticipated war against the American cavalry. Or, possibly, he wanted to improve his people's chances of staying in Canada by seeking a friendship with the powerful chief. If his objective was to gain support for war, Crowfoot was the wrong man to ask.

Crowfoot was every bit the leader that Sitting Bull was. He had demonstrated his bravery on numerous occasions and had a proud collection of scars to prove it. When he received Sitting Bull's offer of tobacco in 1876, he was one of the Blackfoot's three head chiefs. Sitting Bull's efforts to persuade Crowfoot to join in the Sioux cause were unsuccessful. The Blackfoot chief had come to respect the efforts of the Mounted Police in ridding his people of the plague of the whisky traders. He was not anxious to have the Red Coats as enemies. In fact, not many months later in the fall of 1877, he made treaty with the Canadian government.

Spurned in his efforts to establish a military alliance, Sitting Bull pursued the friendship of the Blackfoot chief nevertheless. The two first met in the summer of 1877 when a small hunting party led by Crowfoot encountered a Sioux party led by Sitting Bull, near Fort Walsh. The Sioux invited the Blackfoot to share their camp. Presents were exchanged and the two parties declared peace warmly between their people for all time. There would be no more war or horse stealing. Because the pledge was made while the pipe was smoked, there was no doubt about its seriousness. Sitting Bull, for one, predicted that there was no longer any reason to fear his onetime enemies. To seal the agreement and to show his respect for the Blackfoot chief, Sitting Bull named one of his sons Crowfoot.

As 1878 drew to a close, Sitting Bull was pleased with his foresight. The winter was harsher than the one previous and the Sioux did not find buffalo in great numbers. This shortage presented a great problem to Sitting Bull, who was responsible for ensuring that his increasingly large following was adequately fed. They made their way to the White Mud and Milk rivers, which took them just south of the international border, where they encountered other tribes just as desperate for game. Though there was griping and discontent, especially among the young braves, the peace held.

The efforts of James Walsh also went far towards guaranteeing that there would be no violence on the Canadian plains during the winter. Throughout 1878 and into 1879, Métis leader Louis Riel promoted Native self-determination actively on the plains that straddled southern Canada and the northern United States. Riel was the leader of the successful Red River Rebellion of 1869–70. For his efforts, he was exiled to the United States and, for some years, he wandered from Métis village to Native camp in the territory south of the Canadian border. But the Métis had not forgotten the important role he played in forcing the Canadian government to recognize their rights in what became the province of Manitoba. They hoped he could do the same for them farther west. Riel was willing to try.

Because Riel couldn't enter Canada for fear of arrest, his plan centered on attracting Canadian Natives and Métis to his camp south of the Milk River. To do so, he spread rumors of a plentiful buffalo presence. He also suggested that the American government was sympathetic to his desire to establish a homeland for the Métis and their Native brethren. Rational men would have been doubtful, but for many, clear thinking had succumbed to desperation. His emissaries made overtures to the northern tribes. Crowfoot believed a more promising future lay in remaining faithful to the pledges made to the Canadian government. The Blackfoot would not participate. Riel enjoyed greater success with the Assiniboine, who pledged themselves to support his confederation scheme. However, Walsh successfully convinced Assiniboine Chief Red Stone to abandon his pledge when he visited the camp.

Riel remained convinced. His plan would work if he had the support of the Sioux. He believed that the commitments of Sitting Bull, Spotted Eagle and the other chiefs would go far towards convincing any reluctant Native leaders to participate. Indeed, he managed to draw increasing numbers of Sioux to his camp. Walsh's informants told him of Riel's plan and he dedicated himself to destroying it, without costing the Canadian people a dollar or an hour's annoyance, as he put it. Aware of his influence with the Plains tribes, Walsh spent much of the winter and spring of 1878–79 traveling from band to band and speaking with countless councils. He had not underestimated his standing with them, and before long, had pocketed pledges from all the important Sioux leaders, including Sitting Bull, to remain true to their agreements to obey Canadian law. Then, Walsh turned to his allies in the American cavalry, which had already been active in stopping many Native leaders from visiting Riel's camp. He persuaded them to go to Riel's camp and to demand that Canadian Métis and Natives return north. The two-pronged strategy was effective and soon, Walsh broke Riel's power. There was no more talk of aggressive Native alliances.

Sitting Bull's decision to reject Riel's overtures was likely influenced by another series of events as much as by any deep respect he had acquired for Walsh. The events in question involved the Nez Perces and the Crow. Sitting Bull had discovered a kindred spirit in White Bird, leader of the refugee Nez Perces. White Bird was just as determined as the Hunkpapa chief to exact justice from the Long Knives. The Nez Perces Chief suggested that his long-time friends, the Crow, would be useful allies in a war against the Long Knives. Sitting Bull was uncertain. The Crow had not been friends of the Sioux. In fact, they could regularly be found working for the cavalry as scouts or guides. If the Sioux mentioned the tribe's name at all, it was with great derision

A sketch of the Wood Mountain post; police headquarters
where James Walsh was stationed

and disgust. But White Bird was persuasive, and Sitting
Bull's dreams of routing his white enemies prompted him
to send tobacco to the Crow. The southern Native tribe
responded by raiding the Sioux and taking some 100 of
their horses!

Sitting Bull was incensed; his own kind had embar-
rassed him, humiliated him even. He called for all willing
warriors to visit his lodge to plan a counterattack.
Through the first weeks of winter, many heeded his call.
In late January, there was an unexpected visitor,
Superintendent James Walsh.

Walsh and 22 Mounties had been holed up at the
Wood Mountain post over Christmas. Officially, he was
still the officer in charge of Fort Walsh, but the palisaded post had seen little of him since his return from

the east. Perhaps it was just as well. Since his departure, he had become something of a celebrity at his home fort. The mess was graced with his portrait, and a banner had recently been added to it, declaring him "Sitting Bull's Boss." If he was stationed at the fort, decorum would demand that he have it removed, an unfortunate eventuality, as he rather liked it. But the simple fact was that greater control over the Sioux could be exercised from the more easterly post.

When Walsh entered the camp, there was none of the ceremony or friendship that had been seen previously. In a haughty tone, Sitting Bull outlined the actions of the Crow and then made his demands.

"Long Lance, where is the protection of the Great White Mother that we have been promised? What do you intend to do about these thefts?"

Unknown to Sitting Bull, Walsh was aware of the cause of the Crow assault. His response to Sitting Bull caught the chief off guard.

"You and the Nez Perces are to blame for the Crow raid. If you had not tried to plant sedition in their minds, their warriors would never have ridden into the Queen's country to steal Sioux horses."

"I never deny what I do," replied Sitting Bull, his chin high in the air. "I did send messengers to the Crow, and I did ask them to leave their reservation on the other side and to join with me so that we might defend ourselves against an attack of the Long Knives.

"But now, the Crow have attacked us. They do not act alone. They fight for the Long Knives. I will fight back. I will do to the Americans as they have done to me. I do not wish to fight. I never have. But I must," Sitting Bull asserted. "Meejure, I have never told you that I am a chief. Today I tell you that I am one."

"Then think hard Chief Sitting Bull before you take this course of action," counseled Walsh. "It will surely involve you and your people in a great deal of trouble."

Walsh returned to Wood Mountain and waited to see if his words of advice cooled heated tempers. He was there for a few months when, in late March, he was visited by Sitting Bull and many of the chiefs who camped with him. A council was requested because Sitting Bull wanted to make sure there was no mistake about the sincerity of his words. It was a contrite man who spoke.

"Meejure, I am here to tell you that my intent was not to wage war on the Long Knives. My desire was only to defend myself and my people," Sitting Bull explained.

"I wish to let the Great White Mother know that I have but one heart and it is the same today as when I first shook the Meejure's hand. I said then that I would never again shake hands with a Long Knife. I did so at the urging of the Meejure. I will not do so again," he pledged, his dark eyes unwavering.

"I look to the land of the north for my life. Those of my people who do not are free to return."

Though he hoped he did not show it, Walsh was excited to hear Sitting Bull's comments on this particular matter. Until this point, the Hunkpapa chief had held a tight rein on his people, more or less efficiently controlling what opposition there was with the threat of violence. Finally, he pledged not to interfere with those who wished to surrender. It was an important step towards resolving the greater issue of the Sioux in Canada.

"I'm glad to hear it, Bull."

Sitting Bull nodded.

"For myself and those who choose to remain, we would like some land to till," he continued. "Know, however, that I will not farm. I was raised a hunter and will hunt until there are only mice left on the plains. Where an Indian is shut up in one place, his body becomes weak. But others may wish to farm. The Meejure has long advised of getting our living from the ground. Where can we get the ground here?"

"The country you left is unsurpassed in farming potential, Bull," countered Walsh, who surmised that Sitting Bull intended to establish a legal foothold in the country through ownership of land. Best to crush that idea before it took root.

Sitting Bull ended the council with an olive branch and a pledge.

"There should be no lies between us, Meejure. My people need food. We have traveled below the Medicine Line in search of meat. We have not, we will not, stay south one day longer than necessary," he concluded.

If the Americans find you there, you may not have the choice to return, Walsh thought to himself.

General Nelson Miles was aware of the Sioux presence south of the border before he received orders to march on their camp. Scouts suggested there were as many as 600 of them hunting for buffalo along Beaver Creek, a southern tributary of the Milk River. They were led by Sitting Bull. Miles also knew they'd been hunting south of the border on and off throughout the winter. He considered their presence a significant military threat. In fact, in March, he had proposed a second commission to Secretary of State Evarts to investigate terms of Sioux surrender. It had been rejected. He had later learned that the basis for its rejection was that his government now considered the Sioux as Canadian Natives.

So be it. Whether they were American or Canadian, they were undeniably hostile. In early July, the cavalry set out from Fort Keogh on the Yellowstone River. As they crossed the Missouri River at Fort Peck, Miles was champing at the bit. He'd been wanting another crack at Sitting Bull ever since the Sioux had narrowly escaped his pursuing forces months earlier. To capture Sitting Bull…what a feather in his cap that would be!

The buffalo-hunting Sioux had gone about their business with little, if any, interference. But throughout the spring and summer of 1879, increasing pressure was placed on American government officials by the Indian agents who controlled the reservations. The Sioux were stirring up trouble on the reserves. They were killing buffalo upon which agency Natives depended. Furthermore, Natives who had surrendered were second-guessing their decisions. A forceful example was Crazy Horse's band. The opportunity to live freely with the Sioux, to pursue a lifestyle they had known since childhood, proved too powerful a lure. Despite their commitment to live on the reserve, many of them rode north to the sanctuary of Canada.

The agents were unwilling to admit their culpability in the flight of the agency Natives. Few on the frontier didn't know that much of the restlessness on the reserves was a result of the agents taking advantage of the Natives. Traders, who the agents oversaw, charged exorbitant prices and were always too ready to gouge, ignoring compassion. The agents themselves too often proved dishonest and unnecessarily authoritative or parsimonious when it came to disbursing government funds. Bear Coat Miles, however, was not one to reflect on the immediate reason for his assignment. He was pleased enough that he had been given the go-ahead to ride in search of Sitting Bull.

Though the Sioux were always aware of the possibility of an attack by the Long Knives when south of the Medicine Line, such thoughts were at the back of their minds on this occasion. The buffalo hunt had gone unexpectedly well. Butchering the carcasses had taken longer than expected. Just over 100 Sioux remained to finish the task while the others returned north with what had been prepared. Many of those who stayed behind were women because it was their job to prepare the meat. A few of the chiefs remained as well, including Sitting Bull, Jumping Bull and Long Dog. The men were resting when a group of Natives appeared on the horizon.

"Crow and Cheyenne approach!" called the lookouts. When they heard the cry, the women stopped their activities and waited for direction.

"They have red flags on their rifles," observed Jumping Bull. "Perhaps they want to parley."

"Let them approach, then," advised Sitting Bull.

What neither Sitting Bull nor his chiefs realized was that the advancing Natives were the scouting party for the as yet unseen cavalry unit, commanded by Lieutenant William Clarke. The red flags were not meant to indicate a willingness to talk; they were designed to allow the soldiers to identify their Native allies. The Sioux didn't realize this fact until they were fired on and two of their own lay dead!

No command was necessary to direct the Sioux response. The men spread out and created a makeshift cover to allow the women and few remaining children to flee. Then they returned fire. However, they had few rounds. Their limited supply had nearly been exhausted during the hunt. Pinned down, none had much hope that they could continue to defend themselves. They were not without courage, however, because death in battle was never unwelcome. But this day would not be the one that would see many of them visit their departed ancestors.

In a lull during the exchange of shots, a single rider emerged from the Crow line. He carried with him a white flag, suggesting his desire to parley. A Sioux brave rode out cautiously to determine his intent.

"We have a warrior, Magpie. He wishes to meet Sitting Bull in personal combat," explained the Crow.

The Sioux emissary rode back to his line and relayed the message to Sitting Bull. Although he had not been called upon to fight for some time, the Hunkpapa chief had lost none of his courage. And as a leader, he knew that to meet and defeat the Crow warrior would give his people needed confidence. He agreed.

Spotting his opponent, Sitting Bull could see even from a distance that he was a bull of a man. He had noticed him earlier in the battle, when his efforts to count coup identified him as one in whom courage was not wanting. What Sitting Bull did not know was that Magpie had been known to boast that, if given the opportunity, he would rid the Long Knives of Sitting Bull.

When the eyes of the two warriors locked, each drove his heels into the sides of his mount and charged. Sitting Bull saw Magpie raise his rifle. *Too soon*, thought Sitting Bull, *too soon*. He saw the smoke rise from Magpie's rifle, but heard no crack. The rifle had misfired! With no sense of urgency, Sitting Bull took careful aim. His bullet caught Magpie in the head. Sitting Bull rode to where the fallen warrior lay and cut what was left of the Crow's bloody scalp. Then he mounted Magpie's magnificent horse and rode back to the Sioux line, the scalp held high in the air. He was greeted with greatly animated warwhoops.

Within moments, the Sioux numbers were increased as word of the surprise attack had reached those who had left earlier in the day. With Sitting Bull's brave action fresh in their minds, they fought with renewed vigor. Soon, they were able to turn the tide of the assault and pin down Clarke's men. It appeared as if Sioux victory was certain when General Miles arrived with the main body of the force. Bear Coat quickly positioned the howitzers and, in the face of exploding shells, the Sioux made a hasty retreat. They didn't stop until they reached Rock Creek, just north of the boundary. There they counted their losses: five warriors dead, one woman captured and others injured. It was far from the great cavalry victory at the Battle of Milk River that Miles subsequently reported. But many believed him because they assumed that any battle that saw Sitting Bull retreat simply must be a great victory. Such was the weight of legend.

Above the Medicine Line, Sitting Bull readied his forces for Bear Coat's pursuit. He united with Spotted Eagle and other chiefs and waited, confident that he was not breaking his word to Long Lance. He would defend and not attack. He figured he would not have to wait long because word came from his scouts that Miles neared the border and that it would not prevent him in his mission to bring down the Sioux leader. There was good reason to believe the threat because Miles had long advocated an assault into Canadian territory to defeat the hostile Sioux once and for all.

However, Miles held fast at the border. He had been warned sternly by his superiors that crossing the line to fight Sitting Bull and his followers would result in harsh repercussions. While camped south of the border, James Walsh visited him. Their conversation was tense.

"I've orders to drive all hostile Indians above the border. They simply will not be allowed to enter the United States and conduct hostile raids," declared Miles.

"Quite right. If they're doing that, they should be punished. I'm under orders myself to report any suspected hostilities against Americans to your government," replied Walsh. "But these Sioux went south to hunt buffalo, and I can't see how that's a raid. The poor devils have got to eat."

"We've got our own bloody Indians who need whatever buffalo there is," snapped Miles. "And the Sioux don't stop at buffalo hunting. They raid farms, steal horses, even commit murder. There's a few I want to arrest."

"Of course, you'll have my cooperation. But the matter will need investigation. I'll advise my government, see what they want to do."

Walsh fell silent for a moment and tugged on his goatee. *How far should he go with this man?* Walsh made his decision.

"I don't deny that there might be a murderer or two among the Sioux. Like any people, they've got their share of bad apples. But there's plenty of good in them too. As a whole, they're honest people, fair-minded and willing to listen when they're listened to. Their courage is respected by all the Plains Indians and by more than a few whites. By my measure," Walsh added, "man for man, they're the equal of any white troops."

"Is that so," sneered Miles. "I know of a few white troops who'd like to put that assertion to the test."

Walsh laughed at the response.

"Well, let me assure you that it is my strong belief that the Sioux don't want to fight white people anymore," confided Walsh. "They'll take on your Indian scouts, but that's the most of it. Your Sioux are in the United States to keep from starving and nothing more."

"Let me also be frank," replied Miles. "My position, the position of my government, is that any hostile Indians who cross the line will be able to do so only if they surrender in the process. They'll have to give up their horses and arms and they'll receive food. And as long as the Sioux stay north of the border, they're your problem."

"I'll give the Sioux your message. What's more, I'll return with one of their chiefs who can confirm what I've said about their peaceable intent."

With that, Walsh tipped his hat and rode north. Miles remained uncertain about Walsh's assertion that the Sioux were suddenly peaceful. What's more, he was far from convinced that he'd believe the word of a Sioux, but he reasoned that there'd be no harm in listening. True to his word, five days after his first visit, on July 28, Walsh arrived at Miles' camp with Long Dog.

The Hunkpapa chief joked about the confrontation near Milk River and proved too much of a comedian for Miles' taste. Frustrated, the officer interrupted him in mid-description.

"Have the Sioux chosen their country? On which side of the border do you intend on remaining?"

Long Dog looked to Walsh.

"We intend to remain with Long Lance," he replied. "We come below the line only to hunt buffalo. It is as we have always done. We will not allow our women and children to starve."

"What of your raiding horses and taking scalps?" asked Miles.

"If young braves steal horses, it is only because they do not obey their elders. The young have a mind of their own," he sighed. "Though, too often it is not well used. We take scalps only in battle. And we fight only when attacked," asserted Long Dog.

"Then stay north of the line. It is where you belong. Your own acts have made you Canadian Indians. It is best for all," concluded Miles. Apparently convinced of the sincerity of both Walsh and Long Dog, Miles packed up his camp and returned to his southern post.

Meanwhile, Sitting Bull was busy entertaining American reporters. Through Walsh, who arranged all such meetings, Sitting Bull was often given the unique opportunity to express his views to the American public. Few of the newsmen were not impressed by the man, and what they wrote served to feed the Hunkpapa chief's growing legend amongst their readerships.

On this occasion, when Walsh met with Miles, the American officer asked if John J. Finerty of the *Chicago Times* could visit Sitting Bull's camp. Walsh acceded. Finerty came away extremely shaken by what he had seen and felt. "If he has not the sword, he has, at least, the magic of a Mohammed over the rude war tribes that engirdle him. Everybody talks of Sitting Bull, and, whether he be a figure-head, or an idea, or an incomprehensible mystery, his present influence is undoubted. His very name is potent."

Stanley Huntley of the *Chicago Tribune* was another of the select few to be granted an interview. Like many reporters, he described the chief in a manner that surely heightened American distrust and suspicion. Huntley exaggerated Sitting Bull's role in the destruction of Custer's cavalry. The newsman described him as having dark, piercing eyes, with low hanging lids that looked as if his brain had escaped into them. He noted the stocky, muscular body, appareled in traditional Native garb, though offset by awfully dirty hands. What Sitting Bull had to say to Huntley was a more accurate representation of the man.

"The buffalo are disappearing. What will you hunt?"

"I am a hunter and will hunt as long as there is wild game on the prairies. When the buffalo are gone, I will send my children to hunt mice. Wakan Tanka watches over us, as he does us all. He will never leave me to starve. When the buffalo are gone, he will leave me something else," replied a confident Sitting Bull.

"What of the cavalry, which even now is assembled to keep you from those herds?"

"We will avoid them if we can. If we cannot, we will fight them," declared Sitting Bull.

"Some of your brother Indians have surrendered and settled onto reserves. Will you?"

"I never wanted to go to a gift-house and I never will. They want my people to farm. I never will. As for Red Cloud and Spotted Tail [who had made treaty], they are rascals. They sold our country without the full consent of our people," he said, his dark eyes suddenly cold.

"Do you believe that you will be permitted to stay in Canada?"

"The Sioux have been in the land of the Great White Mother for two years. In that time, more Sioux have been born. Are they not her children? Will she drive them from the country in which they were born? No, she will let them stay. The Great White Mother will protect them and their fathers and mothers."

James Walsh listened. Sitting Bull said nothing he hadn't heard before. He also knew that, despite Sitting Bull's claims, his wishes were not likely to come true.

James Walsh was convinced that the Sioux would return sooner or later to the United States, but as 1879 dragged on, even his faith in the inevitable began to falter. With each passing day, it was evident that any Sioux

surrender would be much later than sooner. As the
Natives' desperation confronted the stubbornness of
Canadian and American government policy, the Mounties
were left holding the bag. It was increasingly difficult to
rein in the young, independent-minded Sioux braves, just
as Long Dog had warned. The Mounties were kept busy
extinguishing the fires of smoldering trouble. But with
winter approaching, the Red Coats were concerned that
the awaiting days of hunger would fan the embers of
Sioux discontent and quickly transform it into a raging
prairie fire.

Already, Walsh had confronted Sitting Bull many times
about Sioux braves crossing the Medicine Line and stealing
the horses of ranchers, farmers and settlers. He was honest
when he spoke to Miles; Walsh did intend to punish those
responsible for such acts. The superintendent had devoted
many hours trying to pacify the angry victims, who were
none too shy about voicing their grievances through the
mail of frontier acquaintances. Valuable hours were regularly
consumed by fruitless searches through the Wood
Mountain region. Invariably, the searches ended with a visit
to Sitting Bull's camp. Walsh seethed at the loss of time he
did not have to spare. The subsequent meetings followed
a common pattern.

"Where are the horses, Bull?"

"Meejure, I tell you that the only horses we have are
ours. Look if you wish. They are tired and weak."

"Do you dispute that your men continue to ride south
of the border?"

"I advise them not to, but I am not their keeper,"
shrugged Sitting Bull. "They are young men and their
blood is hot. They ask me why they should obey the laws
of the Great White Mother if she will not give them
a reserve. I tell them that we have agreed to do so and

that if we do not live by our word, we would be no better than the Long Knives. They say they have agreed
to nothing. They assure me they confine their activities to
the buffalo hunt."

"Hunt hell!" raged Walsh, his face reddening. It was one
thing to defend Sitting Bull before Miles. But when dealing
with the chief himself, it was sound strategy to use a pinch
of bombast and a dash of swagger. "Your men are raiding
American horses. It's cause enough to have your whole
bloody band sent south! You forget who's chief around
here. If those horses aren't returned to me, I will initiate
such a course of action."

Sitting Bull stared at Long Lance, his eyes taking a careful measure of the man. Was he bluffing? He didn't have to
study the Mountie long, for he already well knew that
Walsh was quite capable of acting on his threat.

"Meejure, I will speak to my braves. If they have the
horses, they will be given to you."

The horses eventually showed up at the Wood Mountain
post, where they were meekly given to the Red Coats.

On one occasion, however, when Walsh was enjoying
a brief stay at Fort Walsh, Sitting Bull showed up and his
demeanor was anything but meek. With him were Black
Moon and Four Horns. The first of winter's snow was on
the muddy ground and there was little warmth in their
greetings. It was more than an ordinary call. Walsh called to
one of the constables to get Morin. The translator soon
slipped into Walsh's office.

"We've got some visitors, Cajou. Tell me what they have
to say," directed Walsh.

Walsh had developed a passing ability with Sioux and,
even as Sitting Bull spoke, he got the chief's gist. What
words he couldn't understand were made clear enough by
the tone in which they were spoken.

"They are here for provisions, boss. They want flour, tobacco, tea, bacon…and bullets. They not happy with the Great White Mother. They say she not care if they starve. They know that the Mounties often give them food from their own supplies, but," he carefully added, "they say that not good enough."

The problems the Sioux had caused, their ungrateful-ness, their complaints and threats, they all suddenly coa-lesced and Walsh exploded.

"Holy bloody hell! You come here, into my very office and say that the Canadian government is not doing enough for you. Do I have to remind you that you are American Indians, here only by our good graces! And what do we get in return?" barked Walsh. "No end of goddamned problems. You cross the border and steal. You kill the buffalo that our own Indians need for survival. Your actions keep me and my men so busy that we can't devote the necessary time to our proper duties. Don't you come here and tell me what we have to do for you, Bull!"

Walsh continued on in a tirade with metaphors that were as colorful as a stretch of prairie wildflowers. Finally, his breath weakening, he concluded by advising Sitting Bull and his fellow chiefs to get their supplies from the trading post, just as everyone else did. For good measure, he added that if they stayed in his office and continued to insult him, they'd quickly find themselves in the guardhouse.

Sitting Bull did not like what he heard. He knew some English, but it didn't take mastery of the language to under-stand what Walsh had to say. Nevertheless, he waited for Morin to finish translating.

"Watch what you say, Long Lance. You talk to a Sioux chief." Neither his eyes nor his voice betrayed emotion as he spoke.

"I don't need the likes of you reminding me to whom I speak. Chief or not, if you keep this up, you'll be in irons!"

"No one talks to Sitting Bull like that," the chief replied. His eyes narrowing, his cheeks drawn tight, his hand slipped to the revolver strapped to his chest. Morin, Black Moon and Four Horns stood silently, their breaths frozen.

"My God man!" exploded Walsh in disbelief. "Are you threatening me!? Are you threatening the Mounties!?"

It was too much for the officer. He lunged from his desk and grabbed Sitting Bull by his shirt. Deftly spinning him so that he pinned Sitting Bull's arm behind his back, Walsh pushed the chief towards his door. Throwing it open, he kicked Sitting Bull in the butt and sent him sprawling on the cold, wet ground. Sitting Bull rose slowly, wiped the mud from his face and, with his back to the officer, again reached for his gun. Walsh took one great step into the quad and gave the Hunkpapa chief another boot in the rear.

By this time, Sitting Bull was incensed. The white man had humiliated him. Sitting Bull knew of only one consequence for such an action. Facing Walsh, he placed his hand on the revolver. Whether he would have fired at Walsh will remain unknown because Four Horns and Black Moon darted from Walsh's office and restrained their friend. Sitting Bull was determined, and the fight he put up against his two comrades suggests he was prepared to use his weapon. As the trio struggled, they stumbled into the window to Walsh's office and smashed it. A splattering of blood dripped from small cuts and mixed with the mud. Soon, the great Hunkpapa leader slipped to the ground, resignation plain on his face. He turned and limped slowly from the fort, Black Moon and Four Horns close behind him.

"To arms, men!" bellowed Walsh as the trio passed through the gates of the fort. "Ensure that your rifles are loaded. There might be trouble!"

Soon enough, the war whoops of the Sioux could be heard in the distance.

"Outside the palisades, men," ordered Walsh. "We've got to ensure they don't attack the townspeople."

Quickly, they assembled on the street that was lined with most of the local businesses. In the chaos, there was screaming and confusion. Doors were slammed shut and then there was silence, save for the cries of the approaching Sioux. As they neared the fort, Walsh ordered that two rails be placed near the entrance to the barracks. The Sioux rapidly approached the far side of the makeshift line.

"Tell them that's far enough, Cajou," ordered Walsh.

It's not certain whether the Sioux heard the command, focused as they were on expressing their anger. They waved their coup sticks and rifles and shouted what even those ignorant of Sioux could tell were threats. Walsh looked to Sitting Bull. He had led the Sioux braves in their approach and was now at their center.

"Tell Sitting Bull he caused enough trouble for one day, Cajou," shouted Walsh. "Advise him to return to his camp."

Initially, the words seemed to have no effect. But, as his braves continued on with their threatening ways, Sitting Bull raised his arm suddenly and pulled on the reins to his horse. The animal turned and the chief led his followers back towards their camp. Surely, he knew that he had no other choice. It's likely that, at that moment, he also realized that eventually he would have to lead his people back to America.

It wasn't long after the heated dispute at Fort Walsh in the spring of 1880 that Sitting Bull embarked on a diplomatic mission. He dispatched his nephew, One Bull, to Fort Buford, to discuss terms of surrender with the fort's commander. One Bull let it be known that Sitting Bull was willing to return with his people if acceptable terms were met.

"The terms of surrender have not changed," replied Colonel William B. Hazen. "Sitting Bull must bring his people to one of our forts. They will be required to give up their arms and horses. They will be treated kindly, given plenty of food and taken to an appropriate agency."

When One Bull reported the words to his uncle Sitting Bull the response was predictable. The terms were inadequate. The Long Knives refused to negotiate and the Canadian government was holding fast to its new hard line with the Sioux. One Bull struck out. In early June, he stole a horse from the Wood Mountain trader, Jean Legare. He victimized the wrong fellow because Legare was also the local justice of the peace. Immediately, he deputized two special constables and sent them to arrest One Bull. He refused to return with them and Legare went to see Walsh. Informed of the situation, the superintendent ordered two constables and an interpreter to go to One Bull and demand his immediate presence at the post.

"It'll be easiest for everyone if you come with us," encouraged one of the constables through the interpreter.

One Bull was less certain when confronted with the Red Coats and his resolve began to erode. Sitting Bull spoke.

"If you go, they will tie you up. Better for you to stay," he advised. "Let me go and see Long Lance. Make things better."

Emboldened by his uncle's words, One Bull refused to obey the summons. Walsh's reply was to send out four Mounties with clear orders: take One Bull, by force if necessary. It wasn't. One Bull returned with them to the Wood Mountain post.

Upon arriving, they discovered that 100 Sioux waited for them. The Natives had ridden hard from the Pinto

Horse Butte, eager to present the Red Coats with a sight that might spur the release of their captive. Men brandished their coup sticks and women stood behind them with rifles and cartridge belts. The eerie sound of war cries filled the air.

"One Bull!" called Sitting Bull. "One Bull! Turn! Fight! Run! Do not go with the Red Coats!"

Before his nephew could act, Walsh and a dozen Mounties fanned out before the approaching entourage and their prisoner. The barrels of their Enfield rifles were trained on the angry Sioux. The line of Mounties slipped apart just enough to allow their comrades to slip through. Once One Bull was safely behind the walls of the stockade, Walsh took action.

"You best listen to what I say. I'm the chief in these parts. You've got one minute to leave. One second more than that and I'll order my men to fire," he advised.

Even Sitting Bull took Long Lance's words seriously. Leaving nothing to chance, he waited for precious little of the minute to pass before he called to his people to leave. As they rode back to their tipis, Legare convened court and quickly dismissed the prisoner.

Later that night, some Oglala chiefs visited Walsh. They reaffirmed their commitment to the Queen's laws and went so far as to pledge their braves to fight with the Mounties against hostile Sioux if it came to that. Sitting Bull, meanwhile, was busy defending himself in a hastily convened council at the Hunkpapa camp. His fellow Sioux were blunt in their accusations.

"Today, you acted as a rascal," asserted one.

"And as a rascal, you got what you deserved, to be driven from the post like a dog," added another.

"Today, my heart was bad," Sitting Bull confessed. "It nearly caused my death. I can say that this was the closest escape of my life." Sitting Bull shook his head gently. "Had I raised my arm against Long Lance, I would not be here tonight."

"You are right. Long Lance is like Crazy Horse. He is not afraid to die to make us do what he demands. If we want to live above the line, we must obey."

Suitably chastened, Sitting Bull nodded. But obedience would no longer be enough to stay in the Medicine House.

CHAPTER EIGHT

Diplomacy
and Defeat

John A. Macdonald strode into the Prime Minister's office. Five years had passed since the last time he'd been able to throw the door open and walk in without asking. It felt damn comfortable. It was late October 1879 and his Conservative party had been returned to power. The centerpiece of the Conservative's platform had been Macdonald's National Policy, which had energized enthusiastic voters. It was designed to strengthen the Canadian economy by promoting immigration and industry, and Macdonald was convinced it was the program that would ensure Canada her rightful place at the table of great nations. He, of course, would be the man to take the chair. Or, if his goal took a little longer to obtain than he anticipated, Macdonald knew he would at least be recognized as the man who had made it all possible.

The only problem was that everything depended on the Canadian West. Macdonald was well aware that his National Policy and his vision for the nation would come to naught if western development did not unfold according to his plan. And, while he was mostly an optimist, in his more pessimistic moments he realized that such an outcome was far from guaranteed. First and foremost was the Sioux problem.

Macdonald settled behind his desk, nursed a tumbler of gin and cursed the whole sordid affair. As if he didn't have enough to worry about with Canada's own bloody Indians! The arrival of the Sioux and their continued presence was an unanticipated thorn, deeply lodged. Macdonald couldn't really fault his predecessor Alexander Mackenzie on the matter. He knew that Mackenzie stood hard and fast on the return of the Sioux to the United States. Yet, here they were, some three years after the first of them had started to flee into Canada, and the Dominion government was no closer to resolving the problem. To make matters worse, the American position had hardened over the past year; their officials claimed that the Sioux had become Canadian Natives.

And here on his desk was news of a most troubling episode at one of the handful of trading posts in Wood Mountain. Hungry Sioux had shown up at the establishment of Kendall and Smith demanding food. Apparently, the scene had become commonplace, with hundreds of Native refugees begging for food regularly. As usual, this crowd had nothing to trade, but claimed that the store's manager, a man named Allen, had bilked them so regularly in the past that he owed them supplies. Allen, however, would have none of it and demanded cash or goods. There was plenty of screaming, which no one really understood, and pushing, which heightened everyone's temper, but matters didn't turn nasty until one of the Sioux broke for the trader's house, adjacent to the store. While he was gone, everyone could hear the hysterical cries of the manager's wife. When he returned, the reason for her distress was evident. The Sioux held Mrs. Allen's infant in one arm. In his free hand, he held a steel hatchet, poised above the wailing baby's head and ready to strike.

"My children starve. You give no food. Your child will die too," declared the brave.

Mrs. Allen made one more lunge for her child, but the Sioux calmly kicked her away. Her action provided the necessary diversion for Daniel "Peaches" Davis to grab the loaded Winchester that was kept in the store for just such a purpose. Though still in his early twenties, Peaches was a retired Mountie who'd left the force to find his fortune. Evidently, he retained some Mountie bravado.

"Give the lady back her baby or you'll have a new hole in your head," he demanded.

"I've got a better idea, Peaches," called Allen, who had taken the opportunity to grab his own rifle. He leveled the barrel so that it pointed at a nearby keg of gunpowder. "If anyone makes the wrong move, I'll blow up the whole damn place!"

Peaches swallowed hard, and he wasn't the only one with a dry throat.

"Don't do it boss," advised Peaches. "Give me a minute to go get Major Walsh."

Allen thought for a moment and then gave his head a sharp jerk towards the door. Peaches darted away, the Sioux parting willingly to make way. Only seconds passed before Peaches burst into the Mounties' small post.

"I need Major Walsh right away!"

"He's sick in bed, man," replied Sergeant Hamilton.

"Sick or not, he's needed!" Peaches described the situation and Hamilton quickly made for Walsh's quarters.

Walsh rolled his eyes and sighed raggedly as Hamilton told him of the situation.

"Get some men over there now," he barked. "I want Mrs. Allen and her baby here. And tell those Indians that if they're not over here pronto, and I'm forced to get out of this goddamned bed, there'll be hell to pay!"

Four Mounties hurried to the store. Constable Allen (who was not related to the manager), by far the largest of the four, wasted no time once he arrived. Throwing open the door, he covered the distance to the Sioux with the captive baby in a few giant steps. The surprised brave released the infant when the constable gave him a stiff knee in the back. The Mountie gave the baby back to a much relieved mother.

"You want the Indians arrested, Sergeant?"

"First of all, I'll get Mrs. Allen and her child back to the post. We'll take care of them later."

Hamilton returned to find Walsh, wrapped neck-high in a blanket, perched on a barrel outside his quarters, waiting for him. Hamilton explained what had happened.

"Fine. Get the names of the Indians and then tell them to get the hell back to their camp. Make sure they know they're damn lucky not to be arrested. And tell the trader Allen to get over here."

Allen arrived and was given a tongue lashing the likes of which he hadn't heard since he was an unruly youngster.

"Allen, everyone here knows that your trading is legal robbery. The prices you charge would make an honest man blush. I'd say it's in your best interest to pack up and leave this community. Best we see your behind before something unfortunate does happen," he suggested.

Though he was under the weather, Walsh was still able to pepper his accusations and advice with appropriate expletives so that Allen was under no misunderstanding. In a few days, he was gone.

Macdonald was much relieved to hear the outcome of the incident. All he needed was a story about an Indian killing a white child! The impact of such a tale on his plans would be explosive. Settlement would be deterred and more money would have to be put towards policing the Plains, money the Dominion government simply did not have. Still, Macdonald had to admit that the Sioux had been remarkably well behaved since their arrival in Canada. The problems they'd caused were minimal and uniformly well addressed by the Mounties. However, all reports from his western officials suggested that the conditions that led to the Allen incident at the Wood Mountain post would continue, that bloodshed would be inevitable. The harsh reality was that the land could not meet the needs of the great number of Natives who were suddenly dependent on it. Priorities needed to be established and the few available resources had to go to Canada's own Natives. It was imperative to end the extended sojourn of the Sioux in Canada.

Committed to resolving the matter, Macdonald was left to ponder how it might be done. Clearly, further appeals to the American government would be ineffective. They were content to have Sitting Bull and his followers remain where they were and were unwilling to modify the terms of surrender so offensive to the Sioux. No, the problem had to be handled differently. Macdonald settled on a surprisingly simple solution. If the Americans didn't want the Sioux back, the Dominion government would have to take action to force the Sioux to return. They could be left no other choice. Such an approach required that Sitting Bull and the other chiefs be dealt with in a direct manner. They must be told that there would be no further supplies, no hope of a reservation, and they must be made to believe it.

To achieve the objective, Macdonald was convinced that he must remove the individual he saw as most responsible for the Sioux's continuing presence, Major James Walsh.

Macdonald believed that Walsh was sympathetic to the Sioux cause. He was certain that the superintendent of Fort Walsh enjoyed considerable influence with the Hunkpapa Chief; all reports testified to it. The prime minister believed that the officer used his influence for personal aggrandizement rather than as a lever to have Sitting Bull return to the United States. As his importance was so intimately linked to Sitting Bull—and Macdonald needed to look no further than the American newspaper clippings to see this—Walsh was hardly in a hurry to send the Sioux back to their homeland. To ensure that Sitting Bull went, Walsh would have to go.

James Walsh stood before the window of his quarters at the Wood Mountain post and stared at what lay beyond. The green hills rolled and the trees swayed with the stiff breeze, but he saw none of that, his eyes unable to focus. He stood there silently for some time. Eventually, the frustration became too great and he began to curse. Since he had received orders from Commissioner Macleod that his command was to be transferred to the northeastern post of Fort Qu'Appelle, there was certainly someone towards whom he could direct his anger. But he didn't. He just cursed the whole bloody mess.

He knew a little about Prime Minister Macdonald's position regarding the Sioux presence. Given that Macdonald was also minister of the interior and, as a result of the reorganization of government departments, personally in charge of the Mounted Police, it was inevitable that his position would carry the day. That was confirmed when a government report supporting Macdonald's view that the

Sioux must be made to leave Canada posthaste was quickly formalized into Dominion government policy.

Walsh knew well that his failure to deal with the Sioux in a manner acceptable to the new government was the reason for his transfer, although nothing to that effect had been said. The transfer had been couched as a promotion of sorts. Fort Qu'Appelle was in the heart of quality farming country and was expected to figure prominently in western development. A man was needed who could oversee the inevitable developments, a man with experience. Walsh was perfect for the job. Perfect, hell! His transfer was a result of Sitting Bull's continued presence in Canada. Walsh had his own connections and, through them, a pretty good grasp of what was being said about his efforts. What was being said was exaggerated at best and false at worst.

The latest accusation was that Walsh had been hired by an entrepreneur to convince Sitting Bull to join with a western touring party. It was true Walsh had been approached by any number of such promoters eager to sign the legendary Sioux chief and display him in eastern cities. The officer's response had consistently been, "No." But the accusation seemed to have greater staying power now that fellow officers and government officials blamed him for the Sioux problem and wanted him replaced.

Walsh was certain the Sioux would return eventually to the United States and he never wavered from his belief that such an outcome was in their best interests. One of the greatest obstacles to their return was the Sioux's own unwavering faith that they would be granted a Canadian reservation. That was not to be and Walsh had said so often. But he could have been more forceful in his assertions. Perhaps his actions had even been somewhat counterproductive. For example, while compassionate, it may not have been the most politically sound strategy to provide the Sioux with rations meant for

The killing of buffalo for sport, contributing to the decimation
of the herds and the collapse of the Native cultures
dependent on the buffalo for their way of life

the force. But then, Walsh was no politician. And, whether or
not Sitting Bull realized it, the Sioux would have to return to
the United States. The previous two winters had seen a dras-
tic decline in the number of migrating buffalo. The
Americans had done their best to decimate the herds before
they crossed the border, and there were simply damn few of
the animals left. What there were ranged little farther than

the Milk River in the United States, mostly inaccessible to the refugees. The Americans had made their position on that matter well known by interfering with Sioux hunting parties forced to travel south of the border.

Now that the Dominion government was intent on expediting the Sioux exodus south, Walsh feared for the safety of all those involved: his men, the settlers, the Sioux and the other Natives. Despite occasional outbursts of violence, the Sioux had behaved well while in Canada. There were good, trustworthy men among the Sioux, men whom Walsh would be the first to defend. But there were also troublemakers, those who wanted only an opportunity to sow their discontent. The new government policy to force them south might well provide just such a chance.

Walsh exhaled a great sigh of resignation. He supposed he should visit Sitting Bull in his camp, but he didn't have it in him. The old Hunkpapa Chief would surely know what Walsh's transfer meant for his people. As it happened, he didn't have to ride to Pinto Horse Butte. Despite Macdonald's sarcastic comment that a sitting bull, by its very definition, does not move, Sitting Bull came to see Walsh.

Sitting Bull took the news of Walsh's departure hard. He counted the Mountie as one of the very few white men who had been honest and truthful, whose words were backed by courageous acts. He considered him a friend, as much as he could call any white man a friend. Only the respect he held for the Red Coat had encouraged him to uphold the laws of the Great White Mother. Well…that and his desire to be given a reservation. As he rode with his fellow chiefs to Wood Mountain, he reflected on the number of occasions that he had acted to enforce the new law, even when it might have meant jail or worse for his braves. But the decision had always been made with the best interests of the band at heart.

There was little more Sitting Bull could do to pacify the officials of the Canadian government. Did his actions not demonstrate the truth of his view that his bad thoughts were buried in the land of the Long Knives? Had they not earned a reservation? Apparently not. As his cream-colored cayuse trotted along, Sitting Bull gazed at the open and empty prairie—a land that had once provided for them so well but now, with a cruelty known only to nature, was bringing his people to their knees—the meaning of his most recent vision became all too clear.

In the summer of 1879, the Sioux bands north of the border had gathered for a Sun Dance. Many months had passed since their last ceremony, and everyone felt the need to perform the ritual to strengthen the bonds among them. Sitting Bull had danced, as was his practice, for a message that would reveal the future and show what his people should do. He had danced long, his red blanket well earned, when he finally collapsed. Upon awakening, the message was clear enough. The Sioux could not continue in this way. They had two options. Either they would get a reservation, or they would return to America. With Walsh's departure, it looked as if their fate was sealed. Yet Sitting Bull would press his friend Long Lance one last time.

Walsh was in his office when a constable banged on his door.

"Sitting Bull is here, Major!"

Walsh jumped from his chair and made for the clearing outside the post. There were a handful of Sioux, but none were as imposing as Sitting Bull, who was dressed in his war bonnet.

"Bull, it is good to see you!" called Walsh.

"And it is good to see you, Meejure," replied Sitting Bull as he dismounted. "Though my heart is heavy. Is it true that you are leaving us?"

"'Fraid so, Bull. Let's go into my office and smoke one last bowl."

Nodding, Sitting Bull's face lit up with the smile that was almost as legendary as the man himself. He followed Walsh into the building. Once comfortable, they took out their pipes. Walsh shared his tobacco and soon the upper reaches of the small room were engulfed in a thick haze. They knew enough of each other's language to communicate. And, in this last intimate meeting, a translator would have been out of place.

"I've been reassigned. Going to Fort Qu'Appelle," Walsh informed Sitting Bull.

"Do my people's dreams of staying in the Medicine House go with you?"

"Sitting Bull, you know well, or at least you should know, that a reservation in the Dominion was never anything but a dream for your people. The government was never going to let it happen."

Walsh looked at Sitting Bull. The chief's face betrayed no emotion. For some time, Walsh stared at the man. Finally, his eyes fell and he spoke.

"You know the buffalo are disappearing. Soon, there will not be enough to feed you. The Canadian government will not step in and feed you. Your time grows short." Walsh again put the question to him. "Will you return to your homeland?"

"Those who want to go may," replied Sitting Bull. "You know that many lodges have left and that more talk of going." Indeed, Walsh was well aware that hundreds of lodges had returned since the spring of 1879. He had written letters of introduction to Indian agents and scouts on their behalf. "But I cannot go back. The Long Knives hold me responsible for the death of Long Hair. They will exact their revenge."

Walsh suspected there might be some truth to what Sitting Bull said. The memory of Custer's defeat remained fresh. What he didn't know was that Sitting Bull had investigated the possibility of returning to the Great Sioux Reservation. In the months following the cold, difficult winter of 1879, he had sent a letter to his southern relatives. "Once I was strong and brave; my people had hearts of iron; now I will fight no more forever," he wrote. "My people are cold and hungry. My women are sick and my children are freezing. My arrows are broken and I have thrown my war paints to the winds." The tone of the missive suggested that the Hunkpapa chief was aware that circumstances were slowly choking off his options. He had managed to remain for another year, but he knew that another winter might prove tragic.

After he had puffed on his pipe for a few moments, Sitting Bull continued. For the first time, he seemed to accept the inevitable.

"Perhaps it is time to stand before what must come. If the Great White Mother means to send us away, calves before the wolves, might the Meejure go to the Great Father and ask whether we will truly be treated as the other Sioux who have surrendered? I will believe what you say."

Walsh raised his eyebrow in surprise. Was the end in sight?

"Well, Sitting Bull, I have heard what the Americans had to say and I believe them. But if the government of the Great White Mother will allow me to visit the Great Father on your behalf, I surely will," pledged Walsh.

Sitting Bull nodded.

"I go now Meejure. I will wait for the news you bring."

Sitting Bull stood and slipped the war bonnet from his head.

"Long Lance, I want you to have this," he said, holding the richly decorated headpiece before Walsh. "Know that each feather represents an act of bravery when the Sioux were strong. There was a time when we were very brave," said Sitting Bull as he left the room.

Walsh looked at the war bonnet. There were many feathers. The officer could have been forgiven had he thought that the time Sitting Bull spoke of had not yet passed.

A few days after his meeting with Sitting Bull, Walsh rode north to Fort Qu'Appelle. There, he saw to it that the fort was in order and then made his way east to Brockville, to see his wife and daughter. While there, he was granted sick leave, because his erysipelas flared up again. But the Sioux and Wood Mountain were never far from his thoughts, so he was determined to schedule a meeting with the prime minister in order to fulfill his final commitment to Sitting Bull.

In early October, he wrote Macdonald. He informed the prime minister that Sitting Bull's first choice was to remain in Canada and be accepted as a subject. Failing that, and having no confidence in the American authorities, he noted that Sitting Bull had asked him to intercede with the American president on his behalf. He wanted to be certain of the conditions of the terms of surrender. Walsh also told the prime minister what he thought of the Sioux leader, praising him for his leadership and military abilities. "He is the shrewdest and most intelligent Indian living. He has the ambition of Napoleon and is brave to a fault. He is respected as well as feared by every Indian on the Plains. In war he has no equals, in council he is superior to all, and every word said by him carries weight and is quoted and passed from camp to camp." Civilize him and the prairies will be civilized, Walsh suggested.

The prime minister was none too pleased to meet with Walsh, but clearly, it was time to set the man straight.

Macdonald was particularly hot under the collar because of a letter from Edgar Dewdney, the Minister of Indian Affairs. Dewdney had informed Macdonald of the rumors around Walsh's final meeting with Sitting Bull. Allegedly, Walsh had agreed, at Sitting Bull's request, to meet with the American president to expedite the Sioux's return. It was a poor description of what had actually occurred (as suggested by Walsh's own letter), but Macdonald took the word of his minister. A Mountie conducting diplomatic business! Preposterous! The gall of the man! Macdonald would get to the bottom of the matter.

"Ahhh," said Macdonald. "I finally have the honor of meeting Sitting Bull's Boss."

"No man, certainly not a white one, is Sitting Bull's Boss," replied Walsh.

"I guess our American friends are mistaken, then," suggested Macdonald, as he threw a handful of American newspapers on the desk.

Walsh shrugged. "It wouldn't be the first time. If one seeks accuracy on the matter of Sitting Bull and the Sioux, it's not to those rags I'd be recommending him."

"Well then, how about the reports of our own government officials. How about your own reports?"

Macdonald lifted a folder from his desk and withdrew some sheets from it. He began to read from them.

"'I consider it of the greatest importance to both countries that Sitting Bull be settled in either one or the other'…perhaps that is familiar?"

"Certainly. I wrote it in my year-end report prior to leaving Fort Walsh."

"And presumably you hold to it?"

"Yes, sir."

"Damn it, man. It's this very attitude that has allowed Sitting Bull and his Indian followers to remain here for so long. Settled in America or Canada! Why should he desire to return if he believes that government officials are open to the possibility of his remaining?"

"I have always held that the Sioux should return. I have said as much to Sitting Bull on numerous occasions. The fact remains, however, that unless he is settled, he will continue to have an adverse effect on Indians on both sides of the border. He will attract those who wish to live according to the old ways of Indian life," answered Walsh.

"He'll have an adverse effect on more than the Indians if he remains in Canada!" shouted Macdonald. "We're not in a position to be distributing reserves willy nilly. We can't afford their upkeep; all available land has been set aside for white settlement. He must go!"

"As I say, I agree that to be the best option."

"It's the only option!"

Macdonald paused before continuing.

"And what's this I hear about your agreeing to visit the president—the very president of the United States—on behalf of Sitting Bull."

"As I see it, the greatest obstacle to Sitting Bull's return is his concern that the conditions promised to him by the American government will not be fulfilled. He is particularly concerned about his own safety. I told him that I would visit the American president on his behalf if my superiors permit it," replied Walsh.

"I certainly do not approve of any such undertaking! You're an officer of the Mounted Police, not a diplomat. And it's clear to me now that the greatest obstacle to the Sioux's return is a man who wears a red coat. You're not to have any future contact with him or his followers. Is that understood?"

"Yes, sir."

"Good day." A disillusioned Walsh left the office. He was not to see Fort Qu'Appelle for some time, as Macdonald, in an effort to break Walsh's influence with Sitting Bull, contrived to have him delayed in Ontario. When Sitting Bull finally left the country, Macdonald was determined to have him kicked out of the force.

Sitting Bull sat alone on a grassy bluff, burnt brown by the long summer. The first hint of fall was in the air and the green trees were colored with dashes of red, yellow and orange. As he puffed on his pipe, his eyes scanned the horizon. There were no buffalo. He listened to the birds. They did not speak to him. These were not the only changes, the only losses, in past months. He began to chant, slowly rocking from the waist up, but recent events could not be driven from his mind.

In mid-July 1880, Walsh's replacement as superintendent, L.N.F. (Paddy) Crozier, had arrived. Born in Northern Ireland and raised in Ontario, Crozier had reached the rank of major in the militia prior to signing on with the Mounted Police in 1873. Only 27, he was commissioned as a sub-inspector in the force. Having served in Fort Macleod, Fort Calgary and Fort Walsh, Crozier had attained a considerable body of experience in dealing with most of the Plains Natives. Early in his service, he caught the eyes of his superiors and was marked for promotion, which suited him because he was an ambitious man. He also had a very different approach than Walsh when it came to dealing with Sitting Bull.

Crozier's orders were clear: get the Sioux and their leader out of Canada. Crozier thought that Walsh's approach was seriously deficient, characterized by a coddling of Sitting Bull. He voiced his criticisms to his superiors and

Superintendent L.N.F. Crozier (1846–1901),
who was charged with getting Sitting Bull
and his people to return to the U.S.

then informed them that he would adopt a different, no-nonsense approach more in style with his personality. Perhaps drawing on his military experience, he suggested a strategy of divide and conquer. His plan was to isolate Sitting Bull, ignore him as much as possible and pound home to him that the hunger so many were experiencing was sure to continue. His plan met with enthusiasm from his superiors. In fact, the prime minister strengthened it by directing Crozier to tell the Sioux that there would be no more food from the government.

Crozier first met with Spotted Eagle, the Sans Arc war chief who intimidated so many by his appearance alone. That Spotted Eagle requested the meeting was evidence that Sitting Bull's power was eroding. Their conference went on for the better part of a day. Crozier used the time to make and to emphasize a single point: the Dominion government (or the Queen's Council House as he called it) would not grant the Sioux a reservation. Therefore, the Sioux should pack up and return to live with their brothers and sisters in the United States. But the old fears of Long Knife revenge continued to haunt Spotted Eagle. After all, he had been a conspicuous participant in Custer's defeat. Crozier assured him that his worries were unfounded. The Sans Arc Chief had only to look to his fellow Sioux who had surrendered. Were they not treated well?

Spotted Eagle was a pragmatist. After years of exile and with his band ravaged by hunger and poverty, he accepted the word of Crozier.

"Now that there is to be no more blood spilled below the line, I will shake hands with the Long Knives and live in my own country," he declared. Shortly thereafter, he led his 65 lodges to Fort Keogh, where they surrendered to the American cavalry. Only weeks on the job, Crozier had already enjoyed more success than had Walsh with his many months. But success with Sitting Bull would be a different matter.

Crozier was astute enough politically to know it was necessary to make some overture to Sitting Bull. Despite his waning power among the Sioux, he still commanded enough respect that Crozier's failure to meet with him might be considered a slight to all the Sioux. The two confronted each other in Sitting Bull's lodge. It was a short meeting. Crozier outlined the many arguments Sitting Bull had already heard. When the Hunkpapa chief remained impassive, Crozier added a new twist in the form of a not-so-veiled threat. Should Sitting Bull fail to lead his people south, he might jeopardize the favorable terms offered previously by the Long Knives. Favorable terms! If Sitting Bull had known the Red Coat better, he might have laughed. No. He'd wait to hear from Long Lance.

Sitting Bull's refusal to budge did not surprise Crozier. The superintendent harbored no illusions about the difficulty of his task. However, the meeting had strategic value. Crozier could meet with other chiefs and headmen and claim rightly that Sitting Bull had been consulted. More than that, he could argue that the stubbornness of the Hunkpapa chief would only cause them continued misery. Over the following months, Crozier acted on his plan, meeting either individually with Sioux leaders or with many at councils. More than a few agreed with Crozier's assessment of the situation and his appeals had the effect he desired. Handfuls of Sioux began slipping down over the border.

In an effort to halt Crozier's corrosive influence, in October, Sitting Bull took the remainder of his band to Burnt Timber, just south of the border. He claimed that the reason for the move was a report of buffalo in the region. But as he sat on the bluff, he knew it not to be true. And he had new problems. A Long Knife had arrived in his camp.

Edwin Allison, a scout under the command of Major David Brotherton out of Fort Buford, appeared unannounced. While the possibility exists that Crozier contacted Brotherton to place an agent in the Sioux camp, it's likely that the Americans didn't need much prodding. They were aware of the Canadian government's tough new stand on the Sioux and surely knew a little more pressure might end the whole affair. Furthermore, Sitting Bull and his 140 lodges were camped far too close to the Poplar River Agency and their presence had an immediate and negative effect on the Sioux within its confines. Sitting Bull's Sioux swept down on the agency, begging, stealing and generally causing trouble with the surrendered bands. Some in those bands even rode north to be with him. The situation could not be permitted to continue.

There was a time when the effort of an American cavalry scout to place himself inside Sitting Bull's camp would have surely meant his death. It was a time since passed. Sitting Bull would do nothing to jeopardize his dream of a reservation in Canada. Besides, Allison was known to the Sioux. They called him "Fish" because of his alleged slippery ways. He spoke their language and had a good understanding of their culture. And though they wouldn't trust him any farther than they could throw him, he showed up with a cartload of supplies that he was willing to distribute. Sitting Bull chose to eat his food and then to ignore the man.

Others listened. Most important among those was Chief Gall, Sitting Bull's long-time ally. Gall trusted the Long Knives as little as Sitting Bull did and may have disliked them even more, but Allison's appeals were powerful and heartfelt. Perhaps Gall didn't quite believe Allison's claim that the American government would make him the head Hunkpapa chief if he persuaded Sitting Bull to surrender. But the crafty old scout successfully kindled Gall's desire to return to old hunting grounds and familiar friends. And, despite the Sioux claim that they were raised in the land above the line, hand in hand with their mixed blood brothers, most in Allison's audience responded with recognition to his suggestion that they were but fugitives in an alien land.

Sitting Bull had no control over Gall, but when members of his own band decided they would also return, he became so concerned that he ordered those warriors who remained loyal to him to stop, by force if necessary, those who chose such a path. Through October, the bleeding stopped, but late in the month, Allison returned to the camp. This time, Sitting Bull gave him the hospitality of his own lodge. In the flickering shadows of the tipi's fire, amidst the smell of tanned buffalo hides and pipe smoke, the two spoke late into the evening. Allison's arguments were powerful, but they failed to sway Sitting Bull. Finally, Allison got to the heart of the matter.

"Chief, if you do not surrender and hand over your horses and rifles, the cavalry will ride north into your camp and force you into submission. General Miles waits at Poplar River, but he won't wait long."

"If that is my choice," Sitting Bull replied, "I will return to Wood Mountain and await the return of Long Lance."

He did just that. By November, Sitting Bull and those lodges that remained loyal to him were back in Canada. When he returned, the first Mountie he met was Colonel Irvine, who only weeks before had been appointed commissioner of the force. Irvine, whom the Sioux called "Big Bull," had journeyed from Fort Walsh to Wood Mountain intending to hold council with Sitting Bull. He wanted the Hunkpapa Chief to know that the position of the Dominion government was firm and immutable. The commissioner also wanted to know what he thought of the latest overture of the American government.

Irvine and his entourage met with Sitting Bull and 30 of his headmen on November 23, 1880. The meetings continued on and off for four days. The length of the commissioner's stay was indicative of the progress he made, but such progress did not come easily. Sitting Bull proved stubborn and, from Irvine's perspective, confused about the facts of the situation. Repeatedly Sitting Bull stated that he would not move until he heard from his friend Long Lance. He implored the commissioner to speed Walsh's return.

"Why is it that you wish so desperately to see Major Walsh?" asked Irvine.

"When the Meejure was here, I told him I did not know what to do. I was like the bird on a fence, not knowing on what side to hop," replied Sitting Bull.

"I take it that the fence to which you refer is the border?"

"I was inclined to surrender to the Long Knives. The Meejure told me to wait here for him until he returned, and he would advise me what to do."

"Major Walsh has been reassigned to another post. Currently he is still in the east and the date of his return is unknown and uncertain."

"I can't believe that my friend would desert me so."

"As Major Walsh's superior, I can assure you that he will not be back in these parts. Take my advice. Leave now for your homeland. Walsh would advise the same."

"The Meejure has assured me that the Queen is building houses for my people at Fort Qu'Appelle. He said that if he did not return by the first snowfall, I should travel north to see him," Sitting Bull informed the commissioner.

"Whether or not that was said, I can't be certain. But I am sure that there are no houses being built for you at Fort Qu'Appelle or anywhere else. And Major Walsh is not at that location," Irvine emphatically added.

"Give me time to talk with my council," requested a resigned Sitting Bull.

After a few days of consultation with his headmen, Sitting Bull informed Irvine of his intent. He would leave in a short time, perhaps two months. He would wait that time because he still expected to see Walsh. Failing that, he would let

Irvine know of his plans through Superintendent Crozier. This was good enough for Irvine. He left Sitting Bull's camp certain that the refugee Sioux would soon be back in the United States. Once again, it proved a premature assessment.

At the end of the year, Sitting Bull moved his lodges back into the Milk River region south of the border to hunt buffalo. Wakan Tanka smiled on them and they found some buffalo. As they hunted, they were visited again by Allison. He persuaded Sitting Bull to send a delegation to Fort Buford to meet with Major Brotherton. The hope was that the major could ease the Sioux's remaining fears and clear the way for their return. Among those who attended the meeting at the fort was Gall.

As he had agreed, Gall had returned to the Poplar River Agency in late November. But, rather than surrender, his band set up their tipis near the reservation. Within weeks, his 38 lodges had grown to over 70, as he was joined by others from Canada and Sioux from Fort Keogh who had already surrendered. Among their number were the one-time allies of Sitting Bull, Black Moon and Little Kettle. The growing presence, small as it was, worried the American cavalry, so the contingent at Fort Keogh was increased.

Despite pressure from the Long Knives at Fort Buford, Gall and his fellow Sioux made it clear that they would not move their tipis until the spring. In the meantime, they would hunt as they always did and wait for the arrival of Sitting Bull. Quickly, rumors spread that the Sioux expected bloodshed. Despite the warm words at Fort Buford, the cavalry labeled Gall's band hostile and attacked in early January. Captured, Gall was one of the many Sioux forced to walk to Fort Buford, a humiliating undertaking lasting eight days in harsh weather. Meanwhile, General

Terry, who had lost what little patience he had for diplomacy, ordered an attack on Sitting Bull's camp. News of the impending arrival of the Long Knives reached the camp before they did. More than half of Sitting Bull's lodges decided to surrender rather than flee north yet again. Only 40 lodges, plus some Oglala, followed the Hunkpapa chief into the Medicine House. The violent reaction of the Long Knives to the Sioux merely confirmed in Sitting Bull's mind that there would be no peace for him in the land below the border.

Sitting Bull pulled the blanket tightly around his shoulders and stepped from his tipi. Moving from the warm interior into the cold morning air almost staggered him. Through frosty clouds of his own breath, Sitting Bull's eyes scanned the camp. There weren't so many lodges now, perhaps 50. They formed a circle in the small valley. Snow was thick on the sides of the valley, but it had been trampled down inside the circle. Smoke from the tipis drifted skyward. Save those few signs of life, the camp might as well have been dead. It was a hard winter, the hardest yet experienced above the line. Ignoring the rumblings in his own belly, Sitting Bull looked to the south. The overcast sky gave little hint of a horizon and he turned and stepped back into his tipi.

At least they would eat well tonight. Word had come from the Wood Mountain post that Superintendent Crozier had planned a feast to which the Sioux were invited. It was the second such occasion in February. Sitting Bull knew that the meal was offered so Crozier might make another effort to convince his people to leave. He didn't care why

Sitting Bull, taken in 1883 while he was being
transported to the Standing Rock Agency

they were being offered food. It was enough that they
could go to Wood Mountain and not beg.

Despite having shrunken bellies, the Sioux ate their fill
and more. It wasn't until they were relaxing, smoking pipes
with tobacco graciously provided by their hosts, that
Crozier broached the subject of their return.

"Sitting Bull, you remember that when you were here
last, you suggested that a letter from the commanding officer

at Fort Buford might encourage you to return to the United States."

Sitting Bull grunted.

"I took the liberty of sending a party to Fort Buford for that purpose. They have returned with such a letter. If you'll look at it, I'm sure that you'll see the Americans will receive you well," said Crozier, handing Sitting Bull the letter. "You need not fear for your safety," he added.

Sitting Bull took the letter. A translator read it to him. He was silent for a moment and everyone held their breath.

"I don't believe a word of it!" he declared, throwing the letter to the ground. He turned to leave the hall.

"I don't want to see any of you again!" shouted Crozier, who had finally reached the end of his patience. Sitting Bull's inflexibility was responsible for the continuing presence of hundreds of American Natives in Canada. Despite his efforts to meet with them and to break the chief's influence, Crozier had not been fully successful. Failure grated on him. "I've had far too much trouble with you already. You can go to hell!"

Sitting Bull chose instead to return to Pinto Horse Butte, where his people managed to make it through yet another winter. A few buffalo made it near their encampment, but most of the meat was provided by the Sioux warriors who again rode south into the Milk River country. However, the winter dragged on longer than was usual and the ragged band of Sioux found themselves growing more dependent upon the goodwill of the traders at Wood Mountain. It was not easy for a proud people to beg, so when another opportunity to return was presented, the invitation received a warmer reception.

One of the compassionate traders was Jean Legare. Even he realized that it would be financially impossible to continue providing for the Sioux. Perhaps he wanted some of the glory that would go to the man who brought Sitting Bull back to the United States. He decided to take it upon himself to do what the Mounties couldn't: get the Hunkpapa Chief and his followers to leave. To that end, he planned a great feast. Knowing the condition of the band, he was confident that it would be well attended. When all had eaten, Legare took the floor. He had no problem commanding the attention of those gathered, because his reputation among them was sound.

"My friends, it has been five years since your arrival. Under normal circumstances, I would not take it upon myself to talk to you like this. But things are far from normal, and I believe it is my duty," he suggested in the Sioux language. "The spring is here and you have nothing. Your friends, the Métis and the Mounties, no longer wish to see you. But I will try to help you."

"There is only one good road open to you and it leads south. The Great Father will accept you as friends, as he has accepted your brothers and sisters. You are poor and if you love your children, you will accept my advice and surrender."

"How do we know the Long Knives will be true to their word?" asked one of the headmen. "Can we be sure we will not be killed?"

"I believe them, but I know you remain uncertain. I tell you what I will do. Those of you who trust me, ride with me to Fort Buford. I will provide you with horses, ammunition and food. If you do not receive a good answer there, I will take you back with me."

"What if they will not allow us to return?"

"Then I, too, will remain."

The response met with a chorus of approval. In late April, Legare led a party of some 30 Sioux southwest to Fort Buford. Sitting Bull was not among their number.

Upset at losing more of his band, he sent a handful of warriors after the party. They persuaded about half of the
departing Sioux to return. In early May, the remainder surrendered at Fort Buford.

For his part, Sitting Bull was intent on making one last
effort to meet with his friend Long Lance. He was determined not to ride south until he spoke with Walsh. He
would not be confident in the promises of the Long
Knives until Walsh reassured him. So he set off for Fort
Qu'Appelle.

A journey of 120 miles, it would have challenged even
the very fit, let alone the ragged band of Sioux. They struggled on, without supplies, into unfamiliar territory. Smiles
greeted news of a kill, even if it was only skunk or some
rodent. Smiles faded when they were forced to eat it raw.
Few trees grew on the northern plains and the once
numerous buffalo chips could no longer be found.
Occasionally, they were forced to travel for long periods
without water, tantalized by brackish, alkaline pools from
which they dared not drink. Soon, the hungry Sioux were
reduced to eating their emaciated horses and then dragging
their own travois.

Eventually—no one counted the days—they slipped
into the Qu'Appelle River valley. It had not yet reached
the fullness of summer, but already buds sprang forth from
the trees and tender shoots of grass rolled to the river's
edges. As they passed the small farm plots and the
Hudson's Bay Company post, they must surely have been
a strange sight to the locals. But unlike times past, their
presence did not cause fear or wreak havoc. Perhaps, at
most, those watching might have felt a little pity. When
the white-washed barracks of the Mounted Police came
into view, Sitting Bull must have heaved a sigh of relief.
Finally, he would see his friend Long Lance.

But it was not to be. Prime Minister Macdonald wanted Superintendent Walsh nowhere near the prairies until Sitting Bull was gone. Instead, Sitting Bull met the fort's acting commander, Sam Steele.

"I come to see the Meejure, Long Lance," said Sitting Bull.

"He is not here," replied Steele.

Sitting Bull's brow furrowed.

"The Meejure told me he would wait for me here, that he would give me news of my reservation."

"It is the policy of the Dominion government that the Sioux return to the United States. It is not likely that a reservation will be given to you in Canada," declared Steele.

"This is my land and I do not care to go below the line. My friends are the British, as they have always been," asserted Sitting Bull. "The Long Knives have no right to govern me."

"You've thrown in your lot with the Americans," countered Steele. "Your people have accepted a reservation there. Best you return and receive the benefits given to those at the agency."

"No!' shouted Sitting Bull, shaking his head. "I was told we would get a reservation in Canada."

Steele remained calm.

"It is useless to apply for a reservation. But, if you wish, I will send word to the Indian Commissioner that you desire one," offered Steele. The Major was nothing if not a stickler for following official guidelines. Sitting Bull agreed and a messenger was sent to Edgar Dewdney, who was at Shoal Lake, some 160 miles away. Arriving swiftly, Dewdney confirmed that no reservation would be forthcoming. He suggested that the Sioux return to Wood Mountain. They would be given supplies and a Mounted Police escort for their return journey.

Sitting Bull hesitated. Should he remain and wait for Walsh? Could things be any worse here than in Wood Mountain? Would he even be allowed to remain at the post at Wood Mountain? As he pondered questions such as these, he was approached by a unknown visitor, himself a recent arrival to Fort Qu'Appelle. His name was Louis Daniels, an ex-Mountie.

"Sitting Bull, I come with a message. It is from Major Walsh. He asked me to assure you that your surrender to American authorities will not result in special punishment for you. That is all."

How happy was Sitting Bull to hear from his friend! He had not abandoned him! Walsh, in fact, had been busy trying to get the assurances so desperately sought by Sitting Bull, without going through official circles. He visited New York and Chicago and called upon influential acquaintances. One in particular was General William A. Hammond, an old friend from the general's days in the United States Indian Department. Hammond stated emphatically that Sitting Bull would be fairly treated and that no special charges would be laid against him. Walsh had contacted other high-ranking politicians and received similar assurances. He felt confident that he could advise Sitting Bull to return without fear.

Sitting Bull's mind was made up. He returned to Wood Mountain. Once there, he visited Legare and told him he was prepared to return with him to Fort Buford. Legare was as pleased as anyone with the news. The small community could not continue to maintain the Sioux and he was afraid that there might be violence with the Cree. They decided that they would leave in a week. The Sioux procrastinated. Sitting Bull complained about the short rations Legare provided. He threatened Major Macdonell, the acting superintendent of Fort Walsh, saying that food would be taken by

Fort Buford in the Dakota Territory where Sitting Bull
and his straggling band of Sioux surrendered
to Major Brotherton of the U.S. Army

force if not given willingly. Macdonell ignored him, but
Legare gave him more food. Four Horns moaned that the
Long Knives' bullet lodged in his hip made it too painful to
travel. Councils were held, pipes were smoked. Finally, by
the second week of July, the party was moving south.

There were more complaints along the way, many from
Legare himself, who feared that the Sioux would dispose of
his rations long before they reached their destination. He
did not want to deal with 230 hungry, angry Sioux. He sent
word to Fort Buford of the problem and its urgency. Major
Brotherton responded. There was no way he was going to
lose the legendary Sioux leader when he was so close. Extra
supplies arrived on July 18. The next day, the band reached
Fort Buford.

The first officer to confront the Sioux was not a Long
Knife but a Red Coat. It was Macdonell.

"I am thrown away!" cried Sitting Bull when he saw the man.

"Nonsense. You been given good advice and you'll be well fed when you arrive," replied Macdonell.

On July 20, 1881 Sitting Bull officially presented himself and surrendered to Brotherton. His clothes were tattered and torn, his face deeply furrowed with lines of fatigue and worry. He did not look like the man who had terrified a nation. He slipped from his horse and turned to his son, Crowfoot.

"Give my gun to the major," he asked him. "My son, if you live, you will never be a man because you have neither gun nor pony."

Brotherton took the rifle and listened as Sitting Bull gave his speech of surrender.

"Today, I am home. The land under my feet is mine again. I never sold it, never gave it away. I left it only to raise my family in peace. I always wanted to come back," he declared. "Now, I will bargain with the Great Father, and the officers of the Great White Mother and the Long Knives may hear what is said."

But there was no bargaining. Sitting Bull accepted the terms as they had been laid out by the Terry Commission. On July 29, without ponies or guns, he and his followers boarded the steamboat *General Sherman* for Fort Yates and the Standing Rock Agency.

CHAPTER NINE

A Chief
without a Gun

Sitting Bull's West had changed dramatically during his years of exile. The Dakota Territory was booming. The depression of the early 1870s had played itself out and investors with money were willing to spend it. Railway entrepreneurs, who had been brought to their knees by the hard economic times and the Native resistances, were finally free of all millstones. They attacked the prairies with a lusty vigor, surveying land and laying track at astonishing rates. Initially, the steel lines snaking through the region were built in response to the gold rush in the Black Hills, where, by the end of the 1870s, nearly 20,000 dug or panned with feverish intensity. Soon enough, the railroads triggered a population explosion. In 1880, nearly 120,000 white settlers had settled around the Great Sioux Reservation; 10 years earlier, there had been only 5000.

They came in response to reports that lauded the great agricultural potential of the Dakota Territory. Custer's survey of the Black Hills, his glowing evaluation of the quality of the land and his certainty that even folks new to farming

Deadwood, South Dakota, a lawless boomtown brought
to life during the Black Hills Gold Rush of 1876

could thrive and prosper, had done much to start the influx.
Ideal agricultural weather throughout the early 1870s had
cemented the good reputation of the region in the public's
mind. Those who desired to put their future in their own
hands could do little better and a lot worse, than move to
Dakota. But while the immigrants did well, others suffered.
For the Natives who had called the area home for generations, the popularity of the region introduced changes that
were rarely for the best.

The American government's war against the Sioux throughout the 1870s had culminated with most of them confined to the Great Sioux Reservation. Government restrictions meant they could no longer follow migrating buffalo as in the hunts of yesteryear. Of course, the point was pretty much moot by this time. The once massive buffalo herds that had thundered across the prairies just years before had all but vanished. Eastern factories demanded their hides for leather products. Railways removed the time-consuming and expensive transportation difficulties of beast and wagon. New high-powered rifles, like the .55 caliber Sharps, could bring down the toughest of bulls at 1500 yards. The first half dozen years of the 1870s saw the slaughter of more than a million buffalo a year.

For a time, the Plains were an ugly, smelly place. There was little demand for buffalo carcasses, and piles of rotting meat pockmarked the grassy expanses. Once the scavengers and the elements had done their business, the bones were collected by farming interests. The skeletons were in great demand in the fertilizer factories, an industry that itself enjoyed a boom with the staggering growth in agriculture. Within a decade, the only evidence of the buffalo herds once known to take three or four days to make their way past an astounded bystander was to be found in the memories of the old-timers. For such folks, the buffalo's demise was lamentable. For Plains Natives such as the Sioux, it was catastrophic.

The buffalo had been central to the Sioux way of life and its disappearance had a profound and deeply felt impact, particularly on the Plains people's independence. The buffalo fed the Sioux; without it, they were forced to depend on others for their sustenance. Certainly, they could have farmed, and many of their numbers tried to pursue an agricultural lifestyle. Of those, most found the transition difficult. The sudden change challenged economic practices grounded in the ways of past generations. For even the most determined, the task proved daunting and often impossible.

Though it was not loudly proclaimed, the American government counted on the Sioux facing such difficulties. Officials knew that if the Sioux depended on the government for rations, they would be a more submissive, pliable people. Of course there was a cost involved, but it was a small enough price to pay to eliminate the "Indian Problem." That reason alone was sufficient for the government to advocate the slaughter of the buffalo. What soldiers and bullets couldn't do, a plains devoid of the shaggy beasts could.

With laws requiring them to stay on their reservation and the threat of starvation destroying the resolve of those who might have ignored those laws, the Sioux were vulnerable. The Indian agent made the most of that vulnerability. The agent was the primary government official on the reserve and his word was law. He decided which Natives would be given positions of influence and which would benefit from his paternalism, just as he identified the troublemakers. Invariably, he made those decisions based on the Native's disposition to conform to his demands—a willingness to accept the new rule in the American West and to adapt to its lifestyle.

From the perspective of the Indian agent, his demands were both rational and simple to achieve. He wanted the Natives to transform themselves into the copper-toned equivalent of a white Christian farmer. For the Sioux, this metamorphosis required abandoning their heathen beliefs in Wakan Tanka and the other beings that informed their rich spiritual life. More than that, they had to stop the religious practices honoring the old gods and embrace the missionaries who brought the new religion. As farmers, they were expected not only to learn the skills necessary to till the land, but also to accept the underlying philosophy of an agricultural economy: each man was independent, responsible for the well-being of himself and his family. In that light, links to the tribe were undermining and regressive. They had to be shattered. Those bonds would be replaced by a new loyalty, one to the nation and its government. That objective would be all the more assured by sending their children to the white man's school.

What the Indian agent saw as rational and simple, many Sioux saw as devastating. Even those who accepted the dictates of the new order realized that its intent was their cultural destruction. But, as they looked around and saw the prosperous white settlers and, as they considered their own desperate situation and the impossibility of maintaining the old ways, more than a few accepted the change as necessary, if not desirable. Others continued to resist. The new West to which Sitting Bull returned did not tolerate indecision. No matter; it was not difficult for him to choose his position.

"Ma! Pa!" shouted the young boy as he threw open the door and ran into the house. "They're coming!"

"Land sakes child!" replied his mother. "Be still and tell me who."

"Why, none other than Buffalo Bill! And he's bringing Sitting Bull!" exclaimed the boy. "Can we go to the show?"

It was the summer of 1885 and Sitting Bull had signed on with Buffalo Bill Cody's Wild West show. For four months, they had traveled through the American northeast

Buffalo Bill Cody (1846–1917),
in front of a Wild West Show wagon, was
instrumental in bringing Sitting Bull to the public

and central Canada. Plenty of customers paid to see the
man they believed responsible for the worst of the Plains'
savagery. Many of them left the show wondering if the
small, quiet man who walked with a limp and who wore
a shawl wrapped about his shoulders could really be as violent as they had been led to believe. Ultimately, the tour did
much to rehabilitate Sitting Bull's reputation in the eyes of
white North Americans. As it turned out, it also enhanced
his position among the Sioux.

Two years after returning from Canada, Sitting Bull ended up at the Standing Rock Agency in central Dakota. No longer under army confinement, he was as free as a man restricted to a reservation and under the direction of an Indian agent could be. As soon as he arrived, Sitting Bull was embroiled in controversy. As rapacious as ever, the American government had pressured Sioux leaders into ceding 14,000 square miles, about half, of the Great Sioux Reservation. The official proposal was to divide the reservation into six separate sections, so that each band might have its own territory. The Sioux were not told a huge seventh section would revert to the government. The consent of the Sioux was achieved through a campaign of confusion and fear. The local Indian agent, John McLaughlin, argued that the move would be in the Natives' best interests as it promoted their civilizing, while religious leaders intoned that failure to sign the agreement would displease God.

When the agreement reached the American Senate for ratification, eyebrows were raised. Some elected officials felt guilty enough about the past treatment of the Sioux and wanted to see that future dealings were above board. When it was discovered that the agreement contained far fewer signatures than the three-quarters of adult male Sioux required under the Laramie Treaty of '68, a commission under Senator Henry Dawes was dispatched to investigate. At the Standing Rock Agency, the commission met with several chiefs, including Sitting Bull. Dawes was an advocate of Sioux interests and listened carefully to what the Sioux had to say. However, he noticed that Sitting Bull would not offer an opinion at the meeting. Anxious for both his input and his support, Dawes invited the Hunkpapa chief to speak.

Sitting Bull was angry with the turn of events. He strongly opposed the proposed sale of Sioux territory and he was especially upset at the unfolding of the meeting.

He considered himself to be the Sioux leader, the one to whom questions should be addressed and from whom answers should be received. Government officials were not convinced that Sitting Bull retained much influence among his people. He had led them in a protracted, losing battle; there seemed no good reason for them to continue following him. They were in for a surprise.

"I will speak if you want me to, though it seems those who speak here are only those whose words you wish to hear. Do you know who I am?" he barked impatiently. "You need to know that if Wakan Tanka has chosen anyone to be chief of this country, it is me."

His proclamation was met with silence.

"You behave like men who drink whisky," he continued, "while I have come to give you advice."

With that, he waved his arm and led all the Natives from the room. The commissioners and other onlookers were stunned. Apparently Sitting Bull was still a force to be reckoned with. In truth, he did not hold the authority he once had. Some of the Sioux who did not agree with his action convinced him to return to the meeting. Once there, Sitting Bull re-emphasized his position as chief and then apologized for his behavior. He concluded his speech by protesting the government's plan. Before he sat down, one of the commissioners rose to speak.

"You were not appointed by the Great Spirit, as leaders are not so made. You have no following, no power, no right to control. If it were not for the government's generosity, you and your people would be starving," came the paternalistic rebuke. "If it were not for the government's goodwill, you would now be in jail. Continue to behave as you do and that is where you will be."

John McLaughlin listened to the commissioner's diatribe. The Indian agent concurred with his beliefs and the tone in which they were expressed, but he was concerned. Prior to the meeting, McLaughlin shared the commissioners' belief that Sitting Bull would pose no significant problems on the reservation. His power was spent. Now, he was less sure. He could easily envision Sitting Bull interfering with his program for civilizing the Sioux. There was no reason to suspect that one so long opposed to the white man would suddenly adopt his ways. This reality presented a significant problem for McLaughlin because he was responsible for civilizing the Natives, for ensuring that they shifted their loyalties from their tribe to the American government. Like other government officials, he wanted them to accept the white man's ways—his values, his religion, his culture— as their own. As McLaughlin reflected, he concluded it might be better for the Sioux leader to be as far away from the reservation as possible.

McLaughlin did not have to wait long to rid himself of Sitting Bull, because, as it turned out, the chief was in great demand in the settled West. When the request for Sitting Bull's presence at a public ceremony came from Bismarck, Dakota, McLaughlin agreed to it readily. Bismarck had been chosen as the capital for the territory, and was putting on a grand celebration to mark both that recognition and America's western progress. Many prominent officials, including past President Grant and President Henry Villard of the Northern Pacific Railroad, would be present. They would all meet to lay the cornerstone of the capitol building. Sitting Bull agreed to participate if he could meet with Grant. Assured that such a meeting would take place (which it apparently never did), he set off on his first train ride north.

Sitting Bull never liked trains; he saw them as a hated symbol of the white man's intrusion. But perhaps he enjoyed the irony of riding north to Bismarck, where he had previously helped stop the Northern Pacific in its tracks.

Sitting Bull was treated well upon arrival. Immediately, his celebrity status was confirmed as he was swamped by those seeking his autograph. He was hardly shy about it, charging two dollars a signature. Once he was on the speakers' platform, he was introduced first, following the tradition of beginning such ceremonies with the oldest resident. Finally given the opportunity to speak, he ripped into his audience.

"I hate all those who are white. You are liars and thieves. You have taken our land and made us outcasts," he spat.

He went along in this vein for some time. The officer who had assisted Sitting Bull in the preparation of his speech for the occasion was dumbfounded. When he concluded, the audience burst forth in a thunderous round of applause. The officer had translated Sitting Bull's speech falsely, so that it mirrored the previously agreed upon text, full of greetings and well wishes. The words of the Hunkpapa chief were so well received, he was invited to other ceremonies.

At a similar function in St. Paul, Minnesota, Alvaren Allen witnessed Sitting Bull's enthusiastic reception. Allen was a showman and smelled money. Immediately, he contacted McLaughlin and inquired about the possibility of Sitting Bull joining a traveling exhibition. The idea wasn't a new one; promoters had sought Sitting Bull's participation in such shows since his days in Canada. McLaughlin certainly wasn't opposed to the idea. The key problem was that Sitting Bull wasn't terribly interested. However, with Allen's proposal McLaughlin increased the pressure on Sitting Bull. McLaughlin saw that the Sioux were beginning to adapt more readily to white ways and he didn't want trouble from the Hunkpapa chief. In the late summer of 1884, Sitting Bull accepted the invitation, joining a show that was promoted as the "Sitting Bull Combination."

The exhibition consisted of a troop of Natives and was designed to portray life on the Plains prior to the arrival of the white man. Stages were transformed into prairie settings, complete with tipis and Natives in traditional garb going about their daily business. As they performed, an announcer read a lecture on Native life highlighting Sitting Bull, who was dressed in stunning fur-lined, porcupine-quill decorated clothes. Daily, thousands crammed in to watch the show.

On occasion, Sitting Bull spoke, and when he did, silence descended upon the murmuring crowd. His words came from his heart and illustrated his desire for continuing peace and the need for young Natives to be educated in the way of the white man. Those who didn't understand (almost all, of course) heard different words. The translator told stories of Sitting Bull's victory at Little Bighorn, of his scalping of Custer. It was what the audience wanted to hear; after all, Allen billed his star attraction as "the slayer of General Custer."

The following year, "Buffalo Bill" Cody came calling at the Standing Rock Agency. William F. Cody had come by his nickname honestly. Back in the mid-1860s, he was hired by the proprietors of the Kansas Pacific Railroad to provide buffalo to feed the laborers. He was so good at it, folks began calling him Buffalo Bill. He bragged later that, in any given year, he had killed thousands of the animals. Even Sitting Bull saw the sad irony in his being employed by a man who had done so much to destroy his people's way of life. He didn't, however, let that stand in the way of either a profitable business deal or a friendship with Cody.

Aware of his celebrity, Sitting Bull was able to negotiate favorable terms of employment with Cody. He would tour with the Wild West show for four months, at $50 a week and $125 for expenses, much of which went back to the

Sitting Bull's autograph, which he sold either alone or on his
photo during his stint with Buffalo Bill's Wild West Show

reserve to support his people. At the last minute, he insisted
on a further clause: he wanted the sole right to sell photographs of himself, either alone or with visitors. It was a far-
sighted addition, because he sold hundreds of such
photographs. Cody acceded to the demand grudgingly and
still pocketed a profit of $100,000 during the season! For
the remuneration, it proved to be easy work, as Sitting Bull
was only required to sit on a light gray horse and watch
the proceedings. Whether the audience cheered or booed,
the impassive countenance of *Sedentary Taurus*, as eastern
papers had christened him, never altered.

Sitting Bull took a liking to Cody, whom he began calling
Pahaska, meaning "Long Hair." (Although perhaps too much
should not be made of the friendship; Long Hair was, after all,
the name given by the Sioux to Custer.) The showman didn't
bill Sitting Bull as America's feared enemy. As a matter of fact,
Cody defended him and the actions of his people during the
past decades of Plains warfare. When asked, he readily pointed
out that the Sioux fought to protect women, children and
their very way of life. Of course, Buffalo Bill was careful where
he said such things. Mostly, it was to Canadian reporters during the show's tour north of the border. Sitting Bull was especially popular there, where audiences saw him as a great Native

Sitting Bull with the two eagle feathers
that he earned for his courage in battle

leader rather than the killer of Custer. Cody reinforced the former perspective, pointing out that Sitting Bull did not lead the Sioux against Custer, insightfully noting that his position was less a general than a medicine man or politician who persuaded with sound argument and powerful speech.

Sitting Bull formed other friendships during the tour, but none as deeply as the one with Annie Oakley. "Little Missy," as Cody took to calling her, had only recently joined the show, following a staggering demonstration of her shooting ability. Buffalo Bill signed her on the spot when she shot glass balls out of the air, backwards, with only the aid of a mirror. Sitting Bull, no slouch himself when it came to marksmanship, dubbed her "Little Sure Shot." She found great appeal in the old chief's generosity, informing those who would listen that significant portions of his earnings quickly went from his own hands to those of poor children who took to him in great flocks. Before the tour ended, Sitting Bull adopted her formally.

The following year, Cody asked Sitting Bull to travel with the show to Europe, but he declined. Sitting Bull had heard rumors that the government was resurrecting its failed attempt to take control of Sioux land and he believed that his presence at the reservation was of greater importance. He was right.

In the bottom of the valley that swept up from the Grand River sat a collection of tipis and cabins, enclosed within a patchwork of growing crops. Even the largest of the dwellings, a two-room log house, was marked by the poverty of the encampment. An old man in a tanned buckskin outfit of fringed shirt, leggings and moccasins appeared in the doorway of the cabin and made his way to the shore of the river, chickens scattering with each step. His slow limp and red-hued face, painted to bring good luck, identified the man as Sitting Bull. His eagle feather headband identified him as a warrior still. When he reached the water's edge, he stood there, caressed by the warm prairie winds of fall, lost in thought.

He had been on the reserve for seven long years and, despite all the promises of the white man, the lives of his people had not improved. For the most part, they'd clearly deteriorated. Treaty rations arrived late and, even then, often in reduced quantities. Disease ran rampant and his people, already weakened by hunger, were easy victims. Some Sioux, however, did not suffer as others did. Those who had become friends of the white man, chiefs like Red Cloud and Spotted Tail, dwelt in two-story frame houses and enjoyed lives of comparative luxury. Sitting Bull had vowed never to become an agency Indian, despite the material improvements such a choice would bring. Wakan Tanka made him an Indian, and he would live and die as one.

As poverty and death ravaged his people, Sitting Bull was forced to witness the disintegration of the once great Sioux nation. Intertribal dissent and factionalism had ripped open heaving fissures among his people. For the most part, disagreements emerged over the best way to adapt to the new way of life foisted upon them. Some agreed with the civilizing ways proposed by the Indian agent, who thought it best to make treaties that sold the land and brought more money. Sitting Bull opposed such ideas. He didn't care that those beliefs branded him an obstructionist in the eyes of people like McLaughlin. He held dear the notion that the Sioux must be self-supporting, as much as possible, on their own terms. To achieve this goal required education in the white man's ways and skills for survival. But it also meant that the Sioux must retain their homeland. Above all, it required their unity as a people.

The events of previous years made Sitting Bull's heart grow heavier still because they demonstrated the chasm between the competing visions. The American government had once again sent a delegation intent on buying Sioux territory. When they failed to collect the necessary signatures,

prominent Native chiefs were invited to Washington to continue the negotiations. Sitting Bull was among them. The
chiefs were divided; a minority wanted to make treaty at
minimal cost to the government. Sitting Bull agreed to sell
the land, but only at a price much in excess of the government offer. It was a ploy designed to end the talks, not to
reach an agreement.

As he expected, his proposal terminated the discussions. But to Sitting Bull's surprise, government officials,
under great pressure to end the western Native problem,
showed up on the Sioux reserves seeking signatures based
on the figures Sitting Bull had cited. The Hunkpapa chief
began a campaign against agreement at any price. What
followed indicated that his authority had eroded. Prior to
the commission's arrival at the Standing Rock Agency,
McLaughlin managed to convince the chiefs, including
Sitting Bull's once close ally, Gall, to sign the treaty (or
have their rations cut off). He further solicited promises
from them that Sitting Bull would not be informed of the
commissioners' impending arrival. However, the secret
could not be kept, and when the Hunkpapa chief became
aware of their presence, he rode north quickly to their
meeting place at the agency. Once there, he declared that
no one told him of the meeting. In response the Indian
agent called him a liar. Following that accusation, other
chiefs led their people in the signing of the treaty. The
Great Sioux Reservation was no more.

As Sitting Bull stood on the river's shore, he must have
considered whether the end of the Sioux nation was near.
His recollections and weighty reflections were interrupted
as his eyes fell on a familiar face. The visitor and his companions made their way to Seen-by-Her-Nation, Sitting
Bull's first wife. She directed them to the shore line, where
the leader of the party soon joined Sitting Bull.

Kicking Bear (1850–1890), who brought the
Ghost Dance to Sitting Bull

"Father, I am Kicking Bear," he said.

"Yes, I remember you from the Battle at the Greasy
Grass. I am glad that you are here. Eat and we will talk,"
replied Sitting Bull.

When their bellies were full, the Miniconjou Sioux
Kicking Bear began to tell a tale that captivated the elder chief.

"Father, a messiah has come to save us. His name is
Wovoka, a Paiute from Nevada. He foretells the imminent

arrival of a happy land, one full of bounty and peopled by all the Natives who have long died. There, we will hunt the buffalo and all will live as they once did. It will be a land free of illness and want, one that is peaceful. Father, there will be no white man," he stated with great emphasis.

"It is impossible for a man to die and live again," commented Sitting Bull.

"I have been to the land of the Paiute. I know Wovoka speaks the truth," countered Kicking Bear. "All we need do is to accept his teachings and perform the Ghost Dance. Those who do leave their bodies, join their ancestors. They see the happy future that awaits."

"How will there be no whites?" asked Sitting Bull, still skeptical.

"A great flood will submerge the earth. Wakan Tanka will lift those with eagle feathers above the rising waters. The white men will be submerged and turn into fish."

"The white men will not allow this to happen," stated Sitting Bull. "They will stop the Ghost Dance, just as they have the Sun Dance."

"The Long Knives are not to be feared. Their gunpowder will fizzle. We have sacred garments [the Ghost Dance shirt] to protect the dancers from their bullets. But enough of words, Father. I have a true message from the Native bands of the West."

With that, Kicking Bear's eyes glazed over and he started to chant. "Come here mother; younger brother is walking and crying. Come here mother; here is the father, here is the father."

Kicking Bear began to dance and his companions joined his song. "The father said he brings the pipe for you and you will live. Thus said the father, thus said the father."

Soon, the words reached a high pitch, eerily mournful. Even Sitting Bull was touched. Before his eyes, Kicking

Ghost Dance shirt that was to protect its wearers
from the army's bullets

Bear began to shake and tremble. He struck out with his right arm, transformed suddenly into a weapon. Gyrating crazily, the dancer collapsed. He lay still on the ground.

Sitting Bull sat for some time, content to look at the prostrate Kicking Bear. Finally he rose and moved in for a closer look.

"Do not touch him!" cried one of the dancer's companions. "He is now in the Spirit Land."

Sitting Bull crouched back on the ground and took out his pipe. Uncertain about what to do, it seemed that prayer and reflection were not out of place. With the smoke from Sitting Bull's pipe still rising, Kicking Bear's eyes snapped open.

"I have just seen Wakan Tanka. He has left me with a sign of his visit. He has made my hand stronger than that of the most strong!"

He touched one of his companions, who leaped back as if to escape the goring charge of an enraged buffalo. He spied a china cup on the floor of Sitting Bull's cabin, a gift from a long departed visitor, and crushed it against his palm.

Sitting Bull, the *wichasha wakan*, could not help but respond to the mystical dance. Kicking Bear had given a powerful demonstration, and though Sitting Bull remained uncertain, he was willing to try. For the next five days, his Hunkpapa band performed the Ghost Dance. Sitting Bull joined them until the sweat rolled off his body and his bones ached in pain. Yet no vision came to him. Others claimed greater success, some speaking of visions of buffalo and meals of pemmican. Finally, a dismayed Sitting Bull abandoned the ceremony and retreated to the sidelines. He watched and listened and eventually left.

He made his way to his lodge and retrieved his *wotawe*. Next to his shield, it was his most cherished possession. A cloth nearly three feet long, it had representations of a green dragonfly in each corner and a green, red-spotted elk in its center, all cast against a deep orange-yellow background. It was powerful medicine and Sitting Bull used it only in times of great need. Once it was carefully placed in his pouch, he walked away from his small camp and climbed a nearby hill until he could no longer see or hear the dancing.

He sat down and took out the *wotawe*, along with the two narrow buffalo hide wristlets he always wore during such occasions. Slipping them on his wrist, he took some time to smoke his pipe. He reflected on the puzzling Ghost Dance, desperately seeking an answer as to what it might mean for his people. The pipe ritual complete, he cut his arm, allowing the blood to flow as a sacrifice to Wakan Tanka. Then, he began to sing a sacred song he had composed decades before.

"I have a good friend up there. I have a good friend up there. I have an elk-friend above; on earth, I speak for a nation."

The song complete, he continued to rock and chant, when suddenly, he saw it!

His understanding was as clear as the visions he once so regularly experienced. What Kicking Bear claimed might or might not be true. Perhaps a bountiful land alive with past generations of his people did await. Who knew the limits of Wakan Tanka's power? But Sitting Bull came to see that the real power of the dance did not lie in a happy land in some distant time. No. The value of the dance was that it united the Natives! It linked them in a spiritual bond, one that could serve as a foundation from which to resist the onslaught of the white man's ways. The buffalo were gone, their weapons were taken, the land was overrun, but in the dance, were the seeds of hope.

Others also saw this possibility. One of them was John McLaughlin. When he heard that Kicking Bear was actively promoting the Ghost Dance on his reserve, the Indian agent sent officers to arrest him as an unauthorized intruder. After a few attempts, Kicking Bear and his companions were escorted from the reserve. Their removal was not enough for McLaughlin. He wanted to stamp out the new religion. Not only might it undermine his civilizing mission, it also threatened the security of the West. Many remembered a time when warfare followed the Sioux's dancing. McLaughlin

knew they weren't much of a military threat. They had few
or no weapons and were greatly outnumbered. But it provided him with a good excuse to clamp down on the Sioux.
To achieve his objective, he believed he also had to curtail
the power of the man he considered to be the main advocate of the Ghost Dance—Sitting Bull. McLaughlin found
the prospect most appealing.

Word had blown in on a western breeze and it worried
John McLaughlin. Some 3000 Sioux, from a handful of
adjoining reservations, had gathered in the Dakota
Badlands. There hadn't been that many together since the
days of the Great Sioux War. And as if that wasn't enough,
McLaughlin had a letter dictated by Sitting Bull that promised nothing but trouble. He took the letter up and read it
a third time.

On the surface, there was nothing sinister about the missive. Sitting Bull had written to inform McLaughlin that he
was traveling to the Pine Ridge Reservation to investigate
the Ghost Dance further. If that was all the Hunkpapa chief
was going to do, it was bad enough because the Indian
agent had no doubts about the corrosive effect of the new
ritual. However, McLaughlin suspected that the reason
given by Sitting Bull was an excuse; he was certain the chief
was bound for the Sioux gathering, where he was sure to
stir up unrest. His trip had to be stopped.

It was easier said than done. The problem was that
McLaughlin's hands were tied. Recently, President Harrison
had given the secretary of war responsibility for containing
the Ghost Dance and dealing with the renewed Sioux
problem. Without orders from General Miles, who was

placed in command of the operation, there was little McLaughlin could do. All that changed when a military mail carrier entered his office with an urgent dispatch from Miles. It was just what McLaughlin wanted to read: arrest Sitting Bull.

With his departure imminent, McLaughlin wrote to Sitting Bull, advising that he travel nowhere. Then he contacted the agency police, who were Natives, to carry out Miles' orders. McLaughlin added his own emphasis: Sitting Bull would not be allowed to escape under any circumstances. The last thing he wanted was news that the wily chief had slipped through his fingers. On December 15, 1890, some 40 agency policemen rode to Sitting Bull's camp on the Grand River. Most traveled with little enthusiasm and heavy hearts. Some of them had fought with Sitting Bull at Rosebud and Little Bighorn. Others had followed him to Canada. But while they might respect the man, they no longer cared for his principles. In the peaceful hours before dawn, following a Christian prayer given by their commander Bull Head, the agency police struck.

Pushing in the door of Sitting Bull's cabin and thrusting a candle into the darkness, a handful of police entered the dwelling. Spotting Sitting Bull among the half dozen occupants, Sergeant Shave Head bolted towards him.

"Brother, we come after you," he called.

"How, all right," came the response.

Shave Head grabbed Sitting Bull and pushed the naked man towards the door. In the confusion, some of those who had been sleeping in the cabin left, leaving only Seen-by-Her-Nation, Sitting Bull's wife, and 14-year-old son, Crowfoot.

"This is a fine way to do it, not to let me dress in winter," said Sitting Bull. Seen-by-Her-Nation was permitted to retrieve his clothes.

When he was dressed, they pushed Sitting Bull towards the door.

"Let me be. I will go without your help," he proclaimed.

Stepping out into the morning twilight, Sitting Bull saw that his old gray horse from his days with Buffalo Bill was saddled, waiting for him. He mounted it and was surrounded quickly by the police. Ready to leave, their progress was impeded by Sitting Bull's followers, who had finally been roused by the commotion.

"We expected you," cried Catch-the-Bear to the police. "But you shall not take him! People, let us protect our chief!"

The Hunkpapa were pressing in when young Crowfoot called, "Father, are you not brave? How do you let these police take you?"

Sitting Bull remained impassive, then stated suddenly, "I will not go with you."

Arguments ensued. Some implored Sitting Bull to go peacefully while others demanded they fight for his freedom. As the police tried to force their way through the shouting crowd, Catch-the-Bear raised his rifle and fired at Bull Head. As the stricken officer fell from his horse, clutching his bloodied side, he took a wild shot at Sitting Bull. The bullet found the chief's chest. Red Tomahawk, another of the agency police, followed it with a shot to the back of Sitting Bull's head. Chaos ensued. When the gunfire stopped, eight Natives and four policemen were dead, with two others mortally wounded. One of the Natives was Crowfoot. Discovered while hiding, he was shot begging for his life. Relatives of the men who came to arrest Sitting Bull were so angry at the deaths of their loved ones that they came out of their houses after the shooting stopped, found Sitting Bull's body on the ground and proceeded to beat his head beyond recognition. As for Sitting Bull's followers, they fled the village when the cavalry appeared.

Sitting Bull had foreseen his end. In the spring of the year, while on an early morning walk, a meadowlark had called to him.

"Lakotas will kill you."

The body of the man who considered himself to be the last Native was taken by soldiers and buried without ceremony in an unmarked grave outside the gates of Fort Yates.

Epilogue

On December 16, James Walsh stepped from the lobby of his hotel in Winnipeg and the icy wind stung his cheek. He hurried to a meeting at the Dominion Coal, Coke & Transportation Company, where he was manager. He had held the position for seven years, since he resigned from the North-West Mounted Police.

When Sitting Bull returned to the United States, Walsh took up his appointment at Fort Qu'Appelle. Perhaps sensing that his future as a Mountie was limited because of his role in the Sitting Bull affair, Walsh left the force after a year and established a coal mining operation that found a ready partner in the CPR.

He suddenly heard he raspy cry of a newsboy.

"Sitting Bull dead! Read all about it in the *Manitoba Daily Free Press!*"

Walsh fumbled for a coin and bought a copy of the paper.

"SITTING BULL SHOT.

"Old Sitting Bull is Sent to the Happy Hunting Grounds at Last with Several Followers—Seven Indian Police Killed.

"St. Paul, Dec. 15. Gen. Miles this evening received a dispatch stating that in a fight near Standing Rock Agency this morning Sitting Bull and several Indian police had been shot. The first dispatch was from Pierre, S.D., and said that

Sitting Bull and his son had been killed, but giving no further particulars."

Walsh raised his eyes from the newspaper and stared blankly down the road. Decade-old memories resurfaced, bringing to his face warm smiles and steely grimaces. Back at his hotel he sat down to write a last reflection on the Sioux chief he called Bull.

"I am glad to hear that Bull is relieved of his miseries even if it took the bullet to do it. A man who wields such power as Bull once did, that of a king, and over a wild, spirited people, cannot endure abject poverty, slavery and beggary without suffering great mental pain…and death is a relief.

"Bull's confidence and belief in the Great Spirit were stronger than I ever saw it in any other man. He trusted Him implicitly….

"History does not tell us that a greater Indian than Bull ever lived. He was the Mohammed of his people; the law made him the king of the Sioux.

"I regret now that I had not gone to Standing Rock to see him. There were one or two things I would like to have spoken to him about before he died.

"Bull has been misrepresented. He was not the bloodthirsty man reports from the prairies made him out to be. He asked for nothing but justice. He did not want to be a beggar or a slave….

"Bull, in council and war, was a king of his people. To his superior intelligence in council and his generalship in war every man in his nation bowed. It is a calumny to say he was a coward, or that he ever ran away from a fight….

"This man, that so many look upon as a bloodthirsty villain, would make many members of the Christian faith ashamed of their doubts and weakness in the faith of their god. If they knew him in his true character—he was not a cruel man, he was kind of heart; he was not dishonest, he was truthful. He loved his people and was glad to give his hand in friendship to any man who believed he was not an enemy and was honest with him. But Bull experienced so much treachery, that he did not know who to trust....

"The war between the U.S. and Bull was a strange one. A nation against one man. On the U.S. side there were numbers; on Bull's side there was principle. The one man was murdered by the nation to destroy the principle he advocated—that no man against his will should be forced to be a beggar. Bull was the marked man of his people.

Notes on Sources

As much as possible, the dialogue in this book is accurate and the accounts described are fictionalized as little as possible.

Anderson, Ian. *Sitting Bull's Boss: Above the Medicine Line with James Morrow Walsh*. Surrey: Heritage House. 2000.

Bernotas, Bob. *Sitting Bull: Chief of the Sioux*. New York: Chelsea House. 1992.

MacEwan, Grant. *Sitting Bull: The Years in Canada*. Edmonton, AB: Hurtig. 1973.

Turner, Frank. *Across the Medicine Line*. Toronto: McClelland & Stewart. 1973.

Utley, Robert. *The Lance and the Shield: The Life and Times of Sitting Bull*. New York: Henry Holt. 1993

Vestal, Stanley. *Sitting Bull: Champion of the Sioux*. Boston: Houghton Mifflin. 1932.

Wallace, Jim. *A Double Duty*. Winnipeg, MB: Bunker to Bunker Books. 1997